Mel Bay's
Immigrant Songbook

By Jerry Silverman

Cover illustration by Greg Ragland.

Immigrant Children on the Roof Garden at Ellis Island   *Sherman Collection, National Park Service*

Contents

Introduction

What's in a song? What is there about the marriage of words and music that has proven to be the vehicle through which our deepest feelings have been expressed? Why have some songs endured for centuries and others died a-borning?

The answer is at once simple and complex. In order to survive the test of time, a song must tell us things we already know, things we understand, things we feel. At the same time, like all great art, it must lead us one step further than we have gone before and cause us to examine life through a fresh, new perspective.

So it is with the songs of the people who have come to America from every corner of the earth. When they left their homes they were called "emigrants." When they arrived here they were called "immigrants." With the passage of time they came to be called "Americans."

Along the way they found the time to express the multitude of their thoughts, desires, and feelings in a vast body of song. When we examine this treasure we can begin to fathom what it must have meant to set forth on that perilous journey with "only" hope at journey's end.

What do these people tell us about themselves in their songs? That they left their homelands and came to American for all the "usual" reasons: poverty, oppression, discrimination. Some came as businessmen: for them America was a commercial venture. Others came to make their fortunes and return home — and some actually did return. Some came as indentured servants and worked long years to repay their passage. Some were sent for by other family members who had gone before.

In their songs they also tell us of the people, the land, and the life left behind. Old folks weeping to see the young depart forever. Tragedies at sea and on the land. Intermingled with the wonder and the enthusiasm for the new, we find the terrible nostalgia and heartbreak for the old. We hear, too, from those who chose to stay behind.

Out-and-out "success stories" are relatively few, even though mouth-watering tall tales of gold, pretty girls, handsome men, and cornucopias of plenty are found — usually east of the Atlantic. Harsh realities of adaptation and integration into the strange new society abound in the songs. It is as true here as elsewhere that successful, contented people — people who have "made it" — rarely sing about their lives. Songs protesting against the status quo are infinitely more common than those supporting it.

So far we have spoken only of the people who, for a variety of reasons, desired to come to America. As you read through and, hopefully, sing through these pages, you may find your own family's story refracted through the prism of these narratives. But what of the others: those who had no wish to come to these shores, but who were uprooted, torn away and transported here in chains? What songs did they sing during the long middle passage from Africa? What ballads recount their feelings on arrival on board a Dutch slave ship in Virginia in 1619? What chants were intoned on the "wonders" of the New World by these captive peoples?

In order to attempt to answer these questions, we must first examine the processes by which songs are transmitted and preserved.

The people who came to America from Europe came from societies which had highly developed systems of musical notation as well as written languages. Song writers could put their creations down on paper, and the printing press would guarantee dissemination of their works to a greater or lesser degree. Even if the creator was not capable of or not interested in writing out his or her song, others who heard it could at some point transcribe it.

Collectors, editors, publishers, and musicologists were on hand to notate popular songs. That is to say, they would gather and preserve songs that they deemed **worthy** of being transcribed. This compiling of popular song material in America began toward the end of the 18th century, gained momentum and importance in the 19th century, and really came into its own as a "respectable" field of endeavor in the 20th century.

But the Africans who arrived here early in the 17th century — albeit coming from societies with highly developed musical systems — lacked the means to write down their musical creations, having neither written languages nor musical notation. We can safely assume that they sang songs of yearning and despair, of bitterness and protest: such is the human condition. They **must** have sung their "immigrant" songs. However, to our eternal loss, 17th-century plantations did not have resident musicologists, quill in hand, eager to transcribe this music. Any musically trained whites who may have come into contact with this music must have simply not reacted to it in any positive way — to put it mildly. To them it would have had to have been incomprehensible "savage" chanting.

By the time English-language Negro spirituals and work songs began to be recognized and appreciated — and these have been amply documented and collected — some 200 years or more had passed. The early "arrival" songs had disappeared — vanished from the collective folk memory. They had not been recognized, understood, or deemed worthy of being transcribed.

But eastward, back across the Atlantic, on the West African coast, the collective folk memory of these depredations remained alive — and remains alive to this very day. The oral history of the people has been preserved in a remarkable manner by a remarkable group of people: the griots.

Griots are highly trained, hereditary singer-historians who have committed to memory the detailed history of their village going back hundreds of years — down to specific names and actions of individual people. On important occasions, such as births, weddings, birthdays, and funerals, village griots may be hired to compose songs describing in minute detail the lives of the family members for generations back.

It is thanks to one of the Gambian griots, Alhaji Fatala Kanuteh, that we have an astounding "first-hand eyewitness" singing narrative account of what may be the first sale of slaves to the Portuguese, and then by the Portuguese to the Dutch in 1619. It was collected by folklorist Samuel Charters in Gambia in 1974 and preserved on a recording.*

Accompanying himself on the balafon (a wooden keyed instrument with a calabash resonator), Kanuteh recites a long, detailed description of the arrival of the Portuguese slave ships and the subsequent actions of the Portuguese and the Mandingos. It ends with this extraordinary passage:

> When the Europeans came, when they brought their ship from Portugal, the ship used to start its journey from Banjul, then it went to Sanemunko Joyo to collect slaves there in the presence of Seneke Jammeh, and Mansa Demba Sanko, and Samkala Marong, and Wali Mandeba, and Jata Sela. Anyone who had slaves, they collected them all together and took them to the places called Aladabara and Jufure to sell them to the Portuguese. Then the Portuguese put them in their ship and left there and went to Jang Jang Bure. When they arrived there they went right to the slave house to collect the slaves there, and take them to the Dutch. Then the Dutch collected them and sent them to America. It is because of this that slaves were plenty in America.

> They call them American Negroes.

---

*Folkways Record Album FE 4178

What a pity no such similar oral document exists on this side of the Atlantic!*

With the immense influx of immigrants from Europe in the last decades of the 19th century and the beginning of the 20th, professional American song writers (some of them foreign-born) began to turn out a new genre of popular music: the dialect, pseudo-immigrant song. Unabashedly sentimental tear-jerkers or comic extravaganzas, most of these songs do not stand the test of time. The so-called dialects sound vaguely offensive to our ears today, and the more blatant ethnic stereotypes just don't "play" to our contemporary sensibilities. Yet, in their day, there was a tremendous audience for these songs, and fortunes and reputations were made by their composers and singers. Irving Berlin, to name certainly the most successful of these composers, weighed in with such early numbers as "Yidl, On Your Fiddle, Play Some Ragtime," "Marie from Sunny Italy," and "The Russian Lullaby," to name just a few.

As with the "coon songs" of roughly the same period which purported to described black American life ("Watermelon Time," "At a Georgia Camp Meeting," "Rufus Rastus Johnson Brown, What You Gonna Do When the Rent Comes 'Round," etc.), and which were more often than not composed by white song writers, many of the dialect "immigrant songs" were created by song writers and lyricists of ethnic extractions other than the people described in their songs. This is in contrast with the true immigrant songs which spring directly from the people involved.

The Ellis Island Immigration Museum has a wall display of the colorful sheet music covers of a number of these "dialect" songs. The graphic depiction of every conceivable ethnic and racist stereotype of the characters in these songs clearly shows how we viewed each other "then" — what was acceptable and what was, indeed, expected of song writers and illustrators. That is not to say that all such material is inherently offensive, but it is interesting to note how "others" were seen by the "establishment."

As to the relationship between composer and subject matter, in terms of ethnicity, a few examples will suffice:

---

*Some 200 years after the events described in this narrative took place, a young Irishman named Edward Hollander left his home in Waterford to seek his fortune. In a long ballad entitled "The Flying Cloud," we follow Edward's checkered career from cooper's apprentice, to sailor on board a slave ship, to pirate, and finally to the gallows in Newgate, England. The graphic description of life on the slaver and afterwards forms an eloquent counterpoint to Kanuteh's recitation, which, perforce, ends with the embarkation of the slaves for America.

> . . . When we came unto Bermuda's isle, there I met with Captain Moore,
> The commander of the Flying Cloud, hailing from Baltimore.
> He asked me if I'd ship with him, on a slaving voyage to go,
> To the burning shores of Africa, where the sugar cane does grow.
>
> It was after some weeks' sailing we arrived off Africa's shore,
> And five hundred of these poor slaves, my boys, from their native land we bore.
> We made them walk in on a plank, and we stowed them down below;
> Scarce eighteen inches to a man was all they had to go.
>
> The plague and fever came on board, swept half of them away;
> We dragged their bodies up on deck and hove them in the sea.
> It was better for the rest of them if they had died before,
> Than to work under brutes of planters in Cuba for ever more.
>
> It was after stormy weather we arrived off Cuba's shore,
> And we sold them to the planters there, to be slaves for ever more.
> For the rice and the coffee seed to sow beneath the broiling sun,
> There to lead a wretched, lonely life till their career was run. . . .

"Macaroni Joe"	Stanley Murphy and Percy Weinreich
"Chinatown, My Chinatown"	W. Jerome and Jean Schwartz
"My Pretty Colleen"	B. A. Koelhoffer
"Hello Wisconsin, Won't You Find My Yonnie Yonsen"	Bert Kalman, Edgar Leslie, and Harry Ruby
"Yonkele, the Cow-Boy Jew"	"Kosher words and music" by Will J. Harris and Harry I. Robinson

These long-forgotten, frivolous creations stand in stark contrast to the deeper, heartfelt expressions of the immigrants themselves. The genuine immigrant songs, however, rarely reached audiences outside of their own communities for the simple reason that they were written for and sung to their own countrymen in their own languages — incomprehensible to those "others."

It is ironic to note, as we examine the lyrics of these songs, how closely many of them resemble each other in feelings and sentiments. Too bad that each immigrant community was largely cut off from its neighbors — who had exactly the same problems, joys, and sorrows, and which expressed these common emotions in what should have been the universal language of song.

Which brings us to this present collection.

Many of the songs in this book have lain fallow for generations. Others are of more recent origin, and some were especially written for inclusion here. The great majority of them had never been translated into English and, as descendants of the immigrants lost and continue to lose their "mother tongues," all memory of the older songs was and is in danger of being erased.

In undertaking this compilation, it was necessary first of all to locate the songs — either from individuals' personal recollections, in print, or on recordings. Then, in order to evaluate their contents, a literal translation was necessary. In some cases the printed sources did offer such literal translations. More often than not, however, it was necessary to impose upon the good will and time

National Park Service, Statue of Liberty National Monument

of a great many people who were fluent in one or another for the forty-odd languages which comprise the songs in this book. Without the generous assistance of these contributors and translators, this work could never have seen the light of day.

Once the selection of songs was made, the work of creating singable English translations and piano arrangements began. As far as the piano arrangements are concerned, they have been kept relatively uncomplicated, stylistically in keeping with the character of their national musical tradition and (attention, guitarists!) in user-friendly keys.

Translating raw text into graceful, singable English presented the multiple problems of meter, rhyme, and faithfulness to the meaning and spirit of the original — without coming up with something so stilted and awkward as to render it, finally, unsingable. To that end I have endeavored to retain the original rhyme scheme without getting trapped by it. Some songs virtually wrote themselves in one draft — others required polishing and smoothing.

Now that the cobwebs have been swept away and the songs hopefully have been made accessible to a broader audience, there remains the final question: What to do with them and how to do it?

If you have any familiarity with any of the original languages, by all means sing them that way first. Savor the umlauts, the tildes, the cedillas, the vowels, and the accents that the English language never knew. The original language is presented first on each page precisely to establish the fact that it is the **original** language.

Then move on to the English — perhaps alternating verses if you can, as you sing your way through the verses. More like a gumbo than a melting pot.

Sing the songs to your children, to your parents, to your friends. Sing them to and with people of different nationalities and national extractions. Tell them: "This is the way it was. This is what they thought about coming to America. Some loved it. Some were disappointed. Listen. . . ."

Up to this point we have spoken of the songs largely in the past tense, as historical artifacts of bygone eras. In fact, this is not the entire picture. People are still coming to these shores from all over the world with their hopes and dreams and songs. There is a contemporary immigrant song literature that is still being written. In the songs of these recent arrivals — Cuban, Russian–Jewish, Cambodian, and Philippine, for example — one finds the same human emotions of longing, relief, joy, and sadness as had been expressed in the songs of all those who came before.

Poets have spoken of America's song and tried to define it.

Walt Whitman said, "I hear America singing." Could he ever have imagined the multiplicity of tongues in which America's song would come to be sung?

Carl Sandburg had a vision of "the hallelujah chorus, forever shifting its star soloist."

John Latouche, in his *Ballad For Americans*, wrote, "Our country's strong, our country's young, and her greatest songs are still unsung."

Woody Guthrie said it his way: "This land is your land, this land is my land."

Each of these poets was trying to grasp and express something essential, something vital in the continuing saga of America. Each succeeded in his own way.

Here now we have a kaleidoscopic, multiphonic, polylinguistic view of that same never-ending ballad — of, by, and for Americans.

✴ ✴ ✴ ✴ ✴ ✴ ✴ ✴ ✴ ✴ ✴

The songs in this collection have been presented by country of origin of the singer, although most were, in fact, composed by immigrants in America. It is usually, but not necessarily always, apparent on which side of the ocean the songs originated.

If you know any other songs that you feel should have been included in this collection — particularly from countries not represented here — please send them to me (with an English translation and some background information and pictures, if possible). When we have gathered enough new material, we will present it in a revised and expanded edition.

Jerry Silverman

Photo by David Ranz

Acknowledgments

This book simply would have not been possible without the help of individuals and institutions that contributed songs, translations, and photographs. The fact that I have never met most of the contributors makes the completion of this task all the more amazing. We communicated by telephone and mail; they dug into their personal recollections and institutional archives, and *Immigrant Songbook* is the result. In this way they have helped preserve something of their (and our) cultural heritage. We all owe them a debt of gratitude.

Armenia
George Mgrdichian
Father Karenkin Kasparian

Bulgaria
Dr. Matei Roussan
Ivan Tchanakov,
  Bulgarian Mission to the United Nations

Cambodia
Sam-Ang Sam, University of Washington

Canada
Bernard Ouimet

China
Charlie Chin,
  New York Chinatown Historical Project

Croatia
Daniel Kukich

Cuba
Yolanda del Castillo Cobelo

Czechia
Miroslav Lebeda
Henrietta Grmela Schindler
Martha Viktorin
Anton Smundt
Lilian Chorvat, Czechoslovak Heritage Museum,
  Berwyn, Illinois
Judita M. Prelog, Vice President,
  Slavic Heritage Council of America, New York

Denmark
Robert Wright
Ellen Pittman, Press and Information Department,
  Royal Danish Embassy

Egypt and **Syria**
Dr. Kadri El Araby
Iman K. El Araby

Finland
Lorraine Uitto Richards, Archivist, Suomi College,
  Hancock, Michigan
Molla Kaaria

France
Bibliothèque Nationale, Paris, France

Germany
Lutz Rath
Hans Schaper
Geoffrey and Dorothy Ettlinger
Dr. Otto Holzappel and Uwe Schlottermüller,
  Deutsches Volkslied Archiv, Freiburg, Germany*
Elisabeth Pyroth, Deutsches Haus, New York City

Greece
Michael Kaloyanides
Dino Pappas
Dr. Stavros Sarantakis

Haiti
Joaeuse Macena

Holland
Fried de Metz Herman
H. J. Brinks, Curator, Historical Collections,
  and Zw. C. Janssens, Archivist, Calvin College,
  Grand Rapids, Michigan
Jan Hesseling, Consulate General of the Netherlands
Nicholas Fobe

Hungary
Kalman Magyar
Tom Molnar

Italy
Martha Hodges, Labor-Management Documenta-
  tion Center, Cornell University, Ithaca, New York
Catherine Kosman
Maria del Giudice, Center For Migration Studies,
  Staten Island, New York
Jimmy and Theresa Lionelli
Pino Garreri

---

*The following songs appear in this collection courtesy of Das Deutches Volkslied Archiv (The German Folk Song Archives): "Auf Der Cimbria," "Heil Dir, Columbus," "Lied Vom Mississippi," "Nun Ist Die Scheidestunde," "Nun Ist Die Scheidestunde Da," "Hier Können Wir Nicht Bleiben," "Havre Ist Ein Schönes Städtchen," and "Bald Ist Die Zeit."

Lithuania
Genevieve Meiliunas,
  Lithuanian Alliance of America

Macedonia
George Tomov

Mexico
Halina Rubinstein

Norway
Christina Wright

Philippines
Belen Manuel

Portugal
Eugénio M. Rodrigues

Rumania
Lillian Marcus

Russia
Anatoly Mogilevsky

Scotland
Philip D. Smith

Serbia
Andrea Ader
Milan Opacich

Slovakia
Zdenka Fischmann

Slovenia
Fr. Vendelian Spendov
Jerry W. Koprivsek

Spain
Pedro B. Calero, Assistant Director,
  Casa de España, New York City
Amancio Prado, Madrid, Spain
Nick Spitzer
Sam Armistead

Sweden
Anne-Charlotte Harvey, University of San Diego
Anna Lisa Gotschlich

Switzerland
Professor Leo Schelbert, University of Illinois,
  Chicago, Illinois
Lukas Gloor, Cultural Attaché, Consulate General
  of Switzerland, New York City

Turkey
Dino Pappas
Michael Kaloyanides
Selçuk Yorgancioglu
Murat Atalay, Assistant Educational Attaché,
  Turkish Consulate General
Egemin Bagis, Executive Director,
  Federation of Turkish American Societies, Inc.

Ukraine
Ihor Sonnevitsky
Dr. Oleh Sochan

A special word of thanks must go here to Mr. Barry Moreno of the Ellis Island Library for his help in selecting the rare and beautiful photographs that are such an integral part of this book.

Immigration Museum, Ellis Island   *Brian Feeney, National Park Service*

Armenia

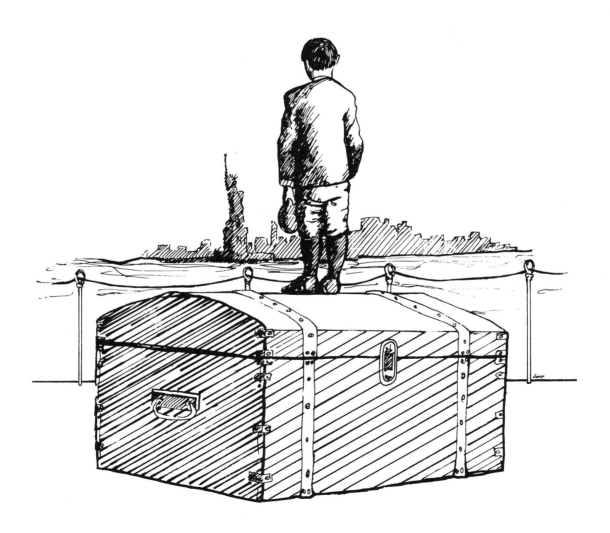

Hay Nazanem Yarer
Hey, My Dear Friends

In the 1870s there were only about 70 Armenians in America. They lived mostly in New York and Massachusetts, engaging in commerce and in the wire mills of Worcester, Massachusetts. In the next decade, word spread among newly arriving Armenian immigrants that the climate around Fresno, California, would be perfect for growing enormous fruits and vegetables. This song was recorded for the Library of Congress by Reuben J. Baboyan in Fresno in 1939.

Armenia

Hay ___ na-zan-em yar-er, Bos-ton-i Hay agh-chig-ner, djan ___
Hey, ___ my dear ___ friends. ___ Ar-men-ian girls of Bos-ton, Oh, ___

___ na-zan-em yar-er. Bos-ton-i Hay agh-chig-ner, hay ___
___ my dear ___ friends. ___ Ar-men-ian girls of Bos-ton, hey ___

___ na-zan-em yar-er, Dok-tor pas-da-pan gou-zen, hay ___ na-zan-em yar-er, Dok-
___ my dear friends, ___ Want doc-tors and law-yers, hey, ___ my dear ___ friends. ___ Want

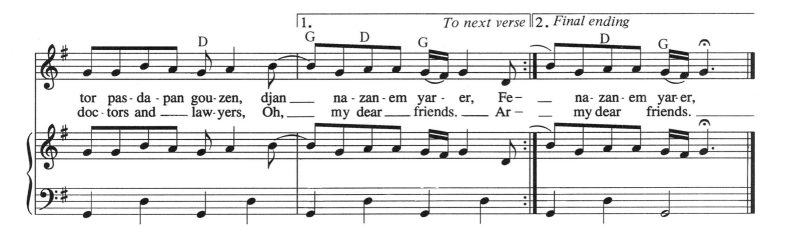

To next verse | 2. Final ending

tor pas- da- pan gou- zen, djan ___ na- zan- em yar- er, Fe— ___ na- zan- em yar- er,
doc- tors and ___ law- yers, Oh, ___ my dear ___ friends. ___ Ar— ___ my dear ___ friends.

Feresnoyi aghchigner, hay nazanem yarer,
Feresnoyi aghchigner, djan nazanem yarer,
Hariur eykernots gouzen, hay nazanem yarer,
Hariur eykernots gouzen, djan nazanem yarer.

New Yorki Hay aghchigner, hay nazanem yarer,
New Yorki Hay aghchigner, hay nazanem yarer,
Khali dzakhoghner gouzen, djan nazanem yarer,
Khali dzakhoghner gouzen, hay nazanem yarer.

Detroiti Hay aghchigner, hay nazanem yarer,
Detroiti Hay aghchigner, hay nazanem yarer,
Fordin kordzavor gouzen, hay nazanem yarer,
Fordin kordzavor gouzen, djan nazanem yarer.

Armenian girls of Fresno, hey my dear friends,
Armenian girls of Fresno, oh my dear friends,
Want one hundred acres, hey my dear friends,
Want one hundred acres, oh my dear friends.

Armenian girls of New York, hey my dear friends,
Armenian girls of New York, hey my dear friends,
Want rug dealers, oh my dear friends,
Want rug dealers, hey my dear friends.

Armenian girls of Detroit, hey my dear friends,
Armenian girls of Detroit, hey my dear friends,
Want Ford workers, hey my dear friends,
Want Ford workers, oh my dear friends.

Museum of the City of New York

Bantookhd Ar Groong
The Migrant To The Crane

In 1894 and 1895, over 300,000 Armenians living in Turkey were massacred by the Turks. A mass exodus of Armenians began, and by 1914 there were about 100,000 Armenians living in America. With the outbreak of World War I, the Turks looked upon the Armenians as a potentially dangerous foreign element within their borders. With the utmost barbarity they attempted to deport the entire Armenian population of about 1,750,000 to Syria and Mesopotamia. An estimated 600,000 Armenians died or were massacred en route in 1915. It was with these atrocities freshly in mind that the Armenian Educational Foundation published a collection of songs of despair and hope, including this one, in New York City in 1919.

Armenia

By Nahabed Kouchag

Groong, oos - di____ goo - kas,____ dza - ra em tzai - nit,____
Crane, where are _____ you from? Your voice en-slaves me.____

__ Gu - roong, mer__ash-khar hen khap - rig_ mi choo __ nis? Mi va -
__ O Crane, do_ you_ have_ word from our_ dear coun - try? Hast-en

zer ye - ra - mit,_____ shoo-dov gah has - nis,_____ Gu-
not, You will soon _____ catch_ up with your flock, O

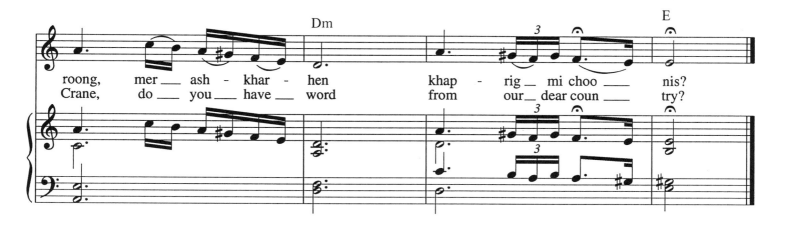

roong, mer ash - khar - hen khap - rig mi choo nis?
Crane, do you have word from our dear coun try?

Togher em'v yeger im mlkers oo aykis.
Kani vor akh ganem goo kaghvi hokis.
Groong, bah mi gatsir, tsynigt i hokis,
Groong, mer ashkharhen khaprig mi choonis?

Krer em mech tghtis teh hohs mnatsi
Orig mi orants zacherus chpatsi.
Sirelik, tsezanits garod mnatsi.
Groong, mer ashkharhen khaprig mi choonis?

Ashoon eh modetser, knaloo es tebdir,
Yeram es joghver hazarner oo pure,
Ents badaskhan chdvir, yelar knatsir,
Groong, mer ahkharhen kna herratsir.

I have left my vineyards and all my wealth.
I've gone so far away — my soul aches as I sigh.
O dear crane, stay a while — let your voice touch my soul.
O crane, do you have any word from our dear country?

In my letters I wrote that while I am here,
Not one single day of joy and happiness I know.
My dear ones, I yearn for you all.
O crane, do you have any word from our dear country?

Autumn now is near — it's time you were gone
With all the other cranes — your flock does fill the sky.
You have left, you are gone — you do not answer me,
O crane, fly away now from our dear country.

Armenian Refugees　　　　　　　　　*American Red Cross (Photo by Capt. G. P. Floyd)*

Bulgaria

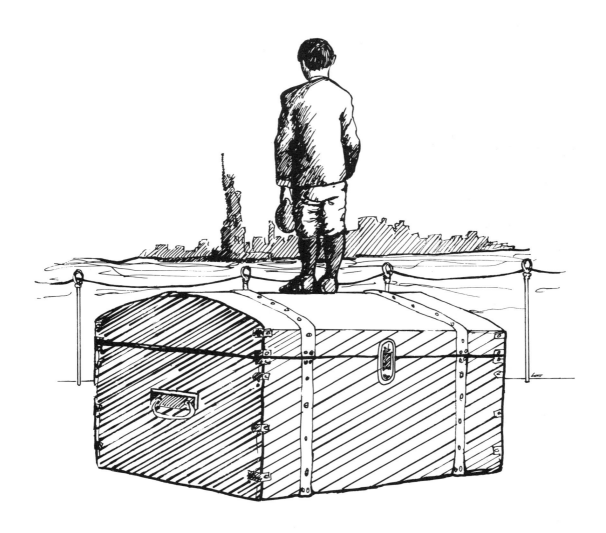

Ya Kazhi Mi, Oblache Le Byalo
Tell Me, White Cloud

On Third and Fourth Street live the Bulgars. There were a good many more than there are today, but, as many of them came here without their families, they were compelled to return home after the outbreak of the war. And even those who remained here for a little while afterward dispersed to other districts, or perhaps other cities. . . . (*Around The World In New York* by Konrad Berkovici, 1924)

Bulgaria

Ya ka - zhi mi, o ___ bla-che le bya - lo, Ot - gde i - desh,
Tell me, white cloud, tell ___ me please, I ask you, Where you come from,

gde ___ ci mi le - tya - lo? Ne vi - dya li ba - shchi-ni mi
say ___ where have you been to? Have you seen the house ___ of my dear

dvo - ri, I ne chu li mai - ka da go - vo - ri
fa - ther, Have you heard the voice ___ of my dear moth - er?

"Shcho li pravi moito chedo milo,
S chuzhdi khora chuzhdi khlyab delilo!"
Ti kazhi i, oblache le byalo,
Che si mene zhiv i zdrav vidyalo.

I kazhi i ot men mnogo zdrave,
Mnogo mina, munichko ostana,
Nablizhava v selo da se vurna,
Da se vurna, maika da pregurna.

"O, my young son, is he safe from dangers,
Is he sharing strangers' bread with strangers?"
Tell her, white cloud, tell her when you see her
That you've seen me — from all worry free her.

Bring her my love, bring her my devotion.
Years have passed by since I crossed the ocean.
I'll be home soon — once again I'll face her,
See my mother — once again embrace her.

"The Story of Bread"

Angel Vassilev

21

Izgnanik
The Exile

And over a former saloon on Forsythe Street . . . the Bulgars, who at home sell that cooling drink brewed from bran and millet, are doing the same thing here, selling *braga* to those who still have a taste for it after many years away from home. (*Around The World In New York* by Konrad Berkovici, 1924)

Bulgaria

By Mikhail Todorov

Ti - kho po - lukh - va ve - cher - nik pro - khla - den,
Cool eve - ning breeze ris - ing o - ver the o - cean foam,

Ga - li vul - ni - te v bez - kpai - na - ta shir.
Rip - ples the waves of the broad end - less sea.

Ei ta - mo lod - ka s put - nik ne - zna - en,
Far off a boat sails bear - ing an un - known

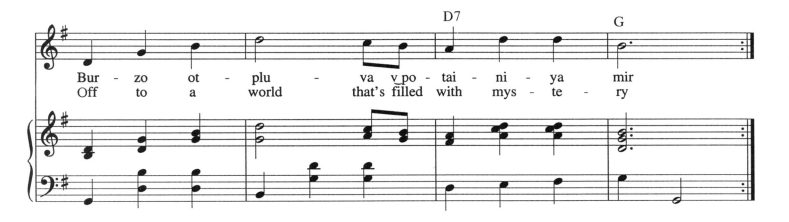

| Bur - | zo | ot - | plu | - va | v po | - tai | - ni | - ya | mir |
| Off | to | a | world | that's filled | with | mys | - te | - r | ry |

Putniko stranen, s neznaina sudbina,
Gde ti dogonvash nesbudna mechta?
Shche li se vurnesh v svoita rodina
Ili shche naidesh otnovo skrubta?

"Tam mozh da svursha v zabvene — ne znaya,
Bez topli sulzi na maika edna,
Mozhe bi pesni — divna omaya —
Veshchayat putya kum tazi strana."

Tell me, o stranger, with your strange destiny,
Where are you chasing your unfulfilled dream?
And your dear homeland, will you again see?
You'll find but sorrow, and your tears will stream.

"Lost and forgotten, I could meet my end there,
Without my mother a-shedding a tear.
Maybe a sweet song, pleasures and no cares,
At journey's end to me will appear."

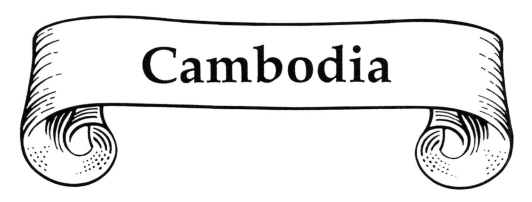

Cambodia

In the river, there is the crocodile.
On the river bank, there is the tiger.
If you go to the forest, there are the thorns.
If you go to the market, there is the policeman.

(Cambodian proverb)

During the second half of the 20th century, the political situation in Cambodia became chaotic. King Norodom Sihanouk came to the throne in 1941, proclaimed Cambodia's independence in 1953, and ruled the country until March 18, 1970, when he was overthrown by Marshal Lon Nol. In 1975 the genocidal Khmer Rouge took power and virtually destroyed Cambodian lives, health, mentality, morality, education, physical properties, culture, and civilization. Then on January 7, 1979, the current government, which is headed by Heng Samrin, chased away the evil Khmer Rouge with the help of the Vietnamese and has since controlled Cambodia.

The United States has received far more refugees from Cambodia for permanent resettlement than any other country in the world. Approximately one quarter million Cambodian refugees have come to the United States with a strong belief that America is the land of opportunity, freedom, and justice. With common language, food, custom, tradition, and religious belief, the Cambodians stay together as a community, creating "Cambodia Towns," the largest being in Long Beach, California, and Lowell, Massachusetts. With little hope of returning home, new songs and poems have been written, conveying different themes — political, revolutionary, patriotic, and nostalgic — as exemplified by the following two songs. (Sam-Ang Sam, University of Washington)

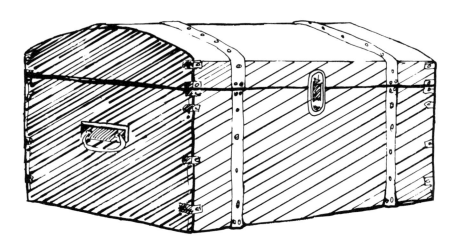

Sranah Srokk Kamnoeut
Nostalgia

Cambodia

By Sam-Ang Sam

Ro-limm takk takk ___ toeuk dakk cheung phnum. ___
The rain drips down ___ a moun - tain pool. ___

Ro-limm takk takk ___ toeuk dakk cheung phnum. ___
The rain drips down ___ a moun - tain pool. ___

A - saur cheat khnhomm sat - trauv ___ chhlean ___
Pi - ty my land, the en - e - mies in —

pean vade, Sat - trauv ___ chhlean ___ pean.
vade, The en - e - mies in - vade. ___

Sranah dey sre
Chamkar phoum than. (2)
Thngai na noeung ban
Vill chaul lumneou?
Vill chaul lumneou?

Khlah kapp russey
Khlah luoh roneap, (2)
Tumraom srokk riep,
Semm sang phteah neou,
Semm sang phteah neou.

Gone lands, rice fields,
Farms, villages. (2)
When shall I go
Back to my land?
Back to my land?

Some cut bamboo
And make long strips, (2)
They wait for peace
To build the house,
To build the house.

Ruoh neou srokk ke
Pi thngai nih teou (2)
Phde phdaim kaun chao.
Oy chaim roeung het,
Oy chaim roeung het.

Ruoh neou sokk san
Pi thngai nih teou. (2)
Bangkoeut kaun chao
Ta phao sasna
Ta phao sasna.

In a strange land
From this day on. (2)
O, children, please
Remember all,
Remember all.

Living in peace
From this day on. (2)
Children are born,
Our people saved,
Our people saved.

Lolork sar euy
Bah puoy tradet. (2)
Rork si tam het,
Tumraom srokk riep,
Tumraom srokk riep.

The snow-white dove
High in the sky, (2)
Feeds where it can,
And waits for peace,
And waits for peace.

U.S. Office of War Information

Kampuchea Aphaop
Poor Cambodia

Cambodia

By Sam-Ang Sam

minn doeung thngai na   minn doeung thngai na   bar chaul _ srokk   vinh. _____

We know not when,   we know not when   we'll see you a - gain. _____

Eylauv akphaop
Reah Khmer soeung slapp
Phott pouch ah nheat
Puok Khmer lngung khlao
Chett khmao chol msiet
Khamm samlapp cheat
Ker pi daun ta. *Chorus*

Neak neou srokk ay
Chett sen khvall khvay
Naom knea thveu kar
Chih rutyun thmey
Prakk chay hoeu ha
Sabbay ahchar
Rouch thveu avey tiet? *Chorus*

Now poor Khmer
People almost die,
Their roots are gone.
Those stupid Khmer,
Black-hearted men
Kill our folk,
Our legacy. *Chorus*

Those who live here
Have troubled hearts.
And they all work,
They drive new cars,
Spend lots of cash.
They're so happy —
And then what next? *Chorus*

3 CAMBODIAN FACTIONS SIGN A U.N.-ENFORCED PEACE PACT; KHMER ROUGE SHARES RULE

The New York Times

Canada

Le Sergent
The Sergeant

During the American Revolutionary War, some young French–Canadian men found their way into the ranks of Washington's Continental Army. They welcomed the opportunity to settle a few old scores against their traditional enemy, England.

Canada

"Mon pa-pa, si vous me bat-tez, oui j'i-rai m'en-ga-ger À
"My pa-pa, if you do beat me, I will join the ar-my. I'm

bord d'un Bos-ton-nais, bat-tre con-tre l'An-glais!" À Bos-ton
off to Bos-ton town, to fight the Eng-lish crown!" At Bos-ton

il s'en est al-lé: "How ma-ny men fi-red a-way? Vou-lez vous
he was heard to say: "How ma-ny men fi-red a-way? May I sign

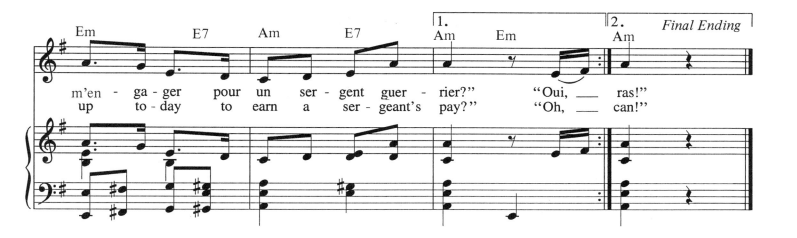

"Oui, nous t'engagerons,
Si tu veux fair' le bon garçon.
Nous irons t'y mener
A la têt' de l'armée!"
Le sabre à son coté,
Et le pistolet à la main,
François marchait devant,
Comme un vaillant sergent.

Dès la première volée,
Les mâchoir's lui ont fêlées.
François tomba en bas,
On s'écria, "Houra!"
Mais il s'est relevé,
How many men fired away?
Il ne faut pas s'arrêter
Pour un sergent blessé."

François se lamenta
A son cher et bon papa,
Qu'il avait été blessé
Par un coup d'grenadier.
"Je n'té l'avais-t-y pas bien dit
Qu'tu périras par le fusil!
A présent t'y voilà,
Ramass'-toi comm' tu pourras!"

"Oh yes, we'll let you join the fight,
If you do what is right.
We'll put you in the van,
To fight the best you can."
So with a sharp saber so grand,
And with a pistol in his hand,
François did what he could —
Just as a sergeant should.

And so he marched away to war.
The first shot broke his jaw.
François fell to the ground,
They cried "hooray' all 'round.
But then he rose from where he lay,
"How many men fired away?
Don't slow the charge a bit,
Although your sergeant's hit."

"Oh my dear and my good papa,"
Lamented poor François,
"I'm wounded, did you hear,
By a British grenadier?"
"It has turned out just like I said,
Think yourself lucky you're not dead.
Just bear it like a man,
And do the best you can."

33

Un Canadien Errant
A Wandering Canadian

An anti-English republican rebellion broke out in Toronto in 1837. The stated purpose of the rebels was: "Never to rest 'til all tyrants of Britain cease to have any domain or footing whatever in North America." The rebellion was soon crushed and its leaders hanged. Many defeated rebels fled to the United States, where they lived in unhappy exile until a general amnesty was declared in 1849.

Canada

Words by M. A. Gérin-Lajoie

Un Ca - na - dien er - rant, ban - ni de ses fo - yers,
A wan - d'ring Ca - na - dian, ban - ished from his dear home,

Par - cou - rait en pleu - rant des pa - ys é - tran - gers.
Weep - ing, was forced to leave, and for - eign lands to roam.

Par - cou - rait en pleu - rant des pa - ys é - tran - gers.
Weep - ing, was forced to leave, and for - eign lands to roam.

Un jour, triste et pensif,
Assis au bord des flots, (2)
Au courant fugitif
Il adressa ces mots: (2)

"Si tu vois mon pays,
Mon pays malheureux, (2)
Va, dis à mes amis,
Que je me souviens d'eux. (2)

"O jours si pleins d'appas,
Vous êtes disparus,
Et ma patrie, hélas!
Je ne la verrai plus. (2)

"Non, mais en expirant,
O mon cher Canada, (2)
Mon regard languissant
Vers toi se portera." (2)

Down by a stream he sat,
Sadly he bowed his head, (2)
And as the current flowed,
To it these words he said: (2)

"If my unhappy land
Some day you chance to see, (2)
Tell all my long-lost friends,
That they are dear to me. (2)

"Oh, days so full of joy,
Lost on the distant shore, (2)
And my country, alas,
I'll see you nevermore. (2)

"But as I pass away,
Oh, Canada, so dear, (2)
My eyes turn toward you,
And shed a final tear." (2)

Library of Congress

La Vie De Chercheur D'Or En Californie
The Life Of A California Gold-Seeker

Canada

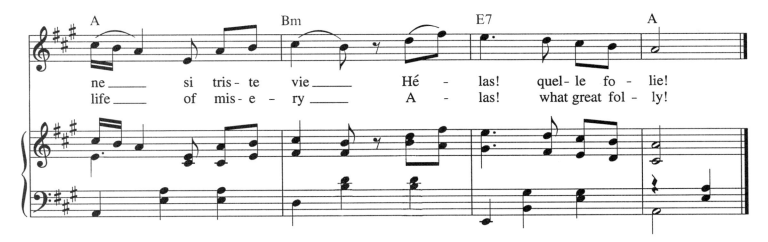

ne ____ si tris- te vie ____ Hé - las! quel- le fo - lie!
life ____ of mis- e - ry ____ A - las! what great fol - ly!

Quand nous somm's sur ces montagnes
À travailler sans s'y lasser,
Regardant vers nos campagnes,
Souvent on fait que pleurer.

Second chorus:
I faut-il donc pour un peu d'or
Subir un si malheureux sort!
Pour une si courte vie,
Hélas! quelle folie!

Les fêtes et les dimanches,
On ne fait que travailler.
Le soir, ils nous mett'nt dehors;
Sur le champ, il faut s'coucher. *First chorus*

Quand nous somm's dans ces cabines,
Nous pensons à notre maison;
Et souvent on se chagrine
De se voir parmi ces nations. *First chorus*

Quand l'heur' d'la grand messe arrive,
Dans les *saloons* nous les voyons
Au jeu de cartes, à boire, à rire
Comm' du mond' sans religion. *First chorus*

When we are on those high mountains,
Working with no chance to sleep,
Looking back towards our country,
Often we must stop and weep.

Second chorus:
And must we, then, because of gold,
Suffer a fate that can't be told?
For a life of misery —
Alas! What a great pity.

Holidays and every Sunday
We just work without respite.
After work we have no shelter,
So outdoors we pass the night. *First chorus*

When we are in those poor shanties,
To our homes our thoughts do race.
Often we do feel great sorrow
To be in this foreign place. *First chorus*

When the time for mass arrives,
We see them in the saloons,
Playing cards and drinking, laughing;
No religion — just buffoons. *First chorus*

Library of Congress

Les Chantiers Aux États-Unis
The Lumber Camps In The United States

Hélène Noël was born in the town of Petite-Lamèque in New Brunswick in 1900. She sang this song about the young men of her village who came down across the border looking for work. From the wealth of detail describing the life of an itinerant lumberman, we may infer that Mme. Noël herself may have been one of those *bien-aimées* mentioned in the last verse.

Canada

Nous somm's par - tis,_____ ces jeu - nes vo - ya - geurs, Nous somm's par-
We're on our way,_____ these youth- ful vo - ya - gers, The U. S.

tis pour les É - tats___ U - nis,_____ Sans dire a - dieu_____ à
A. will be our jour - ney's end. _____ We did - n't ev - en

nos pères, à nos mères, Sans dire a - dieu aux pa - rents, aux a-
say a fond fare - well to fa - thers, moth - ers, rel - a - tives and

Les chars nous mèn'nt quarant'-cinq milles à heure,
Quarant'-cinq mill's sans jamais modérer.
Pendant vingt heur's, nous marchons sans relâche
Pour arriver à notre destinée.
En arrivant à cett' ville étrangère,
Tout aussitôt nous nous somm's t-engagés
À un monsieur d'au nom d'René Springer,
Pour les chantiers où nous devons bûcher.

En arrivant à cett' triste cabane,
En arrivant à ce triste chantier,
Thomas Corbett, le *boss,* souffl' la *Wingagne*
Et il nous donn' des haches à amancher
En nous disant: "Après cet ouvrag' fait-e,
Vous irez dans ces ch'mins-là travailler."
Là, il s'en va trouver ses autres hommes
Sans nous offrir un' bouchée r-à manger.

Jour après jour, nous allions t-à l'ouvrage,
À tous les jours sans jamais nous lasser.
Et après quelque temps de dur ouvrage
Nous commencions à être fatigués.
Voilà bientôt les jours de fêt' qu'arrivent,
Il faut passer ces beaux jours au chantier.
Grand Dieu! qu' c'est trist' quand on pense à l'église.
À nos parents qui y vont pour prier.

Par un beau jour un de notre brav' gang
Tomba malade, il lui faut s'en aller.
Chacun de nous on lui donne un message
Et tous chagrins de se voir séparés:
"F'ras des respects à ceux de ma famille,
Tu iras voir ma très chèr' bien-aimée,
Tu lui diras après cet dur hiver-e
Que j'espèr que je la reverrai."

Bientôt hélas! finira le *skidage,*
Il nous faudra encor' recommencer.
Nous somm's pas las-se de notre esclavage,
Il nous faudra que nous chargions les *sleighs.*
Il nous faudra remuer le *cant-hook-e*
Lever bien fort sur ces pesants billots;
Il nous faudra travailler dans la neige
Et dans la pluie comm' quand qu'il fera beau.

Bientôt hélas! finira le mois d'mars
Et le printemps, bientôt z-il fera beau.
Le beau soleil consommera la neige
Et nous aurons fini nos durs travaux.
Nous retourn'rons au villag' de Lamèque
Voir nos parents, aussi nos bien-aimées.
Nous retourn'rons à notre beau village
Et tous ensembl', nous passerons l'été.

The cars drove us forty-five miles an hour,
Forty-five miles — and never slowing down.
For twenty hours we drove without relief,
'Til we arrived at our lumber town.
On getting to this city far away,
We were engaged as soon as we did stop.
'Twas by a man, by name, René Springer,
Straight to the camps where we would have to chop.

When we arrived at this mournful work camp,
When we arrived at the broken-down shacks,
Thomas Corbett, the boss, hummed a refrain,
And gave us handles to put on our axe.
And then he said, "After this job is done,
You'll work the roads until the job's complete."
Then he took off to find his other men,
Without proposing us a bite to eat.

Day after day we went to do our work,
And every day we barely did perspire.
After a while, though, it became so hard,
That we began, despite ourselves, to tire.
And when the holidays, they did at last arrive,
We worked the job like any other day.
My God! It's sad when one thinks of the church,
And of our parents, who go there to pray.

And then one day a fellow in our gang
Fell ill, and so he had to go away.
Each one of us, we gave him a message,
And we were sad to see him leave that day.
"Give my respects to all my family,
And go and see my own sweetheart so dear.
And tell her after this hard winter's work,
That I'll see her again — and not to fear."

But soon, alas, the skidding will be done.
We'll have to go back up along the road.
Our slavery, it never seems to end,
For then the lumber sleighs we'll have to load.
The cant-hooks then we'll have to move with force,
Onto the sawing blocks to hoist the logs.
We'll have to work in snow and in the rain.
The weather doesn't matter — we just work like dogs.

But soon, alas, the month of March will end,
And in the springtime the weather will turn fine.
The warming sun will melt away the snow,
And we will finish working all the time.
We'll see again the village of Lamèque,
See our parents and also our girlfriends.
We will return to our village homes,
And we will be together once again.

Library of Congress

Weaver Aux États-Unis
Weaving In The United States

This song is known and sung in Ontario, Quebec, and New Brunswick, as well as among Americans of French–Canadian descent in New England. "Weaver," pronounced *à la française,* is of course an English word. The French equivalent is *tisser*.

Canada

Quand j'ai par - ti du Ca - na - da, C'é - tait pour mon - ter aux É - tats, Aus - si -
From Ca - na - da I went a - way, To tra - vel to the U. S. A. Just ar -

tôt qu'nous fûm's ar - ri - vés, L'on a com - men - cé à *wea* - ver, Et en a -
rived, now would you be - lieve, We start - ed, right a - way to weave. So, here we

vant nous autr's, nos gens! Et en a - vant, nous au - tres.
go, friends one and all! So, here we go, my bud - dies.

42

Et aussitôt qu'nous fum's arrivés,	Just arrived, now would you believe,
L'on a commencé à *weaver*.	We started right away to weave.
Mais on a joué d'la rissonnette	It wasn't easy — what a battle,
Pour l'enfiler c'saudit' navette! *Chorus*	To thread that blasted weaving shuttle! *Chorus*
Mais on a joué d'la rissonnette	It wasn't easy — what a battle,
Pour l'enfiler c'saudit navette!	To thread that blasted weaving shuttle.
Le lundi, l'mardi se passe,	Monday, Tuesday came across,
Et on voit de second *boss*. *Chorus*	And we saw the second boss. *Chorus*
Le lundi, mardi se passe,	Monday, Tuesday came across,
Et on voit de second *boss*.	And we saw the second boss.
Mais à la fin de la semaine,	When the first week came and went,
On r'tir' pas une maudite cenne! *Chorus*	We didn't have a bloody cent! *Chorus*
Mais à la fin de la semaine,	When the first week came and went,
On r'tir' pas une maudite cenne!	We didn't have a bloody cent.
Mais on arrive au p'tit logis	We went to the landlady,
Pour payer tout' notr' *groc'rie*. *Chorus*	To pay up our "grocery." *Chorus*
Mais on arrive au p'tit logis,	We went to the landlady,
Ah! la bonn' femm' veut mettr' la chicane:	But then that woman said to me,
"Va t'assir, viens pas m'bâdrer!	"Come sit down and don't go away!
Tu sais bien qu'j'ai pas 'té payé!" *Chorus*	You know that you just have to pay!" *Chorus*
"Va t'assir, viens pas m'bâdrer!	"Come sit down and don't go away!
Tu sais bien qu'j'ai pas 'té payé!"	You know that you just have to pay!"
Mais on arriv', les Canadiens.	But here they come, the Canadians.
Comment ça va, les Américains? *Chorus*	And how's it going, Americans? *Chorus*
Mais on arriv', les Canadiens,	But here they come, the Canadians,
Comment ça va, les Américains?	And how's it going, Americans?
A Woonsocket, ç'a bien été,	At Woonsocket it wasn't bad,
Mais on a sacrement *weavé!* *Chorus*	But boy, did we all weave like mad! *Chorus*

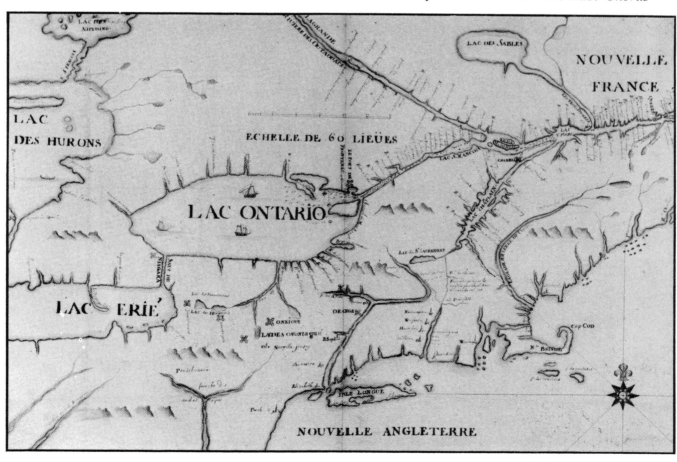

J'Aime Mieux Les États Que L'Alberta
I Like The States Better Than Alberta

Mathilda Gauthier, wife of Joseph Plamondon, wrote this song sometime between 1907 and 1910. She was a native of Lake Leelanau, Michigan, and it was there she met her husband. They were requested by Catholic missionaries to come to Alberta and establish a French-speaking parish.

Canada

Pour moi j'aim' mieux les É- tats qu'l'Al-ber- ta, parc' qu'on ré – colt' plus de fruits par i-
I'd rath – er live in the States than Al- ber- ta, For you har - vest more fruit on this

ci, Mais il faut bien suivr' son ma – ri. Pour moi, j'aim'
land, But I must fol – low my hus – band. I'd rath – er

2. bien suivr' son ma – ri. *Chorus* Je vas re – tour – ner
fol – low my hus – band. To Ca – na – da

Il faut laisser notre fill' par ici	We have to leave our daughter here,
Car son mari aime trop son pays.	Because her husband holds his land so dear.
Parlez-lui pas du Canada.	Don't speak to him of Canada.
Il faut laisser notre fill' par ici	We have to leave our daughter here,
Car son mari aime trop son pays,	Because her husband holds his land so dear.
Et elle aussi suit son mari. *Chorus*	She follows her man, just like me. *Chorus*

J'ai rien à dir' contre mon mari	There's nothing I'll say against my husband,
Car quand je m'ennuie, il m'emmène par ici,	For when I'm bored he takes me to this land.
Mais c'est sa bours' qui en pâtit.	But it's his purse that suffers so.
J'ai rien à dir' contre mon mari	There's nothing I'll say against my husband,
Car quand je m'ennuie, il m'emmène par ici,	For when I'm bored he takes me to this land.
Je m'en retourne avec lui. *Chorus*	It's back with him that I must go. *Chorus*

45

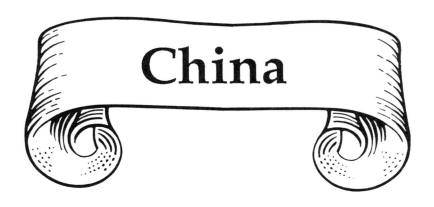

China

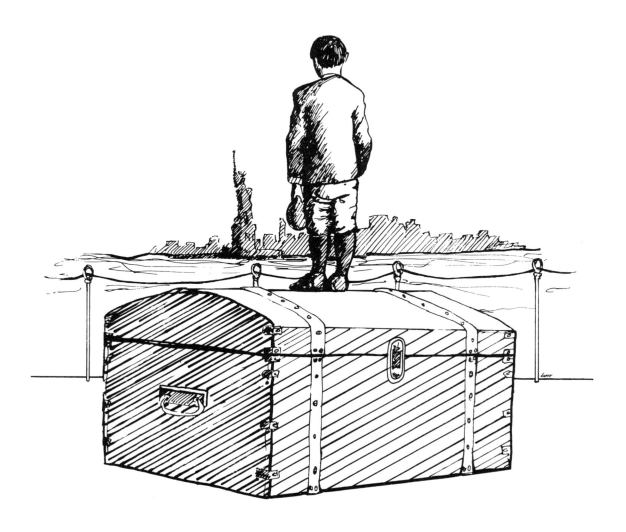

Dig For The Gold

Oh, workmen dear, and did you hear the news that's goin' 'round?
Another China steamer has been landed in the town.
Today I read the paper and it grieved my heart full sore,
To see upon the title page, oh, just "Twelve Hundred More."

Oh, California's coming down as you can plainly see;
They are hiring all the Chinamen and discharging you and me.
But strife will be in every town throughout the Pacific shore,
And the cry of young and old shall be, "Oh damn Twelve Hundred More!"

(Excerpt from an 1870s broadside, *Society of California Pioneers*)

    In 1852, there were an estimated 22,000 Chinese in San Francisco. Those who had hoped to strike it rich working the gold fields found themselves up against an impenetrable system of discrimination. They were shunted to the poorest, worked-out diggings and if, by chance, a Chinese miner actually struck gold, his claim would be invalidated and jumped by some American prospector.

China
                                                    By Charlie Chin

I was on—ly a boy in old Can-ton town, When I first heard the sto—ries that were go—ing a—round. Un-cle made his for—tune, and he wore a gold ring; If you

asked him a - bout it, he glad - ly would sing.

Chorus
Dig for the gold, Dig for the gold, I'll be a
rich man in Chi - na be - fore I grow old

Well, I boarded a ship, it was all made of wood.
The bedding was lousy and the food was no good.
Six companies met us on Frisco's long pier —
Of three hundred started, only two hundred here. *Chorus*

Well, I walked to the hills my fortune to find,
Of hardship and want, well, I paid it no mind.
But the jumpers were waiting, and they wished us all dead.
They took all our claims and put lumps on our head. *Chorus*

Well, I headed for Hangtown, the biggest of camps,
There was gambling and murder by the light of the lamps.
Of the money I had, it was gone in a wink,
I spent it on women and foul whisky drink. *Chorus*

Brandy Gulch was my next stop, but who should I meet,
But a crazy old miner they called One-Eyed Pete.
I picked up a six-gun and put down the spade —
By robbing and killing our fortune was made. *Chorus*

Vigilantes, they caught us at the place called Pig Hill.
Old Pete with a hangnoose the miners did kill.
They banged me and beat me 'til they thought I was dead,
But I lived 'til the morning and I ran off instead. *Chorus*

Well, I ran to the place where we hid all our loot,
I bought me some new clothes and a pair of new boots.
Took a trip back to China on the next swelling tide —
When they asked me about it, I turned and I lied.

Last chorus:
It was digging for gold, digging for gold,
I was a rich man in China before I grew old.

Yat Wah Soon Dou Mei
Immigration Lament

The Angel Island Immigration Station in San Francisco Bay was opened in 1910 to process immigrants coming from Asia. Although Angel Island was sometimes called the Ellis Island of the West Coast, the comparison between it and the famous immigration reception center in New York Harbor is not entirely accurate. Chinese immigrant hopefuls who arrived at Angel Island were considered detainees — virtual prisoners — and some remained there incommunicado for weeks, and in some cases over a year. Many of these people vented their feelings of anger and frustration by writing poems — yes, poems! — on the wooden walls of the barracks in which they were confined. In time the walls came to be covered with hundreds of these graffiti.

In order to convert some of these poems into true songs, I enlisted the aid of Charlie Chin of the New York Chinatown History Project. He sent me a tape recording containing "a song done in the 'mok yee' or wooden fish style. This is the style heard in the villages of the South of China. It is called 'Wooden Fish' because it is often sung to the beat of a wood block that has been carved in the shape of a fish, a good luck symbol. There are hundreds of these songs which have been popular since the 1700s. They are printed in cheap pulp song books which were sold along with face powder and combs to women. Meant to be a way to pass along the stories from history and the latest news to illiterates, i.e., women and poor farmers, they are showing up in the streets of the Lower Eastside as new immigrants arrive from the rural areas of China."

I have set the words of two of these immigration laments to a melody in the "mok yee" style.

U.S. Geological Survey

China

Mei lai ho yo fu.
Yun kwan ban bic dou.
Saw low hao sum sow jai mor.
Lew yat gum long jit tai dou.
Cham mok sau.
Fu ting tan mo lou.
Kwan gou gum moon lan yuk chee.
Bow serong fung mei fuie ban dou.

Cruel are the laws here.
The people are jailed,
Tortured like birds in a trap.
To whom can I complain?
No way out!
I shout to heaven.
I can't pass the Golden Gate.
Why did I come here? It's too late!

Angel Island, California

The Wandering Chinaman

China

By Charlie Chin

I left my home and my par - ents at the age of twen - ty one; In a

fam - 'ly of eight chil - dren, I was the young - est son.

Lit - tle choice was left to me but to go to a for - eign land. Oh,

who will mourn the pass - ing of this wand - 'ring Chin - a - man?

53

I arrived in this country in nineteen twenty-five.
A sixteen-hour day just to try and stay alive.
When I'd saved enough and thought I was doing fine,
I lost everything I had in the crash of twenty-nine.

Seven long years, gambling was my trade,
I'd wander from city to city on the money that I made.
When I'd saved enough and thought that I was done,
Then came a terrible world war in nineteen forty-one.

Oh lonely and lonely, and lonely was my life,
I decided to marry and sent away for a wife.
I settled down to a family, no longer could I roam,
I gave up my dreams of ever reaching home.

I lost my precious wife in nineteen sixty-five.
Without her loving strength, how do I stay alive?
And as for my daughter, she's gone to sleep with a red-haired man,
And I lost my youngest son in the war in Vietnam.

The letter said he died to protect democracy,
But why he had to go is still a mystery to me.
And as for my eldest son, for him there is no hope.
He turns all his money to the man who sells him dope.

So I sit in this park until the night-time comes,
And I worry for my daughter, and I mourn for my sons.
I sit inside this park and stare into my hands,
Oh who will mourn the passing of this wandering Chinaman?

Library of Congress

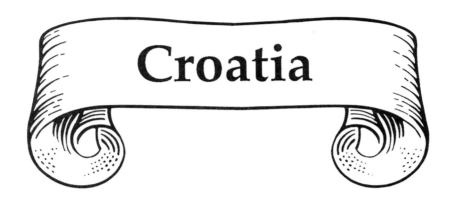

Croatia

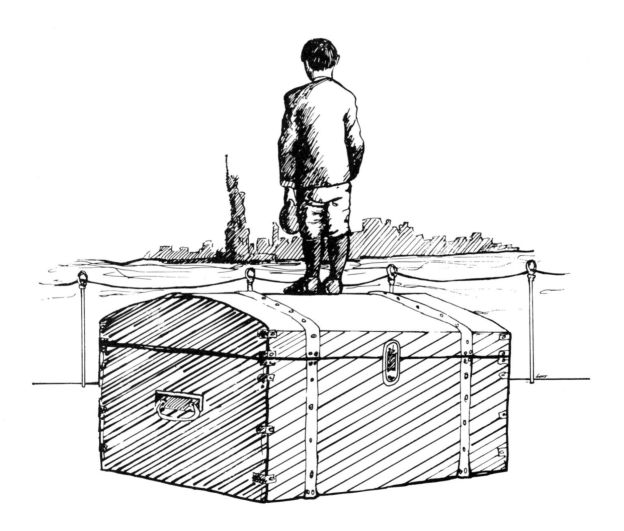

Zavičaju Mili Kraju
My Dear Homeland

There is also in that part of the city a heterodox mixture. There are also Poles and Hungarians and Slavs and Croatians and Macedonians. . . . What a relief when suddenly coming into Tompkins Square, with the wide acres that once were dangerous salt marches, and the big inviting houses all about the square. Children of the neighborhood play together in the sand . . . learning to appreciate each other's qualities between two vigorous punches and a dozen curses. Immigrants without children are not an asset to America. . . .
(*Around The World In New York* by Konrad Berkovici, 1924)

Croatia

Zavičaju mili kraju, U kom sam se rodio.
O, my own land, my dear home-land, It's the place that gave me birth.

Duše moje slatki raju Ko te ne bi volio. volio.
It's sweet heaven to my soul, And who could not love its dear earth? its dear earth?

U tebi mi sve poznato —
Svako drvo svaki kam
Sve me gleda umiljato, (2)
Jer ja tamo sve poznam.

Everything there is familiar —
Every tree and every stone
Looks upon me with affection. (2)
Everything to me is known.

Otac mati misle ne me,
Brat se seća brata svog,
Mila seja pozdrav šalje, (2)
Cuvao te brate Bog.

Father, mother, think about me,
Brother cares for brother too.
Sister greets me — she's without me. (2)
May the Lord watch over you.

A ja jadna u tudjini,
Često gledam na taj kraj.
Molim Boga sa visine (2)
Da mi čuva zavičaj.

Often I look back in sadness,
It is more than I can stand.
And I pray that God will keep watch (2)
Over my dear native land.

Sherman Collection, National Park Service

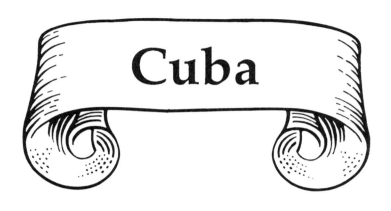

Cuba

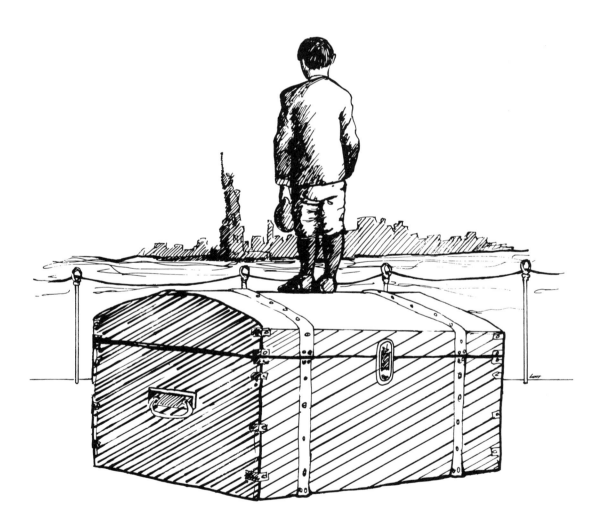

Miami

In a period of less than six months in 1980, about 125,000 Cubans left Cuba in a boatlift of massive proportions — from Mariel to Miami. On arrival some moved elsewhere in the United States, but the overwhelming majority remained in the south Florida area. Their impact on this region — socially, economically, and culturally — has been significant.

Cuba

By Yolanda del Castillo Cobelo

Hoy que han pa - sa - do__ ya vein-te a - ños de es-pe - ra,__
The years have passed by,__ It's twen-ty long years of wait- ing,__

Que he-mos an - da-do lar-gos ca - mi- nos__ de nie - ves y pra-
And we have wan- dered a–long strange high-ways__ of snow and broad green

de - ras,__ En — tre tan-ta nos — tal- gia y tan - to deam-bu—
mead — ows.__ We're caught be—tween nos - tal - gia and wan—der—ing so

lar, en — tre mil es—pe — ran-zas que vie-nen y se van. Pa—ra to—dos no—
much, Our hopes we count by thou-sands they come and then they go. But for all of us

58

Cuban Refugees   *American Red Cross*

Vendedores
Street Vendors

The street vendors that appear in Miami, a few months after came people from Mariel, gave me the inspiration for the song. This song was my tribute to those men honest and hardworkers . . . good Cubans that only wanted to come to this land of opportunity and live with freedom. (Yolanda del Castillo Cobelo)

Cuba

By Yolanda del Castillo Cobelo

Me en can – tan los ven-de – dor-es que han sur – gi-do __ en Mi – a-mi. Se vén lo mis-mo en West-ches-ter, el South-west que en Hi-a – le-ah. Lle-van su mer-can-cí – a, un no sé que de re –

I real – ly like the street ven-dors who have sprout-ed up – in Mi – a-mi. They're al – so seen in West-ches-ter, at South-west or __ Hi-a – le-ah. Car-ry-ing in their push-carts who can say how man-y

63

*A farinaceous root considered a great delicacy in Cuba (*Arum sagitæ folium*).

can‑to.
bring‑ing.

Pa – ra – do en el Ca – lle O – cho,
I've got my push‑cart down on Eighth___ Street,

Lle –
I'm

van – do mi mer – can – cí – a:
sell – ing such good things to eat:

Li – mon – es, ma – lan – ga y
Fresh lem‑ ons, *ma–lan – ga* and

chu – rros.
pas‑try.

Me en‑cuen‑tras to – do los dí – as, sí___ se – ñor. Ven – de___
You'll find me here ev – 'ry day,___ *sí___ se – ñor.* O, you

flor – es,
flow‑ers,

Mi Cu – ba ha – cen re – cor – dar.
Bring me back Cu – ba's hap – py hours.

Chorus 2:
Del Mariel y muy honrado,
Paso los días vendiendo.
Traigo rico granizado,
Y así me voy defendiendo,
   Ya lo ves!

Chorus 3:
Y dedico este cantar
A esos buenos vendedores,
Que con sus frutas y flores,
Mi Cuba hacen recordar.

Chorus 2:
I'm proud to be from Mariel, sir,
And every day I'm here to sell, sir.
My living I make selling ices,
There's no better ice at these prices,
   You can see!

Chorus 3:
I dedicate my little song now
To those men who wander along now,
Who with their fruits and their flowers,
Bring back Cuba's happy hours.

Library of Congress

Czechia

Czech is the native language of Bohemia, Moravia, and Silesia, all within the Czechoslovak Republic. The Czech term for this western part of Czechoslovakia is *Čechy* ("Czechia" in English). I have used this term to distinguish the songs in this section from those of Slovakia (the eastern region of the country), which are found under their own heading in this book.

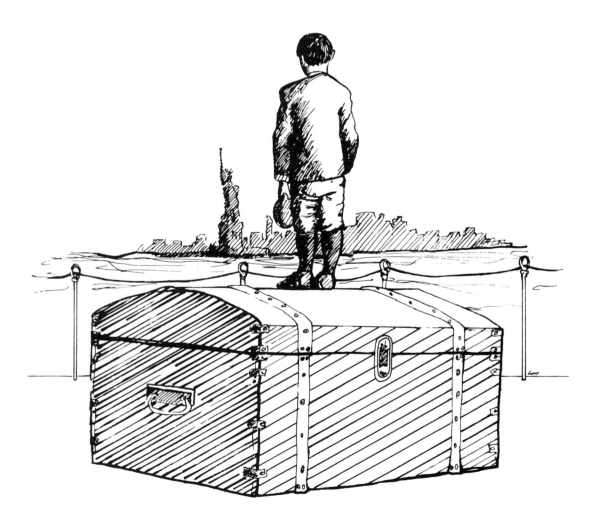

Zasvit' Mi, Ty Slunko Zlaté
Brightly Shine, O Golden Sunshine

This song was sung at funerals, but I haven't heard it for this occasion in many years. I emigrated from Bohemia in 1905, age 3. On my visit this summer to Czechoslovakia (Czech & Slovak Federal Republic) I received a song book . . . song #118, "Zasvit mi, ty slunko zlate" . . . it is a Farewell to Bohemia. Copy enclosed. (Anton Smunt)

Zas - vit' mi, ty slun - ko zla - té, na po - sled - ní z vla - sti krok,
Bright - ly shine, o gold - en sun - shine, as I bid my last good - bye.

Za–hřej v pr–sou ci–ty sva–té, U–suš v o–čích sl–zí tok.
I shall miss the land that was mine; Dry the tears that cloud my eye.

Ne–za–zli mi, dra–há má–ti, Po–že–hná–ní své mi dej,
Dear–est moth–er, do not chide me, Bless me, for I'll soon be gone.

Ač ti mu–sím s Bo–hem dá–ti Za sy–na mě vždy–cky měj.
Though great pain wells up in–side me, I will al–ways be your son.

Zas – vit' mi ty, slun – ko zla – té, Na po – sle — dní z vla – sti
Bright-ly shine, o gold – en sun — shine, As I bid my land good-

krok, Za – hřej v pr – sou ci – ty sva – té.
bye. I shall miss the land that was mine;

U – suš v o – čích sl – zí tok, U – suš v o – čích sl – zí tok.
Dry the tears that cloud my eye, Dry the tears that cloud my eye.

Květné luhy, hvozdy černé,
Nikdy vás již nespatřím,
Nikdy víc své děvče věrné,
Věrné druhy neuzřím.
    Český hlahol, české zpěvy,
    Nebudu víc v duši ssát;
    Toužit budu bez úlevy,
    V cizně pro vlast svou lkát.

Flowers, meadows, mountains, forests,
Nevermore shall I see you;
Nevermore, my faithful sweetheart,
Nor my friends who were so true.
    Nevermore to hear Czech spoken,
    Nevermore to hear Czech song;
    Longing with a heart that's broken,
    To be back where I belong.

Repeat first 4 lines

Repeat first 4 lines

Krasná Amerika
Pretty America

I've had no formal education in the Czech language. As a child it was the first language I learned, as both my parents came from a heavily populated Czech community in Texas, and their parents were the immigrants. I married a man of German descent and have just recently found out that his grandparents immigrated from almost the same area of what is today Czechoslovakia near my ancestors' homes. It was Austria then. (Henrietta Grmela Schindler)

Czechia

A, kras – ná, to je kras – ná to je kras – ná A – me – ri –
How pret – ty, you're so pret – ty, you're so pret – ty A – me – ri –

ka. A, ka.
ca. How ca.

Do A – me – ri – ki po – jed –
To A – me – ri – ca we will

me, Tam se vše – ci sej – de – me. A,
go, There we'll be to – geth – er, you know. How

V Americe tam je hej,
Po krika teče petrolej. *Chorus*

V Americe jsou slepice,
A nejsou vajca jak čepice. *Chorus*

V Americe tam je blaze,
Tam teče pivo po podlaze. *Chorus*

V Americe su děvčata,
Hezké jsou jako poupata. *Chorus*

In America, land of dreams,
Oil flows in all the streams. *Chorus*

In America the chickens
All lay eggs as big as the dickens. *Chorus*

In America there's good cheer,
All washed down with plenty of beer. *Chorus*

In America there are girls,
Prettier than flowers or pearls. *Chorus*

National Park Service

Hora Šhinerská
The Hills of Shiner

In 1849, thirty-six Czechs arrived in Baltimore on three ships: the *Martha,* the *Ann,* and the *Goethe.* Leaving from the German ports of Bremen or Hamburg, other immigrant ships headed for New York City and Galveston. Large-scale immigration of Czechs into Texas started in 1850 and continued until about 1910. Shiner, Texas, lies approximately mid-way between San Antonio and Houston. Neighboring towns bear names like Cestohowa, Panna Maria, Rosanky, and Moravia — not to mention New Berlin, Breslau, and Cologne.

Czechia

Ho — ra Šhin-er–ská, Kras — né, mes-teč–ko, Jest tam
Oh, you Shin-er hills, Charm — ing lit-tle town. There's a

pi – vo–var, Do — bré pi – več–ko. Do — bré pi – več–ko.
brew-er–y, Drink the good beer down. Drink the good beer down.

Chorus

Pi – jem, pi – jem, pi – vo ra – di, Pro – to že jsme ka – ma – ra – di.
We will drink our beer to – geth – er, friends, in fair and storm-y weath-er.

A co jste sedlaci,
Co jste dělali?
Že jste pivovar
Nepodporovali? *Chorus*

And oh, you farmer boys,
What is all this noise?
Why don't you support
Shiner's brewery? *Chorus*

Denmark

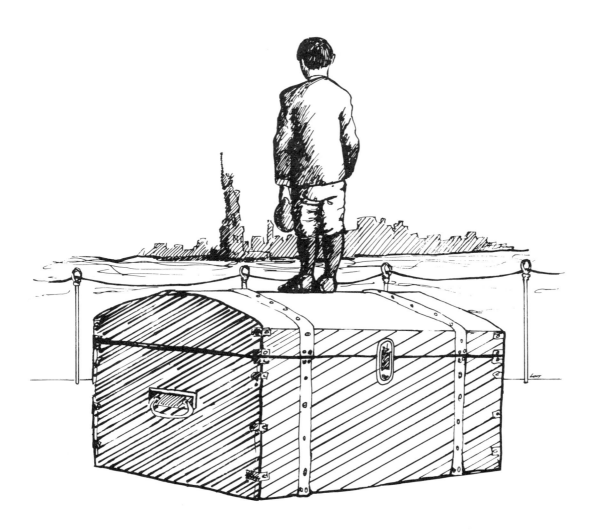

Danebrog Og Stjernebanner
Danish Flag And Starry Banner

In 1871, Niels Pedersen (1848–1931) emigrated from Denmark to Racine, Wisconsin. He changed his name to Adam Dan, and it was under that name that he wrote this hymn-like song in 1887. He was one of the founding fathers of the Danish Church in America, and edited its newspaper, *Kirkelig Samler (Church Chronicler),* where this song was first published.

Denmark

Da – ne–brog og Stjern–e–ban – ner, en – es kan I godt,
Dan – ish flag and Star – ry Ban – ner, you make quite a pair,

Her i Sko – vens hø – je, ly – se, grøn – ne Som – mers – lot!
Here in the tall for – est man – or, in the sum – mer air!

Hvil – ket, Flag der er vel skøn – nest, ved vi næst – en ej, Beg – ge
Which flag has the great–er glo – ry? No one here can say. When it

har til æd – el Stor – daad vin – ken–de vist Vej. Beg – ge
comes to free – dom's stor – y, both have led the way. When it

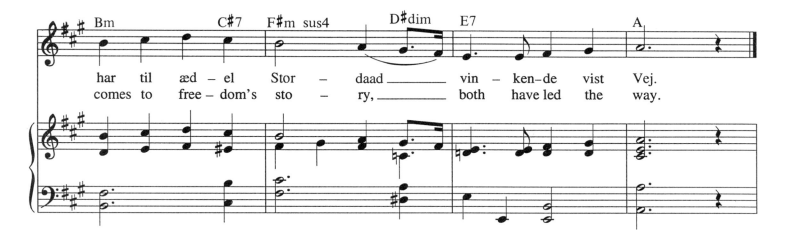

har til æd – el Stor – daad _____ vin – ken-de vist Vej.

comes to free – dom's sto – ry, _____ both have led the way.

Fjered Julidagens Minder
Synes glemt i Knald
Og i Optog, tomme Taler,
Narreværk og Skrald;
Vi, der kom fra Bøgelunde,
Vil paa Fædres Vis
Her, som ved de danske
 Sunde,
Synge Friheds Pris.

Her er større Ting at vinde
End den gode Farm,
Ej blot til at bruge Øksen
Løftes skal vor Arm,
Og til mer end Guld at tjene
Tanken skærpes skal;
Det var ædle Mænd, der
 rejste
Landets Frihedshal.

Kan vi møde med de
 Bedste,
Tage Kampen op
Mod hver Uaand, som sig
 breder,
Pege paa den Top,
Hvor os Idealet vinker
Al Tid længer frem,
Vise, at i Aandens Rige
Har og vi et Hjem.

Ja, kan vi vort Eget hævde
Ret i god Forstand,
Da har vi en Plads at fylde
I det store Land,
Hvor en Washington har
 kæmpet
Og en Franklin talt,
Hvor en Lincoln Trældom
 knuste,
Hvor en Garfield faldt.

Vær velkommen, fjerde
 Juli,
Glade Frihedsdag!
Bort med kaade Drenge-
 streger,
Vilde Drikkelag!
Danebrog og Stjerne-
 banner,
I os minde om,
Hvor vi har vor Arne
 plantet,
Og hvorfra vi kom.

Real July Fourth memories
Are rarely given voice.
Speeches vanish with the breeze,
Tomfoolery, and noise.
We, whose fathers crossed the
 ocean
In the good old days,
Shall as Danes, with great emo-
 tion,
Sing in freedom's praise.

Here are greater things in season
Than to have a farm.
Chopping wood's not the sole
 reason
That we raise our arm.
More than just to earn a living,
Shall we give our all.
Noble men, our freedom giving,
Built Liberty Hall.

With good people we surround us,
And take up the fight
'Gainst the evils that confound us,
Strive for mountain's height.
May the ideal always guide us,
Calling us to roam
And with noble thoughts inside
 us,
We will build a home.

We can make a contribution,
As we understand.
Strengthening the constitu-
 tion
Of this wond'rous land.
Washington fought here with
 bravery,
Franklin served us well,
And where Lincoln did crush
 slavery,
And where Garfield fell.

To July Fourth we give our
 thanks,
Day of Liberty.
No more silly, juvenile
 pranks,
Drinking noisily.
Danish flag and Starry Ban-
 ner,
We do you acclaim.
To this land we sing hosanna,
And from whence we came.

Amerikansk Humbug
American Humbug

William Rantzau, who wrote this song sometime during the 1860s, chose wisely in his use of the word "humbug" to describe the flim-flammery and sharp practices that one could expect in the New World. Hard work had its rewards, but there was nothing like a million-dollar line of credit at the bank!

Denmark

By Wilhelm Rantzau

Jeg hav – de le – vet, ja lov – ligt flot, Det var Sag – en, Be –
I lived the life and I car – ried on rath – er gai – ly. Just

stan – digt dre – vet og ik – ke blot He – le Dag – en. Nei!
goof – ing off in a ma – ra – thon, Not just dai – ly. No!

Nat – ten munt – re – de jeg i – sær tit mit Sind op, I
When night came I'd es – pe – cial – ly cheer my – self up At

Num – mer ty – ve, de veed nok der Hos Hr. Gin – rup.
num – ber twen – ty, you fol – low me? Mis – ter Gin – rup's.

Jeg skulde læse til Artium
Og studere,
Men helst i Phønixs Collegium
Jeg polkered,
Jeg dandsed' lystigt og gjorde Griin,
Gav Partiet,
Det sidste Sted blev, hvor jeg kom hen,
Slutteriet.

Min Onkel hjalp mig, De kjender vel
Brygger Mule?
Den pæne Mand klarede min Gjæld
Hver en Smule,
Men paa det Vilkaar, at jeg stak a'
Ganske roligt,
En lille Tour til Amerika
Snarest muligt.

Han sa'e, vi har her en vis Falent
Og Grosserer,
Der rendte bort, men nu har han tjent
Summer svære.
Den samme Dag han derover kom
Med Bagage,
Han tjente strax, før han saae sig om,
En Plantage.

Nu har han indkaldt hver Creditor,
Han er sjælden,
Og han har lovet paa Æresord
Klare Gjælden.
Han har bragt med sig en heel Portion
Creditiver;
I Banken faaer han en Million,
Blot han skriver.

Et Dampskib har han og hver Kahyt
Separatis,
Paa Edderduun kan Du hvile blødt,
Ja og gratis,
Du bli'er barberet ombord, reis med,
Sagde Onkel,
Din Udsigt her er, saavidt jeg veed,
Mørk og dunkel.

I should have worked on the artium* —
School advancing,
But much preferred Phoenix Collegium —
Polka dancing.
I gaily danced and I had a ball —
Full of gism.
The place I landed the last of all
Was in prison.

My uncle helped me, you know his name,
Mule the brewer.
Paid all my debts and erased my shame —
No man's truer.
He only said I should sail away,
Not to worry.
A little tour to Americay,
And to hurry.

I know a bankrupted merchant there —
Rather stealthy,
Who disappeared into the thin air,
Now he's wealthy.
The very day his feet touched the ground
In that nation,
He earned at once, before looking 'round,
A plantation.

His creditors, now they all have heard —
(This'll slay 'em.)
He's given them his most solemn word,
To repay 'em.
He's brought with him a portfolio —
Notes of credit.
The bank will lend a million or so —
He has said it.

He owns a steamship — the cabins are
Separatis.
You rest on eiderdown without par —
Yes, and gratis.
You will be barbered once you're on board,
Uncle said so.
Your prospects here are, in one short word,
Less than zero.

*A-level university entrance exam

Jeg fulgte Raadet, og meldte mig
Paa Contoiret,
Og fik Billet til New York, men nei
Knapt De troer'et,
Hvor jeg blev proppet og det i Hast
Om den Lykke,
Jeg vilde gjøre, derpaa jeg fast
Kunde bygge.

Der blev mig lovet ti Tønder Land,
Saadan lød'et,
Og naar blot Jorden blev gjort istand
Rigtig gjødet,
Gav Kornet tusinde Fold igjen,
Naar man saaer'et;
Titusind Dollars Fortjenesten
Blev om Aaret.

Og Huse bygges af Arbeidsde-
Partementet,
Ja! Med Altan, hvis man blot vil be'e
Og forlange 'et.
Aviser faaer man til Gjennemsyn
Næsten daglig,
I selve Urskoven sendt fra By'en,
Hvor behag'lig!

Jeg løste Passet, gik glad i Sind
Hjem og laa mig,
I skjønne Drømme jeg slumred ind,
Alt jeg saae mig
Tilbage vende som riig Nabob.
Men tilfældigt
Var Skibet gaaet før jeg stod op;
Hvor uheldigt!

Jeg stod paa Skibsbroen, jeg var gram,
Ja, som Fanden.
Men Lykken bedre dog var, min Skam,
End Forstanden.
Jeg hørte Chefen var kneben ud,
Tænk, hvor dreven,
Med hele Kassen, jeg takked' Gud,
Jeg var bleven.

Hans Creditorer skreg' Vee og Vok,
Deres Penge
De vente paa, ja, og de kan nok
Vente længe.
Til Cautionisten hans Venner sa'e,
Du var dum, Du!
Du burde vidst, fra Amerika
Kommer Humbug.

I took his counsel, his words of pity,
And set out
To buy a ticket for New York City,
And get out.
I got all puffed up with dreams of glory
So lurid.
I started feeling my success story
Assuréd.

Ten-acre farms I would get — just be
Enterprising.
The only work on it there for me —
Fertilizing.
The grain would give you enormous profit —
Just plant it.
Ten thousand dollars I would take off it —
For granted.

The houses are all built by their
Labor Department.
With balconies — each one gets his share,
By apartment.
And the newspapers are all sent down
Nearly daily.
The virgin forest is sent from town,
Very gaily.

I got my passport without a care,
And retired.
And in my dreams I was standing there,
So inspired.
I was quite rich — on my homeward trip,
With a fortune.
When I awoke, I had missed the ship —
What misfortune.

I watched the ship leaving with the tide —
I was blazing.
But good luck turned out upon my side —
How amazing.
I heard the boss, he had run away
(It was crazy)
With all the funds — I thanked God that day
I'd been lazy.

His creditors, they were stunned to hear
He'd absconded.
And they will wait many a long year
Unrefunded.
The people said to the guarantor
With a sad shrug,
America sends us more and more
Of pure humbug.

Kalifornien
California

Only a mere handful of Danes ever tried their luck at prospecting for gold in California in the 1850s. Nevertheless, fantastic songs and stories of untold wealth abounded in the popular imagination. Street ballads hawked as broadsides sold throughout Denmark in the tens and sometimes hundreds of thousands — feeding these wondrous tales to a delighted public. This one was written by Eric Bøgh in 1850.

Denmark

Det Ka – li – for – nien er dog et Land U – den Li – ge! Ak, var at der, Kun – de
Oh, Cal – i – for – nia it is a land Like no oth – er! Its riches are found at

al – le Mand Bli – ve ri – ge. I Fald man blot ken – der Sand fra Guld – Det er
ev – 'ry hand, Lis – ten broth – er. If on – ly one can tell sand from gold – That's the

Sag – en – Saa kan man hen – te en Po – se fuld Hjem om Dag – en.
tick – et – Then you take all that your sack can hold, Just go pick it.

Det gaar hver en Stodder med Port d'Epe
    Og Galoner;
Og vil han gifte sig, faar han tre,
    Fire Koner.
Der kan man leve, hvordan man vil
    Uden Ris'ko.
Ja, var jeg Pige — jeg rejste til
    St. Francisko.

Sin Slave har man, som paa et Vink
    Straks parat er.
Og sine Børn la'er man spille Klink
    Med Dukater.
Og den, det sparer det mindste blot
    Kaldes kneben
Og gerrig — Herre, du großer Gott
    Hvilken Leben!

Der er den fattigste Millionær —
    Jo jeg takker;
Og selve Rotschild man regner der
    For en Prakker.
Det er et Land, som kan svare Skat
    Til Finansmænd.
Der maa jeg over! God rolig Nat,
    Mine Landsmænd!

And there all beggars lead happy lives,
    Without worry.
And when they marry, take many wives,
    There's no hurry.
There one can live as it pleases you,
    Without risk-o.
Were I a girl I would travel to
    San Francisco.

Yes, every man has a slave today,
    It's quite funny.
And even children are used to play
    With real money.
And if a fellow decides to save,
    He's demented.
Why, you can have everything you crave —
    Be contented.

And there a poor man's a millionaire,
    Yes indeedy!
And even Rothschild cannot compare —
    He'd be needy.
It is a land where you pay your tax
    To financemen.
And so I'm off — may you all relax,
    My dear landsmen.

Sherman Collection, National Park Service

Ny Vise Fra Udvandrene
New Song From The Emigrants

The subtitle of this song reads: "About the Journey from Copenhagen to Liverpool and Thence to New York Aboard the *William Rathbone,* Commanded by Captain Braett." The *William Rathbone* was built in Connecticut in 1849 and came into the Atlantic service just as the first groups of the over 300,000 Danes who were to come to America between 1850 and 1914 began moving west. The song was published in Copenhagen in 1855. It employs the typical literary devices of exaggeration and overstatement to make the serious point about the difficult conditions aboard this and most other immigrant ships of the period.

Denmark

En Sang jeg her vil sen – de, Hjem fra A-me-ri – ka, Og
A song I will send wing – ing, Home from A-me-ri – ca, And

la – de E – der vi – de, Hvor Rei – sen den stod an. Fra
let you know by sing – ing, Just how the voy – age was. We

Kjø – ben-havn vi to – ge, Kom vel til Li – ver – pool, Paa
left from Co – pen – ha – gen, To Liv – er-pool␣ we␣ came; And

86

Wil – li – am Rat bo – ne Om – bord vi der – paa kom.
got on board a ship, *Wil – liam Rath – bone* was its name.

Jeg vil kun Sandhed skrive,	Matroserne med Knipler	I'll only write what happened,	The sailors came with cud-gels,
Mine Venner dette bød.	Ned under Dækket kom,	The truth to you I'll tell.	We all feared a shipwreck.
Den første Dag til Middag	Og skreg til os paa engelsk:	The first day for our dinner	They yelled at us in English,
Var al vor Kost lidt Grød.	"Op paa Dæk alle Mand,"	We'd porridge — nothing else.	"All men get up on deck!"
Vi Morgenen derefter	Saasnart de skulde røre	And then, the morning after,	To trim the sails a little,
Fik Sukker, Thee og Brød,	En Smule ved et Seil;	Came sugar, tea, and bread,	The captain did command.
Hvoraf vi otte Dage	Og drikked' Brændeviin	And that, my friends, is just how	They drank their brandy daily,
Maa leve, men med Nød.	hver Dag	For eight days we were fed.	As long as they could stand.
	De stod paa deres Been.		

Jeg vil kun Sandhed skrive,
Mine Venner dette bød.
Den første Dag til Middag
Var al vor Kost lidt Grød.
Vi Morgenen derefter
Fik Sukker, Thee og Brød,
Hvoraf vi otte Dage
Maa leve, men med Nød.

En halv Tvebak om Dagen
Det skulde her forslaa.
Med Længsel otte Dage,
Før Proviant vi faa,
Vi vented' og bekom da
Den samme Quantitet,
Samt et Pund Riis, et halvt
Pund Flæsk
Og ei en Smule meer.

Til Kjøkkenet vi skulde
Nu for at koge Grød,
Vort Liv vi resikeerte
For Puf og Slag og Stød;
Thi der var saadan Træng-
sel,
Vor Kok stod med en Tamp
Og slog Enhver for Fode,
Ret, som han fik Behag.

Enhver kan vistnok tænke
Vi var ei glad i Sind,
Dertil paa hele Reisen
Vi havde stærk Modvind;
Saa vi sex Uger vare
Om Reisen til New-York,
Blev jaget op om Natten
Udi den værste Storm.

Matroserne med Knipler
Ned under Dækket kom,
Og skreg til os paa engelsk:
"Op paa Dæk alle Mand,"
Saasnart de skulde røre
En Smule ved et Seil;
Og drikked' Brændeviin
hver Dag
De stod paa deres Been.

At puffe, slaae og drille
Var stedse deres Lyst.
Gud skee Lov, Priis og
Ære!
Den amerikanske Kyst
Vi saae med hele Lemmer,
Gud! skjærm den til vor
Død,
Og giv os Held og Lykke,
At tjene for vort Brød.

Farvel jeg nu vil sige
Forældre, Frender kjær.
Gud skjærme Danmarks
Rige
For Ild, Pest, Hunger,
Sværd.
Gid vi maa Alle vandre
I sand Lyksalighed,
Indtil vi hisset samles
Hos Gud i Evighed.

I'll only write what happened,
The truth to you I'll tell.
The first day for our dinner
We'd porridge — nothing else.
And then, the morning after,
Came sugar, tea, and bread,
And that, my friends, is just how
For eight days we were fed.

They gave us half a biscuit —
That was our daily lot.
For eight long days we waited,
I'll tell you what we got.
The same starvation rations,
Exactly as before.
A pound of rice, a half pound
pork,
And not a morsel more.

We went down to the galley,
Our porridge to prepare.
But it was risky business,
For they did beat us there.
I never saw such crowding,
The cook stood with a whip.
He snapped it at the people —
We all did feel its nip.

I'm sure you can imagine
Our feelings of unrest.
What's more — for the whole
voyage
The wind blew from the west.
For six long weeks we travelled,
Until we reached New York.
The nightly storms that struck us
Just tossed us like a cork.

The sailors came with cud-
gels,
We all feared a shipwreck.
They yelled at us in English,
"All men get up on deck!"
To trim the sails a little,
The captain did command.
They drank their brandy daily,
As long as they could stand.

To prod and strike and beat
us,
Was what they did the most.
But praise to God on highest,
We saw the Yankee coast.
Our limbs as yet unbroken,
God save us 'til we're dead,
And give us the good fortune
To work here for our bread.

Farewell, I will now bid you,
I send you all this word,
May God save Denmark's
kingdom
From fire, plague, hunger, and
sword.
And in peace may we wan-
der,
Wherever we may be,
Until we meet in heaven,
For all eternity.

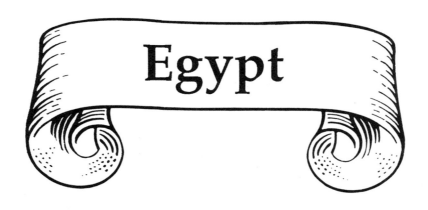

Egypt

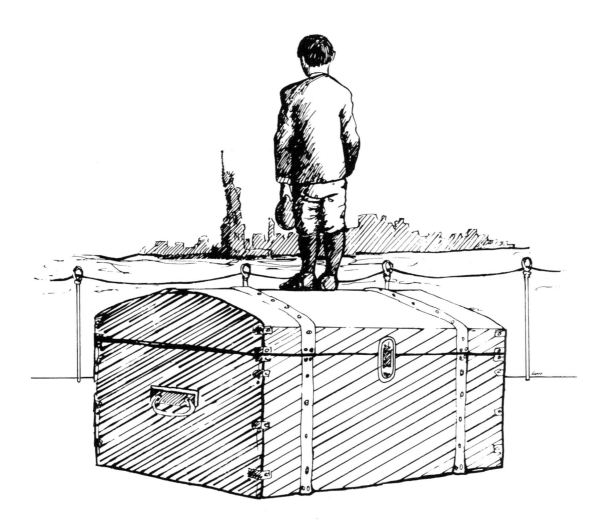

Salma Ya Salama
Safely, With Safety

Sayed Darwish (1892–1923), known affectionately as El-Sheikh Sayed because of his early religious training, was an innovator in the world of Arabic music. He altered the musical form of traditional song and dealt with subjects, such as drugs and alcohol, that were previously thought to be inappropriate. He composed the words and music to the Egyptian national anthem.

Words by Badee Khairy
Music by Sayed Darwish

Egypt

Sal – ma ya sa – la – ma Roh – na wi geen – a ___ bil ___ sa – la – ma. ___
Safe – ly, with safe – ty we have ___ gone a – way and now ___ have ___ come back safe – ly.

Sal – ma ya sa – la – ma, Saf – far ya wa – bour or – bot aan – dak naz –
Safe – ly, with safe – ty, O, train blow your whis – tle and please let me

zill – ny ___ fil ___ ba – lad – dy. Ba – la A – mer – ka, ba – la O –
off ___ in ___ this, ___ my ___ ci – ty. For – get A – me – ri – ca, don't think of

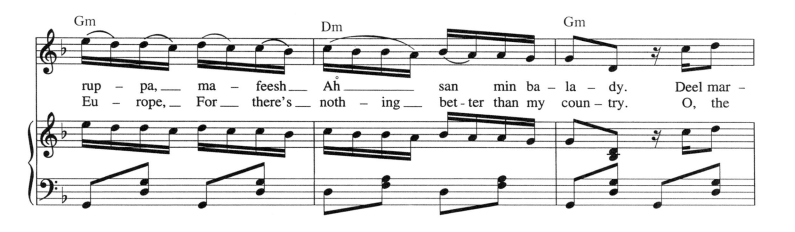

rup — pa, __ ma — feesh __ Ah __ san min ba — la — dy. Deel mar -
Eu — rope, __ For __ there's __ noth — ing __ bet — ter than my coun — try. O, the

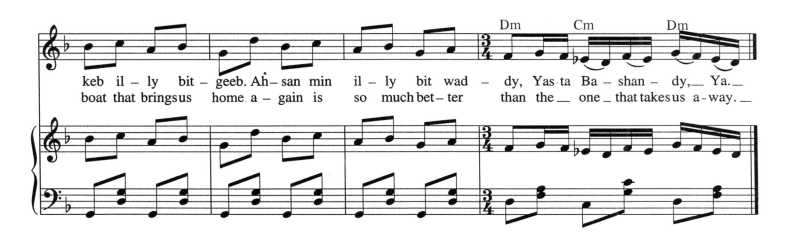

keb il — ly bit — geeb. Ah — san min il — ly bit wad — dy, Yas — ta Ba — shan — dy, Ya. __
boat that brings us home a — gain is so much bet — ter than the __ one __ that takes us a — way. __

El-Ghorba yama bit warry,	Estrangement — what does it show us?
Bit khally el-saanayee beyorton.	The laborer must speak strange languages.
Matraĥ ma beerooĥ el-Masry,	Wherever is found an Egyptian,
Bardo tool omro zoo tufoonon.	He always is very creative.
Wahyat Rabina el-maabood,	I swear by the God that we worship,
We are very good, Yasta Mahmud,	We are very good, Mister Mahmud,
Adaha wi edood.	Able and capable.
Sallat el nabby aal shakhs minna,	May the prayers of the Prophet be upon one of us.
Forset meh, balla afya.	Is this good? Please excuse me.
Illy fee geybo, yefangarbo,	What he has in his pocket he spends,
Wil baraka fil ein wil aafya.	With thanks for our eyes and our health.
Hat-akhod eh min el-donya,	What are you going to get from life,
Gheyr el-sattre ya sheikh khaleeha sayrra.	Except, o sheikh, to keep moving.
Donya fanya.	Life is but a moment.
Solta ma solta, kollo maksab,	Power, no power — it's all gain.
Ĥawishna mal wi geyna.	We saved money and returned.
Shofnal ĥarb wil shofnal darb,	We saw war and we saw fighting,
Wi shofna el deenameet baa neyna.	And we saw dynamite with our own eyes.
Rabbak Waĥed, omrak waĥed,	God is One, your life is one,
Addeĥna aho roĥna wi geyna.	And here we are. We went, we came.
Eh khass aaleyna.	What did we lose?

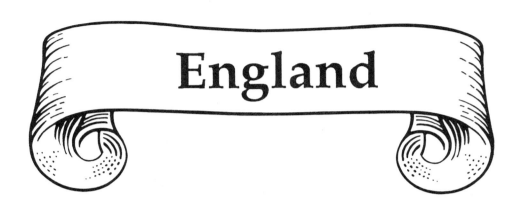

England

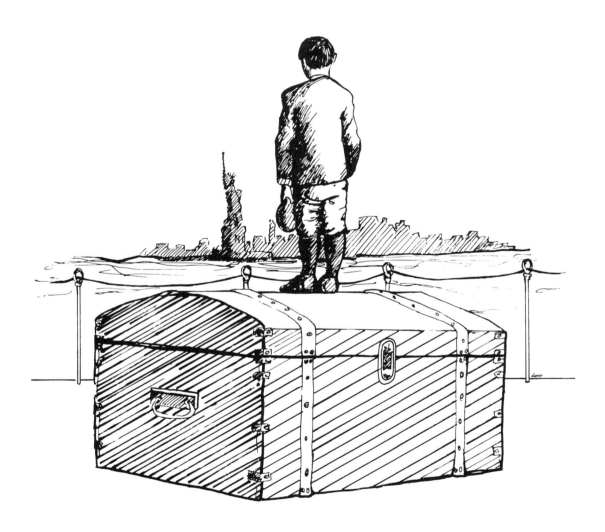

An Invitation To North America

In 1687, Henry Purcell wrote one of the inspired melodies of all time — "Liliburlero." Since then it has been used in countless variants, both in its tune and words. It is safe to assume that everybody in 17th and 18th century England could at least recognize it, if not sing it. The anonymous poet who set his "invitation" to this melody was assured that it would be familiar to all who heard it. However, his musical instincts were sharper than his political insights. The line in verse 7, "But we'll have no taxes in North Americay," was tossed overboard with the tea into Boston harbor.

England

Come all you bold Brit-ons, Where-ev-er you be, I would have you draw near, and lis-ten to me. The times they get hard-er in Eng-land ev-'ry day; It is

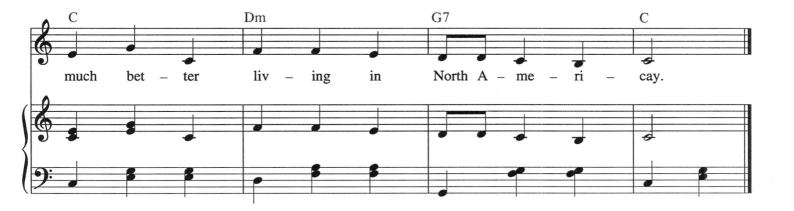

much bet — ter liv — ing in North A – me – ri – cay.

There is many a family of late that has gone
Away to New York, father, mother, and son;
Let us likewise follow and make no delay,
For 'tis much cheaper living in North Americay.

The farmers in England sell their corn so dear,
They do what they can to starve the poor here.
They send it to France, which sure is not right,
To feed other nations that against us do fight.

Why do we stay here for to be their slaves,
When in Nova Scotia we can do as we please;
For who'd work in England for ten pence a day,
When we can get four shillings in North Americay.

The landlords in England do raise the lands high,
It forces some farmers abroad for to fly;
If times grow no better, I'll venture to say,
Poor men had better go to North Americay.

Observe then good people what to you I've told,
What a plague is in England by short weight of gold.
With bad silver and halfpence, believe what I say,
There's nothing of this in North Americay.

The priests in England come into the field,
They tithe as they please, you dare not but yield;
This is a great hardship, you believe, I dare say.
But we'll have no taxes in North Americay.

There's many a farmer you very well know,
That went to New York but a few years ago,
Have bought land and houses; who now would here stay —
But go and make fortunes in North Americay.

Manufactures in England are grown very bad,
For weavers and combers no work's to be had.
But let's go abroad, I dare venture to say,
They'll find us employment in North Americay.

So here's a health to George our gracious king,
I hope none will take amiss the song that I sing;
Then lads and lasses now come away,
And ship yourselves to North Americay.

The Distressed Damsel

The life of an indentured servant girl in the Virginia colony was certainly as hard, if not harder, than the life she had left behind in England. Yet, despite her "invitation to stay away," more and more young people sought passage under the terms of indenture, where they had to work for years to pay off the cost of their passage.

England

Give ear un – to a maid that late – ly was be – trayed, And sent _____ in – to _____ Vir – gin – ny, O; In brief I shall de – clare, what I have suf – fered there, When that I was wea – ry, wea – ry, wea – ry, wea – ry, O.

When that first I came
To this land of fame,
Which is called Virginny, O,
The axe and the hoe
Have brought my overthrow,
When that I was weary, weary, weary, weary, O.

Five years served I
Under Master Guy,
In the land of Virginny, O.
Which made me for to know
Sorrow, grief and woe,
When that I was weary, weary, weary, weary, O.

When my dame says, "Go,"
Then I must do so,
In the land of Virginny, O.
When she sits at meat,
Then I have none to eat,
When that I was weary, weary, weary, weary, O.

The clothes that I brought in
They are worn very thin,
In the land of Virginny, O.
Which makes me for to say,
Alas and well-a-day,
When that I was weary, weary, weary, weary, O.

Instead of beds of ease,
To lie down when I please,
In the land of Virginny, O,
Upon a bed of straw,
I lay down full of woe,
When that I was weary, weary, weary, weary, O.

Then the spider she
Daily waits on me,
In the land of Virginny, O.
'Round about my bed
She spins her tender web,
When that I was weary, weary, weary, weary, O.

So soon as it is day,
To work I must away,
In the land of Virginny, O.
Then my dame she knocks
With her tinder-box,
When that I was weary, weary, weary, weary, O.

I have played my part,
Both at plow and cart,
In the land of Virginny, O.
Billets from the wood,
Upon my back they load,
When that I was weary, weary, weary, weary, O.

Instead of drinking beer,
I drink the water clear,
In the land of Virginny, O,
Which makes me pale and wan,
Do all that e'er I can,
When that I was weary, weary, weary, weary, O.

If my dame says, "Go!"
I dare not say no,
In the land of Virginny, O.
The water from the spring
Upon my head I bring,
When that I was weary, weary, weary, weary, O.

When the child doth cry,
I must sing, "By a by,"
In the land of Virginny, O.
No rest that I can have,
Whilst I am here a slave,
When that I was weary, weary, weary, weary, O.

A thousand woes beside,
That I do here abide,
In the land of Virginny, O.
In misery I spend
My time that hath no end,
When that I was weary, weary, weary, weary, O.

Then let maids beware,
All by my ill-fare,
In the land of Virginny, O.
Be sure you stay at home,
For if you do here come,
You all will be weary, weary, weary, weary, O.

But if it be my chance,
Homewards to advance,
From the land of Virginny, O,
If that I once more
Land on English shore,
I'll no more be weary, weary, weary, weary, O.

A New England Ballad

Just like his compatriot, the indentured servant girl in Virginia, the singer in this early 18th century complaint has nary a good word to say for New England.

England

Will you please to give ear a while un-to me, And straight I will tell you where I have been. I've been to New Eng – land, but now have come o'er; I think they shall catch me go thith – er no

more, I think they shall catch me go thith – er no more.

Before I went thither, Lord how folk did tell,
How wishes did grow and how birds did dwell,
All one 'mongst t'other in the wood and the water,
I thought that was true, but I found no such matter.

When first I did land, they 'mazed me quite,
And 'twas of all days on a Saturday night;
I wondered to see strange buildings were there,
'Twas all like the standings at Woodbury Fair.

Well, that night I slept 'til near prayer time,
Next morning I wondered I heard no bells chime;
At which I did ask and the reason I found,
'Twas because they had ne'er a bell in the town.

At last being warned, to church we repaired,
Where I did think certain we should have some prayers;
But the parson there no such matter did teach,
They scorned to pray for all one could preach.

The first thing they did, a psalm they did sing,
I plucked out my Psalm-book I with me did bring;
And tumbled to seek it, 'cause they called it by name,
But they'd got a new song to the tune of the same.

Now this was New Dorchester, as they told unto me,
A town very famous in all that country;
They said 'twas new buildings, I grant it is true,
Yet methinks Old Dorchester's as fine as the new.

Across The Western Ocean

This song was sung by both the English and Irish. Liverpool was the great port of exit for countless emigrants, not only from Britain, but from all over Europe. My father's family was part of the great tide of humanity that sailed down the Mersey into the broad Atlantic.

England

The land of promise there you'll see,
   Amelia, where you bound to?
I'm bound across that Western sea,
   Across the Western Ocean.

Similarly:
To Liverpool I'll take my way. . . .
To Liverpool that Yankee school. . . .

There's Liverpool Pat with his tarpaulin hat. . . .
And Yankee John, the packet rat. . . .

Beware these packet ships, I say. . . .
They steal your stores and clothes away. . . .

We are going away from friends and home. . . .
We are going away in search of gold. . . .

Fathers and mothers, say good-bye. . . .
Sisters and brothers, don't you cry. . . .

100

National Park Service

The Leaving Of Liverpool

By the middle of the 19th century, an Englishman might dream of sailing off to California — around Cape Horn — to seek his fortune. He promises to return, but we are not sure if he ever does.

England

Fare you well, the Prin – ce's ___ Land – ing stage, Riv – er Mer – sey, fare you well. ___ I'm ___ off to Ca – li – for – ni – a, A ___ place I ___ know ___ right well. ___

Chorus So it's fare you well, my ___ own true love, When

I'm off to California
By the way of the stormy Cape Horn,
And I will send to you a letter, love,
When I am homeward bound. *Chorus*

Farewell to Lower Frederick Street,
Anson Terrace and Park Lane,
Farewell, it will be some long time
Before I see you again. *Chorus*

I've shipped on a Yankee clipper ship,
Davy Crockett is her name,
And Burgess is the captain of her,
And they say she's a floating shame. *Chorus*

The tug is waiting at the pierhead
To take us down the stream,
Our sails are loose and our anchor secure,
So I'll bid you good-bye once more. *Chorus*

I'm bound away to leave you,
Good-bye, my love, good-bye,
There ain't but one thing that grieves me,
That's leaving you behind. *Chorus*

Finnish–American Historical Archives

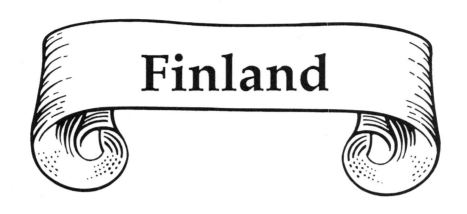

Finland

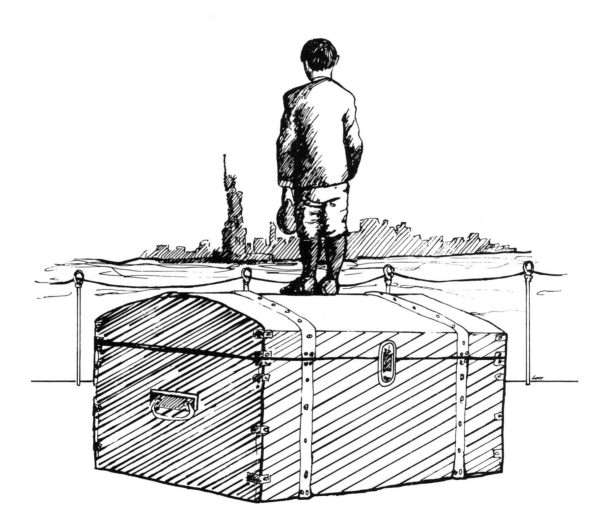

Värssyjä Sieltä Ja Täältä
Verses From Here And There

Singer and song writer Hiski Salomaa was born in Finland in 1891 and died in New York in 1957. He worked as a tailor in Michigan and Massachusetts, where there were large groups of Finnish immigrants. He gained wide popularity throughout the Finnish community by his witty and insightful musical commentaries on Finnish–American life, which he performed at labor union meetings.

Finland

by Hiski Salomaa, 1931

Nyt työ – tä mi – nä o – len taas kat – sel – lut, Piek – sun
poh – jat – kin ___ ha – jal – le as – tel – lut. Ja kan – rat – kin men – nyt on
lin – tal – leen, Kär – jet si – mi – hin ___ kat – soo jo tar – kal – leen. Et – tä

I have been look – ing for a job all 'round town, And the
bot – toms of my boots they are all worn down. And both of my heels, they are
worn like – wise, And the toes, they are ___ curl – ing up to my eyes. Ev – 'ry

mis – sä – hän mah – taa vi – ka taas ol – la, Kun uus – i – a ei a – la
bod — y is won — d'ring what has gone bad here, For there are – n't an — y new

jal – koi – hin tul – la, Ku – rj – al – ta näyt – tää ai – ku ja tää, Ja
boots to be had here. Times are get – ting hard, the peo – ple all say, And

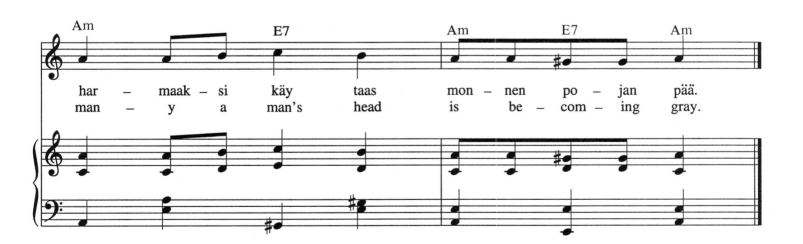

har – maak – si käy taas mon – nen po – jan pää.
man — y a man's head is be – com — ing gray.

Wall Streetti se nauraa partaansa,
Kun kaikki se on saanut alle valtansa.
Paavikin huutaa nyt Herrassa,
Että kirkotkin vastaa jo kerrassa.
Bolshevikit museoita niistä nyt laittaa,
Se pappien unta hieman kai haittaa.
Kun niitäkin alkaa jo loppua työ,
Kaikk' synkältä näyttää kuin syksyinen yö.

Now Wall Street is a-laughing up its sleeve,
For whatever they do say the people believe.
The Pope cries out in the name of the Lord,
And the churches are all in accord.
The Bolsheviks are turning them into museums,
Disturbing the priests and giving them bad dreams.
Even they're out of work — what a sight.
Everything looks dark as an autumn night.

Jos Englannin työläiset lakkoontuu,
Yrjö yskähän aina silloin sairastuu.
Ja prinssin horsikin kompastuu,
Ja nenä hältä joka kerta loukkaantuu.
Sotakorvaukset Saksalla puree jo vatsaa,
Espanja kuninkaansa laittoi nyt matkaan.
Ei Ranskassa työttömyys kai haittaa se tuo,
Kun maailman rikkaat siellä mässää ja juo.

Setä Sami se on myös viisas mies,
Se pisneksen kyllä hyvin tarkoin ties.
Neillä puhuvat kuvatkin on vallassa,
Moni taiteilija on ollut pannassa.
Masina se heidänkin paikkansa otti,
Ja työttömäks' kadulle se tuhansia johti
Moni soittaja halvalla pillinsä möi,
Ja lunssina viimeiset tinansa jo söi.

Meitä finnoja on täällä setä Sämin maass',
Noin viitisen sataa tuhatta.
Ja täällä me elämme kuin taivahass',
Vaikk' moni on tullut tänne luvatta.
Meillä puoluehommat on suuria,
On haalit kuin Paapelin muuria.
Moness' paikassa niitä on meilla jo kuus',
Ja riita kun syntyy niin tehdään uus'.

Vaikka republiikki meitä nyt hallitsee,
Silti demokraatin aika se vallitsee.
Ja kaikki on postuun partaala,
Hyvää odotamme mielellä hartaalla.
Moni poika lyönyt on jo rukkaset tiskiin,
Ja juonunna nykyajan huonoa viskii.
Että töppöset ylös aina keikahtaa,
Ja viimeisen kerran veisatann.

If merry England's workers go on strike,
Then good King George's temperature begins to spike.
And even the prince's charger stumbles,
And hurts his royal nose when the market tumbles.
Meanwhile Germany can't its war debts pay,
And the King of Spain has been sent on his way.
Unemployment doesn't seem to hurt France —
The wealthy carouse and drink champagne and dance.

Our dear old Uncle Sammy is clever too,
For he really knows his business and what to do.
Talking pictures are out everywhere now,
And many artists have lost out, and how!
Their jobs have been taken over by machines,
And unemployment is what it means.
Many a musician has felt the crunch,
And sold his horn to buy himself a lunch.

There are five hundred thousand Finns living here
In Uncle Sam's country as of this year.
It's just like heaven here, living free,
Although many of us came here illegally.
In political activities we like to dabble,
And our halls sound just like the old Tower of Babel.
In many places there are six Finnish centers,
And when a fight starts, a new one enters.

Republicans are ruling now over the land,
Though the time of the Democrats is at hand.
Oh, everyone's begging for nickels and dimes,
And waiting patiently for better times.
Many a man's thrown his work gloves away,
And is now drinking bootleg whisky, they say.
That goes on until he turns up his toes,
The last psalm is sung for him, and out he goes.

Elämän Varrelta
In The Course Of Life

Two young Finnish immigrant boys head west to seek their fortune. In this instance, the west is Canada.

Finland

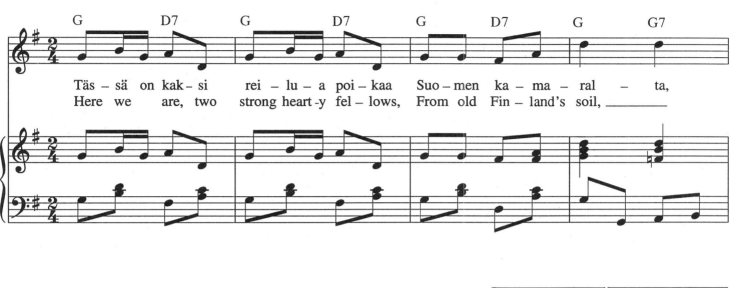

Täs – sä on kak – si rei – lu – a poi – kaa Suo – men ka – ma – ral – ta,
Here we are, two strong heart -y fel – lows, From old Fin – land's soil, _____

Pie-noi-sen ky–län _ lai-dal – ta ja_ Mä–en _ kuk-ku lal – ta. lal – ta
In the_ out-skirts_ of a small vil-lage,_ High on a hill did toil._____ toil._____

Myrsky kun laivaa keinutteli ja Ulvoi taklingeissa, Pikkasen meitä huoletti mäissä (2) Meren mainingeissa.	Crossing the ocean our ship was rocking, The wind howled around us. We were so worried, we were so frightened, (2) The tall waves, they nearly drowned us.
Astumme kunnaita vierahan maan, Korvet meile soittaa; Poikansa pitää kultala, (2) Et voi sinä sitä voittaa.	As we passed over the hills of a strange land, Forests sang to greet us. These boys just think there's gold for the taking, (2) Nothing on earth can beat us.
Harvestihoopona lännen mailla, Mainissa mokkarina, Tyttäret usein kiusailee, (2) Kas tummaa kulkuria.	Harvesting out west or trying mining, Every job does please us. "Just take a look at those dark vagabonds, now," (2) How all the girls would tease us.
Suuri on tämä haaveiden maa ja Toiset täälä nääntyy, Poikia moitä ei huoleta vaikka (2) Tukkamme harmaaksi kääntyy.	Some in this land of dreams are defeated, Hear what we are saying. But we don't worry and we'll just repeat it, (2) Though our hair is graying.

Reisaavaisen Laulu Ameriikan
Song Of A Wanderer To America

In true classical ballad style, the singer recounts the long and arduous journey, step by step from Finland through Sweden and England, and finally across the stormy Atlantic to America.

Finland

A - lo - tan mi -nä lau - lu - ni Taas täl - lä - kin ta - val - la. Ja
I'll start sing -ing my song to you, Once a - gain its words re - sound. And

ai - jon läh - te - ä rei - saa - maan si - tä maa - il - ma la - vi - aa.
I will start all my wan - der - ing through this whole great wide world a - round.

Ameriikkaan mennä meinaan	America is the place I'm bound,
Ja sinne nämä pojat muuttaa	And it's there the boys will roam.
Me katselemme mailman avaruutta	We will be searching the open world,
Ja asuntoa uutta.	Just a-looking for a new home.
Kun Suomen rannasta lähdettiin	When we left from the Finnish shores
Niin maistettiin maljasta,	There were drinks in every hand.
Hurraa huuto kuuluu,	And we could hear all the loud hurrahs
Isänmaasta armaasta.	From our dear fatherland.
Tukholmin sillalla ensi kerta,	First we came to Stockholm's bridge —
Meitä vastaan otettiin	They met us at the pier.
Kun kuulivat mihin reisaamme	And when they heard where we were bound,
Niin värkkimme korjattiin.	They fixed all of our gear.
Siitä me läksimme ajamaan	On gallant wagons we then did mount,
Niillä vaunuilla uljailla	And we started in to drive.
Kahden päivän reisattua	And after a journey of two days,
Gööteporiin tulimme.	At Gothenburg did arrive.

Englannin meri kaupunki
Jota Hulliksi sanottiin
Sepä nyt ensiksi
Meitä vastaan tuleepi.

Siitä me läksimme ajamaan
Englannin maata pitkin
Että se kuuluisa Liverpooli
Jo nähdä saataisiin.

Atlantin meri aukeni
Iso ja lavia
Vaan kyllä Herra laivamme
Vielä laittaa haminaan.

Irlannin järven saaret
Jotka ensiksi kierrettiin
Mitä niillä reisaavilla
Siinä liene mielessäkin.

Laivat on raudasta rakettu
Ja ne on niin pitkiä
Niin ettei tartte reisaavaisen
Pelvosta itkeä.

Atlantin aallot on korkeita
Ja välit on pitkiä.
Monen raukan reisaavan
Täytyy pelvosta itkeä.

Kymmenen päivän reisattua
Meiltä huolet jo väheni
Kun tuo kuuluisa Ameriikka
Meitä jo läheni.

Ei siellä helssata herroja
Ei pappia palvella
Vaan niinkuin vertaisellensa
Saa asiansa toimittaa.

Union Pacific R.R. Co.

An English seaport we then struck —
The one that they call Hull.
That was the one that they told us
Would be our next port of call.

Our journey it picked up from there
Along the English roads.
Up to the city of Liverpool
We bore our heavy loads.

And there we saw the Atlantic sea,
And it was so large and wide.
We knew the Lord would guide our ship
Safely to the other side.

The islands of the Irish lake
Were the ones that we first spied.
I wonder what those wanderers
Then felt deep down inside.

The boats are made of iron,
And they are so very long.
So travelers don't have to fear
That something might go wrong.

Atlantic waves they are so high,
They toss the ship about.
So many of the vagabonds
In fear must still cry out.

After the trip of ten long days,
Our sorrows turned to cheer,
When that famous America
We realized was so near.

There you don't bow down to a master,
You are not bound to priests.
Instead, as among equal men,
You can do just as you please.

Ameriikan Siirtolaisen Laulu
A Song Of An American Immigrant

The Finnish community of Michigan, in an effort to preserve their language and culture and to document their experience in North America, founded Suomi College in Hancock in 1896. The college archives contain oral family histories, manuscripts, artifacts, books, periodicals, and recordings. This song comes from that collection.

Finland

A - me - riik ka___ Suo - men poi - kain mie - le - hen nyt___
Fin - nish boys have A - me - ri - ca now in their thoughts and _____

kään - tyy, Voi! kun ra - kas ko - tin-sa näin
in their mind. Oh, those love - ly. Fin - nish homes that

kau - vas jät - tää täy - tyy. täy - tyy.
they must leave so far be-hind. far be-hind.

Valtameri lavealta
Silmissämme siintää,
Suomen poikain silmät vuotaa (2)
Eron kyyneleitä.

Ameriikka Suomen poikain
On nyt paras turva,
Kun ei saata veljellänsä (2)
Oleskella orja.

Pappan talo vahvistettu
On mun veljelläni,
Amerikkaan kuuluu täältä (2)
Suomen poikain ääni.

Amerikkaan Suomen pojat
Tuhansia seilaa,
Ameriikan kultamaassa (2)
Rikastua meinaa.

Ameriikan kulta on niin
Maailmassa mainittuna
Suomen pojat Ameriikan (2)
Matkalle hankittuna.

Ameriikan kulta on niin
Loistavata lajia,
Kaikki Suomen neitosetkin (2)
Ameriikan naidaan.

Matkustamme vierahalle
Ameriikan maalle,
Vaikka siellä siirtolaisna (2)
Majaella saamme.

Monta kertaa mielehemme
Suomi vielä miustuu
Kun nuo aallot laivan eessä (2)
Kohisee ja truiskuu.

Höyry vaan kuin voimallansa
Propellia vääntää
Eikä meidän enää salli (2)
Takaperin kääntää.

Piljetit on lunastettu
Ameriikkaan asti,
Eronhetki kyynelillä (2)
Poskiamme kasti.

Eipä tässä itkeminen,
Parempi on laulaa,
Ehkä sydän kuumempi kuin (2)
Masuunissa rauta.

Hyvästi jää sä Suomen maa
Sä kallempi kuin kulta,
Et sä taida ikänänsä (2)
Unhoittua multa.

Oh, the ocean, it is so wide,
Bearing us away from here.
And the eyes of Finnish boys
Are brimming full of farewell tears. (2)

Finnish boys know America
Does offer freedom they all do crave.
Even for your own brother
You cannot live here as a slave. (2)

My own brother has taken over —
Father's old house he now enjoys.
All the way to America
Now goes the voice of Finnish boys. (2)

Finnish boys to America,
In thousands strong they all sail away.
Golden land — America —
They'll strike it rich without delay. (2)

Gold and wealth in America
Is so well known the whole world around.
Finnish boys to America,
This very moment are all bound. (2)

Gold and wealth in America
Is shiny and oh, so glittery.
All the young girls of Finland
Are married to Ameriky. (2)

We are travelling o'er the sea
To America, and we have no care.
Even though as immigrants
From now on we'll be living there. (2)

Many times our minds will turn back.
Finland, we will remember thee
When those waves before the bow
Do foam and splash as we sail the sea. (2)

The steam engine with strength
Turns the propeller ever upon its track.
And it will no longer let us
Turn around and sail on back. (2)

We have bought our tickets
To America, and we must depart.
When at last we took our leave,
We cried so hard it broke our heart. (2)

But it's not time for us to shed tears.
Better that we should sing a song.
Hearts inflamed like molten iron —
Now's the time to move along. (2)

Farewell to you, dear land of Finland,
Dearer to me than any gold.
Never will you be forgotten,
Memories of you I'll hold. (2)

Kasvakohon kankaillasi
Vapauden kukka,
Valmistukoon hedelmäsi
Tasarvoisuutta. (2)

Että saisi suomalaiset
Täällä sekä siellä
Toisiansa kätellä he
Veljeksinä vielä. (2)

Eläköhön tasa-arvo,
Kuolkohon raha-valta,
Sitten eivät Suomen pojat
Lähde kotomaalta. (2)

Let your moors always grow with flowers,
Flowers showing that man is free.
Let the fruits in your green orchards
Be filled with equality. (2)

So that all of the Finnish people,
Living here and living there,
Might shake hands once more as brothers,
Living freely everywhere. (2)

And so, long live equality —
And death to money's cold, icy hand.
Then the boys of our dear Finland
Never will leave their homeland. (2)

Sherman Collection, National Park Service

114

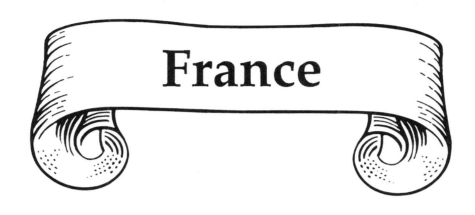

France

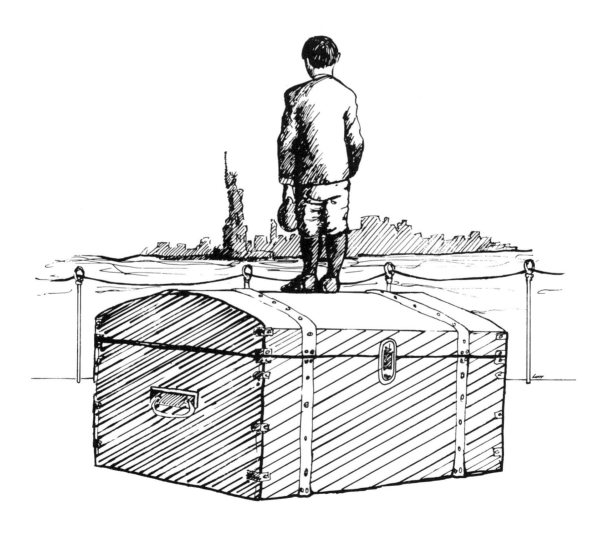

Le Mississippi
The Mississippi

In 1719, when this song was written, the Banque Royale had greatly expanded its overseas activities by successively absorbing the China, Guinea, and Santo Domingo investment companies. "Mississippi," that is, Louisiana, was looked upon as a potential gold mine for investors. Fortunes were made. Fortunes were lost. It is interesting to note that the author of this song had a somewhat inaccurate notion of the geography of the region: The Spanish (verse 6) were actually in Texas.

France

116

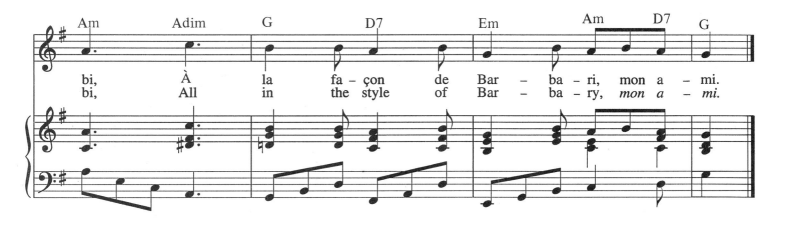

bi, À la fa – çon de Bar – ba – ri, mon a – mi.
bi, All in the style of Bar – ba – ry, *mon a – mi.*

C'est un roman que ce qu'on fait	It's like a novel how they act,
Dedans le Ministère;	The Ministry's in motion.
Non, non, l'on ne croira jamais	You don't believe me? It's a fact,
Tout ce qu'on y voit faire.	Just look at the commotion.
A l'avenir avec raison,	There'll come a day — it won't be long,
La faridondaine la faridondon,	*La faridondaine la faridondon,*
On rira du Mississipi,	We'll laugh at the Mississippi,
Biribi,	Biribi,
A la façon de Barbari mon ami.	All in the style of Barbari,* *mon ami.*
Les uns se sont fait une idée	Now, some of them have the idea
D'augmenter leur finance,	To better their condition.
Les autres d'avoir leur lippée	And others want **theirs** — don't you see?
Dedans cette occurrence;	And join the competition.
Chacun s'abuse à sa façon,	Everyone's ready to be gone,
La faridondaine la faridondon,	*La faridondaine la faridondon,*
Je le suis du Mississippi,	I, too, am from Mississippi,
Biribi,	Biribi,
A la façon de Barbari mon ami.	All in the style of Barbari, *mon ami.*
Ces Messieurs vont donc voyager	These gentlemen all want to go
Dedans la Louisiane?	To visit Louisiana.
Chacun courre s'y engager.	Each one is hoping — don't you know?
C'est une courtisane	To find a pollyanna.
Qui attire les vagabonds,	They're just a bunch of vagabonds,
La faridondaine la faridondon,	*La faridondaine la faridondon,*
Ce que j'en pense je le dis,	I say what I think, don't you see?
Biribi,	Biribi,
A la façon de Barbari mon ami.	All in the style of Barbari, *mon ami.*
C'est certainement voyager	It's certainly just like a trip
Dans l'île de Chimère,	That is called a wild goose chase.
Cela s'appelle aller chercher	They might as well all take a ship,
Dans les Cieux, la terre.	And search for earth out in space.
Tôt ou tard nous les reverrons,	Sooner or later we'll see them,
La faridondaine la faridondon.	*La faridondaine la faridondon,*
Chargés d'or du Mississippi,	Full of gold from Mississippi,
Biribi,	Biribi,
A la façon de Barbari mon ami.	All in the style of Barbari, *mon ami.*

---

*A possible reference to the "adventurous" behavior of the Barbary pirates, who flourished in the Mediterranean during this period.

Puis enfin, c'est aller brusquer
La fortune contraire,
Et vouloir aller débusquer
L'Espagnol de sa terre.
La poudre de projection,
La faridondaine la faridondon,
Vient tout droit du Mississippi,
   Biribi,
A la façon de Barbari mon ami.

Pour moi, j'en attends les effets
Assis dedans ma chaise,
Et je ris de tous ces projets,
Ici fort à mon aise.
Pour connaître l'illusion,
La faridondaine la faridondon,
Faut aller au Mississippi,
   Biribi,
A la façon de Barbari mon ami.

And finally, to take a chance,
And challenge fickle fortune.
To kick out Spain and put in France,
I fear we may have war soon.
Here comes the big ex-plo-si-on,
La faridondaine la faridondon,
Which comes straight from Mississippi,
   Biribi,
All in the style of Barbari, *mon ami.*

Well, as for me, I'll wait and see,
Here seated in my armchair.
I laugh at this activity,
It's castles in the thin air.
Would you join in the senseless fun?
La faridondaine la faridondon,
Then go straight to Mississippi,
   Biribi,
All in the style of Barbari, *mon ami.*

La Fayette En Amérique
La Fayette In America

Cornwallis led a country dance,
The like was never seen, sir,
Much retrograde and much advance,
And all with General Greene, sir.

Greene, in the south, then danced a set,
And got a mighty name, sir,
Cornwallis jigged with young Fayette,
But suffered in his fame, sir.

("Cornwallis' Country Dance")

France

Words by Pierre Jean de Béranger (1780-1857)
Music by J. B. M. Braun

Ré-pub - li-cains, quel cor-tè - ge s'a-van - ce? Un vieux guer-rier dé-bar-que par-mi nous. Vient-il d'un Roi nous ju-rer l'al-li-an - ce? Il _ a _ des _ rois al-lu-mé le cour-roux. Est il puis-

Re-pub - li-cans, what cor-tege - is ad-vanc-ing? An old cam-paign - er comes up-on the path. Is it a king that he is rep-re-sent-ing? He _ has _ caused _ kings to feel an — ger and wrath. And is he

sant? Seul il fran-chit les on-des. Qu'a-t-il-donc fait? Il a bri-sé des
strong? A- lone he crossed the o-cean. What has he done? He has smashed all the

fers. Gloire im - mor - telle à l'hom - me des deux mon-des! Jours_ de_ tri-
chains. Im - mor - tal__ fame - two worlds owe him de - vo-tion! Oh,_ days_ of_

om-phe, jours_de_tri - om-phe, jours_de_tri - omphe, é - clair-ez l'un-i-
tri-umph, oh,_ days_ of _ tri-umph, Tri - um-phant_ days light_ the world with your

vers. Jours_de_tri - omphe é-clair-ez l'un-i-vers._____
rays. Oh,_ days_ of_ days light the world with your rays._____

Européen, partout sur ce rivage,
Qui retentit de joyeuses clameurs,
Tu vois régner, sans trouble et sans servage,
La paix, les lois, le travail et les moeurs.
Des opprimés ces bords sont le refuge.
La tyrannie a peuplé nos déserts.
L'homme et ses droits ont ici, Dieu pour juge. *Chorus*

Mais que de sang nous coûta ce bien-être!
Nous succombions; La Fayette accourut,
Montra la France, eut Washington pour maître,
Lutta, vainquit, et l'Anglais disparut.
Pour son pays, pour la liberté sainte,
Il a depuis, grandi les revers;
Des fers d'Ollmutz nous effaçons l'empreinte. *Chorus*

Ce viel ami qui tant d'ivresse accueille,
Par un héros ce héros adopté,
Bénit jadis, à sa première feuille,
L'arbre naissant de notre liberté.
Mais aujourd'hui que l'arbre et son feuillage
Bravent en paix la foudre et les hivers,
Il vient s'asseoir sous son fertile ombrage. *Chorus*

Autour de lui, vois nos chefs, vois nos sages,
Nos vieux soldats se rappelant ses traits;
Vois tout un peuple, et ces tribus sauvages
A son nom seul sortant de leurs fôrets.
L'arbre sacré sur ce concours immense,
Forme un abri de rameaux toujours verts.
Les vents au loin porteront sa semence. *Chorus*

L'Européen, que frappent ces paroles,
Servit des Rois, suivit des conquerants;
Un peuple esclave encensait ces idoles,
Un peuple libre a des honneurs plus grandes.
Hélas! dit-il, et son oeil sur les ondes
Semble chercher des bords lointains et chers:
Que la vertu rapproche les deux mondes! *Chorus*

Oh, European, all over these shores,
Which echo with such joyous refrains,
It's you will reign — in bondage no more,
With peace and laws and with work — no more chains.
All the oppressed will now here find refuge,
For tyranny has peopled our deserts.
Man and his rights, they are here — God will judge. *Chorus*

But for this freedom, how the wars did bleed us.
We did succumb; then La Fayette appeared.
He showed how France, with Washington to lead us,
Could battle, conquer — make England disappear.
And for his land, our liberty most holy,
He has since then increased in many ways.
The chains of Ollmutz,* we'll erase the memory. *Chorus*

That dear old friend who's greeted by such cheering,
A hero he, adopted by the free,
He once did bless, with its first leaves appearing,
The tender tree of our liberty.
But nowadays, since it has grown and flourished,
And braves in peace the lightning and the storm,
He seeks the shade of that which freedom nourished. *Chorus*

Around him flock our leaders and our wise men,
And our old soldiers, who remember yet.
You see the people and the savage tribesmen,
They leave their forests — they cannot forget.
The sacred tree, above the people towering,
A shelter forms, with branches always green.
The winds will carry far and wide its flowering. *Chorus*

The European whom this appeal inspires,
Still serves his kings and lords against his will.
A people enslaved, did flatter all these liars,
A people free, has honors greater still.
"Alas!" says he, while gazing o'er the ocean,
He seems to seek shores, dear, yet far away —
"Would that the two worlds join in their devotion!" *Chorus*

---

*Site of a French defeat, in what is now Czechoslovakia, by the Austrians in 1742 during the War of the Austrian Succession (1740–1748).

Adieu, Je Pars Pour L'Amérique
Farewell, I'm Bound For America

This classic ballad of love and parting is widely known in Quebec, Acadia, and France.

France

A - dieu, je pars pour l'A - mé - ri - que, Ma bien - aim -
Fare – well, I'm bound off for A – me – ri - ca, My dear - est

ée, y vien - drez vous? Ell' me ré - pond: "Non, non," dit
heart, won't you come too? She an - swered me: "No, no," says

el – le, "Je n'i - rai pas, _____ Car tous gar -
she to me, "I will not go, _____ For all the

çons qui vont dans l'A - mé - riq' en re - vienn'nt pas."
lads gone to A - me - ri - ca nev - er come back."

122

J'ai de l'argent dans mon gousset,
Ma bien-aimée en voulez-vous?
Elle me répond: "Non, no," dit-elle, "je n'en veux pas.
Tous garçons qui vont dans l'Amérique en ont besoin.

"Quand tu seras dans l'Amérique,
Bien loin de moi, tu m'oublieras.
Tu voiras une, tu voiras l'autre, tu m'oublieras.
En attendant de tes nouvelles, je languirai."

Quand je serai dans l'Amérique,
Ton blanc portrait, je le voudrais.
Je le mettrai dedans ma chambre bien enfermé.
Cinq ou six fois dans la semaine l'embrasserai.

I have some money in my pocket,
My dearest heart, don't you want some?
She answers me, "No, no," says she, "I don't need it,
For all the lads who go to America need all they have.

"And when you'll be there in America,
Far, far from me, you'll forget me.
You will see one, you'll see another, you'll forget me.
Waiting to hear from you, my heart will ache."

When I will be there in America,
A portrait of you I'd gladly have.
I'll lock it up safely where I will live.
Five or six times during the week a kiss to it I'll give.

National Park Service

Je Suis Sur Mon Départ
I'm Getting Ready To Depart

In the mid-19th century, long ocean voyages to Australia and California had about them an air of uncertainty, of finality. Despite promises to return "in two years," both singer and listener knew that the chances of their ever seeing each other again were slim.

France

Je suis sur mon dé - pa - - re pour chan -
I'm get - ting read - y to de - part, to change

ger de pa - ys. J'en - tre - prends le voy - a - ge
my coun - try. I'm un - der - tak - ing a voy -

de sou - cis et d'en - nuis R'a -
age of trou - bles and of mis - er - y. Fare -

Moi qui es jeune encore, qui n'aime guèr' l'argent,
J'm'en vas chercher de l'ore en mon âg' florissant.
Si Dieu vient à mon aide, j'espèr' bien dans deux ans,
Au retour du voyage, de voir tous mes parents.

Dans un vaisseau de mer je me suis embarqué.
Surpris par la tempête, je manqu' de m'y noyer.
On vient dedans ce monde pour chercher des trésors.
Souvent dans les voyages, on rencontre la mort.

Qui a fait la chansonnette, c'est un vieux paysan.
Sur la mer il navigue avec deux de ses enfants.
Il dit que dessus la mer on a bien du bon temps.
Et parmi les poissons on peut vivre cent ans.

And I, who still am young, and love not money,
In the prime of my life I'm seeking gold in Californy.
If God will be my aid, I hope that in two years
I will return back home and see again my dears.

Aboard an ocean ship I soon was outward bound.
A tempest struck us then and I was nearly drowned.
We come into this world — to seek great wealth we're led,
But often on our trips it's death we find instead.

The man who made this song, an old-timer is he,
And with his two brave sons he sails upon the sea.
He says beneath the waves there are no cares or fears,
And down among the fish you can live one hundred years.

Nun Ist Die Scheidestunde Da
The Hour Of Parting Is Now Here

Despite its German text, this is in fact a French song. It comes from Alsace and dates from a period when Alsace was part of France. It was collected in Hunspach in 1937 by Th. Wolber, who had this to say about it (in French):

> In the middle of the 19th century many people from Alsace and Lorraine emigrated to America, because there was an economic crisis in our region. This song describes the exodus of a family to America. The song itself allows us to fix the time of its creation. We see that the inhabitants of the Hunspach region loaded their belongings onto a wagon, but from Strasbourg they took the railroad train. The Wissembourg–Strasbourg Line was, therefore, not yet inaugurated. Since the Strasbourg–Sarrebourg–Paris Line was opened in 1851 and the Wissembourg–Strasbourg Line in 1855, the song could only have been composed after 1851 and before 1855.

France (Alsace)

Jetzt ist die Zeit und Stun – de da, Wo wir fah – ren nach A –
To – day's the day and now's the hour when we trav – el to A –

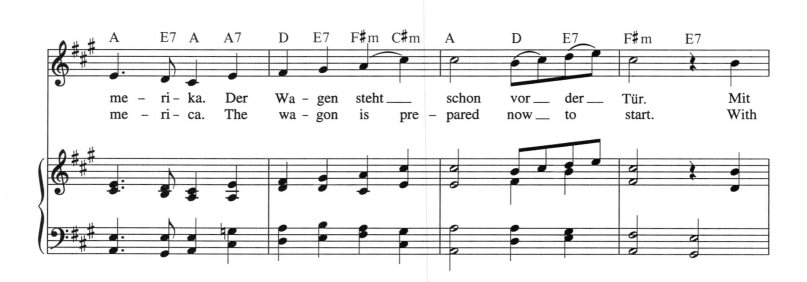

me – ri – ka. Der Wa – gen steht schon vor der Tür. Mit
me – ri – ca. The wa – gon is pre – pared now to start. With

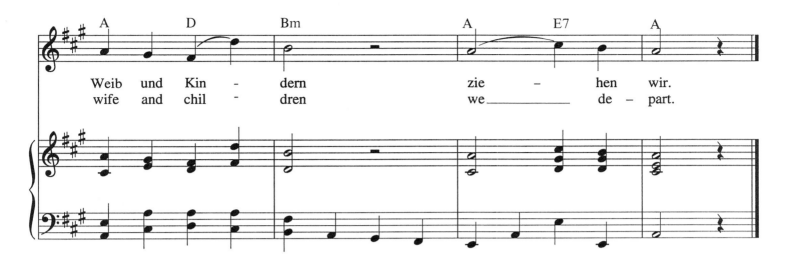

Weib und Kin - dern zie — hen wir.
wife and chil - dren we_____ de - part.

Und als wir kamen in Strassburg an,
So steigen wir ein in die Eisenbahn.
Wir fahren fort schnell wie der Wind
Mit Knecht, mit Magd, mit Weib und Kind.

Und als wir kamen in Havre an,
Da heißt es, Bruder, geh' voran!
Und schwing dein Hütlein hoch in die Höh
Und sag dem Frankreich nun ade.

Und als wir kamen aufs hohe Meer,
Da heißt es, Bruder geh einher!
Wir fürchten keinen Wasserfall,
Wir denken, Gott lebt überall.

Und als wir kamen in New-York an,
Da trafen wir Bekannte an.
Wir reichen einander die brüderliche Hand
Und fragen gleich: Aus welchem Land.*

And when to Strassbourg then we came,
We climbed aboard the railroad train,
The train sped down the track so wild,
With servant, maid, with wife and child.

And when into Havre the train roared,
They called out, "Brothers, get on board!
And toss your cap high in the sky,
It's time to bid old France good-bye."

And when we were on the high sea,
The ship sailed on so speedily.
The stormy sea we do not fear,
Because we know our God is near.

And in New York at journey's end,
We greeted our dear old friend.
We grasped each other's outstretched hand,
And asked then: "You are from what land?"*

---

*It is a pity that the song ends abruptly on this curious note. Apparently the collector's source did not remember any more of it, since a sixth verse is implied by a dotted line after the number "6" in the handwritten copy found in the Deutsches Volksliedarchiv (German Folk Song Archive) in Freiburg. There is a strikingly similar Swiss song (not included in this collection) which ends with the same question, leading us to assume that *Land* in this context might refer to a specific locale rather than a country.

Hier Können Wir Nicht Bleiben
We Cannot Remain Here

Another Alsatian song, collected in 1918 from the singing of an old woman who remembered hearing it sung by emigrants as a child. From the year of the French Revolution (1789) until 1870, Alsace was under French control. From 1870 to 1918, Germany took over. After the Treaty of Versailles (1918), France regained control until the period of German occupation during World War II (1940–1945). After the war, it once again reverted to France.

France (Alsace)

Ich ver – kauf mein Gut und Häus – chen wohl
I sell my house and po – ses – sions wohl for

um ein ge – rin – ges Geld, Wir wol – len aus Frank – reich
hard – ly what they are worth, From France we will be

rei – sen in ein an – dern Teil der Welt.
leav – ing for the far side of the earth.

Als wir in Havre kamen,
In die schöne feste Stadt,
Da gehn wir zum Präfekt,
Legen unsere Schriften ab.

„Herr Präfect und Herr Präfect,
Wir haben eine Bitt an Euch,
Und den Paß sollet ihr unterschreiben,
Wir wollen aus Frankreich."

„Was habt ihr für eine Ursach,
Was habt ihr für eine Klag,
Euer Leben zu riskieren
Im Land Amerika?"

„Hier können wir ja nicht bleiben,
Hier können wir ja nicht sein,
Denn die Huissiers und Notarien
Haben unseren größten Teil."

Als wir über's Meer 'nüber kamen
In's Land Amerika,
Da kamen sie mit Kreuz und Fahnen,
Sagen uns den Willkomm an.

Seid willkommen, seid willkommen
Ihr schöne junge Leut.
Wollet ihr uns etwas geben,
Lasset uns nicht lange stehn.

Sung to last four measures:
Denn die Nacht die kommt zu schleichen
Und wir haben noch weit zu gehn.

And when we came to Le Havre,
In that city all secure,
Then we went straight to the prefect
To depose our signature.

"Mister Prefect, Mister Prefect,
Won't you please give us just a chance?
Our passport won't you please sign now,
For we want to go from France."

"Tell me what could be your reason,
And why are you dissatisfied?
Your lives you are really risking,
Sailing to the other side."

"Well, we can no longer stay here,
We just simply can't remain.
The bailiffs and the notaries,
They cause us endless pain."

And when we cross the wide ocean
To America's fair land,
They'll come with cross and banner,
And extend a welcome hand.

You are welcome, you are welcome,
You handsome, fine young folk.
Can you give us a little something?
Don't let us stand here so.

Sung to last four measures:
For the night will soon be on us,
And we still have far to go.

National Park Service

Lafayette and Rochambeau were brave Frenchmen who fought for us. Baron Steuben, a brave German officer, and Kosciuszko, a gallant Pole, also helped the American cause. General Burgoyne surrendered at Saratoga in 1777, while General Howe and Sir Henry Clinton found conquering America was hard work, and Lord Cornwallis surrendered his entire army. Tarleton was a cruel British cavalry leader.

1166

130

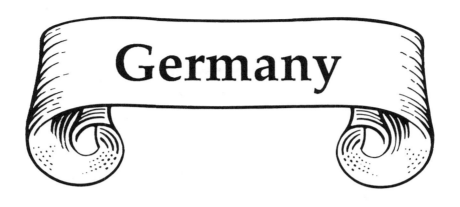

Germany

Wir Reisen Noch Amerikâ
We Are Traveling To America

In 1830, Samuel Friedrich Sautter, a schoolmaster in Wurttemberg, Germany, wrote this song, which he included in his 1845 publication *Collected Poems of a Poor Village Schoolmaster*. Over the years it has achieved the status of a true folk song, with many variant versions. It found its way into Pennsylvania Dutch country, where it is sung to this day.

Germany

Jetzt is di Zeit un Schtun-de dâ, Wir reis - en
To - day's the day and now's the hour, we tra - vel

noch A - me - ri - kâ; D'r Wâj - je schteht schun fa d'r
to A - me - ri - ca; The wa - gon is pre - pared to

Dier, Mit Weib un Kin - ner ____ zie - jen wir.
start, With wife and chil - dren ____ we de - part.

Di Ferde sin schun eingeschpannt
Un alle die mit mir verwandt;
Di Ferde sin schun eingeschpannt,
Reich mir zum letschtenmâl di Hand.

Ach Freinde, weinet nicht so sehr
Wir sehen einander jetzt nimmermehr,
Ach Freinde, weinet nicht so sehr
Wir sehen einander nimmermehr.

Un wenn das Schiff aus dem Hâfen schwimmt
Do warren Lieder angeschtimmt,
Un wenn das Schiff aus dem Hâfen schwimmt
Do warren Lieder augeschtimmt.

Wir firchten keinen Wasserfall
Un dencken Gott ist iwwerall,
Wir firchten keinen Wasserfall
Un dencken Gott is iwwerall.

Un kommen wir noch Baldimor
Do schtrecken wir di Hende vor,
Un rufen aus, "Victoriâ,
Jetzt sin wir in Amerikâ."

The horses are hitched up in place,
There's many a familiar face.
The horses are hitched up in place,
Reach out your hand in last embrace.

Dear friends, don't cry and don't complain,
We'll never see you all again.
Dear friends, don't cry and don't complain,
We'll never see you all again.

And as the ship sails out to sea,
We sing our songs so heartily.
And as the ship sails out to sea,
We sing our songs so heartily.

The stormy seas we do not fear,
Because we know our God is near.
The stormy seas we do not fear,
Because we know our God is near.

And when we come to Baltimore,
We raise our hands and loudly roar.
And then cry out, *"Victoria,*
Now we are in America."

National Park Service

Lied Vom Mississippi
Mississippi Song

Only the text of this enthusiastic song has come down to us, accompanied by the vague indication, "1844 — Nach einer Negermelodie" (to a Negro melody). In seeking to find an appropriate tune that would do justice to the rhythmic bounce of the text, "The Patriotic Diggers" (which dates from the War of 1812) seemed a perfect fit, although it is not a "Negro melody." It is interesting to compare the sentiments expressed in this song with those of the French "Le Mississippi," which was written over 100 years earlier.

Music by Samuel Woodworth
The Patriotic Diggers
Adapted by Jerry Silverman

Germany

zei   Täg-lich kom-mer-sier-en   Hier am Mis-sis-sip-pi.
lice   Stop us from ca-rous-ing   On the Mis-sis-sip-pi.

Freies Denken gilt	Our thoughts are free,
So wie freies Sprechen,	Freedom of expression.
Nirgend, nirgend hier	Nowhere, nowhere here
Für ein Staatsverbrechen.	Political repression.
Hier macht kein Gendarm	Here there's no *gendarme*
Jemals uns Bedrängnis,	That will give us trouble.
Und kein Bettelvogt	Here no beadle leads us
Führt uns ins Gefängnis	To prison on the double —
Hier am Mississippi.	On the Mississippi.
Adel, Ordenskram,	Nobles, medal-junk,
Titel, Räng und Stände,	Title, rank and standing,
Und solch dummes Zeug,	And such stupid stuff,
Hat allhie ein Ende.	Here does find its ending.
Hier darf nie ein Pfaff	Here there are no priests
Mit der Höll uns plagen,	Threatening hell to curb us,
Nie ein Jesuit	And no Jesuits
Uns die Ruh verjagen	Are here to disturb us —
Hier am Mississippi.	On the Mississippi.
Früher lebten wir	Formerly we lived
Gleichsam nur zur Strafe,	Lives of constant fearing,
Und man schor auch uns	And we were like sheep
Eben wie die Schafe.	Led unto the shearing.
Brüder, laßt uns drum	Brothers, let us go
Singen, trinken, tanzen!	Where our fortunes land us.
Keiner darf und kann	Singing, drinking, dancing,
Hier uns je kuranzen,	None to reprimand us —
Hier am Mississippi.	On the Mississippi.
Michel, baue nicht	Michael, do not sow
Ferner deine Saaten	Your seeds anymore now,
Fürs Beamtenheer	For the bureaucrats
Und die Herrn Soldaten!	And the men of war now.
Michel, faß ein Herz,	Michael, listen here —
Endlich auszuwandern:	Leave with all your brothers.
Hier gehörst du dir,	Here you're your own man,
Dort nur stets den andern,	There you are another's —
Hier am Mississippi.	On the Mississippi.

Heil Dir, Columbus
Hail To Thee, Columbus

After the political upheaval of 1848, thousands of disappointed Germans left their homeland for America. The best-known song among these people was this so-called "Columbus Song." The figure of Christopher Columbus assumed the stature of a patron saint and religious symbol.

Germany

Heil dir, Co - lum - bus, sei ge - prie - sen, Sei hoch ge - ehrt in
Hail thee, Co - lum - bus, glo - ry to you, Hon - ored for all e -

E - wig - keit! Du hast mir __ den Weg ge - wie - sen,
ter - ni - ty! Thou hast shown __ me what I must do

Der mich von har - ter Dienst - bar - keit Er - ret - tet hat, wenn
To flee from hard - est sla - ver - y. You res - cued me, I

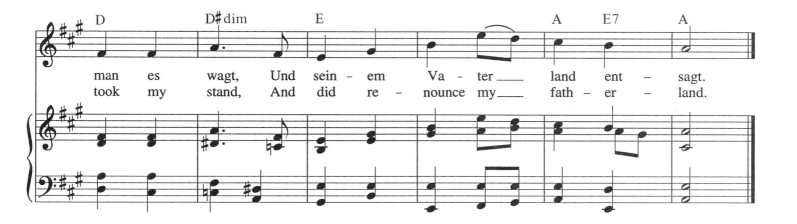

man es wagt, Und sein-em Va-ter___ land ent – sagt.
took my stand, And did re – nounce my___ fath-er – land.

Hier ist der Mensch an nichts gebunden,	Here may a man live life contented,
Was er erwirbt, gehört auch sein,	And he can keep what he does gain.
Die Steuern sind noch nicht erfunden,	Taxes have not yet been invented,
Die unser Leben machen zur Pein.	That cause our life such constant pain.
Wer redlich schafft, der hat sein Brot,	The man that works will have his bread,
Er leid't kein Mangel und kein' Not.	He'll have no lack and know no need.

Wann Ich Vun Dem Land Rei Kumm
When I First Came To This Land

In the great tradition of the humorous, cumulative song is this Pennsylvania Dutch "success story." William Penn had guaranteed religious freedom in his corner of the New World, and the German Amish and Mennonites responded to his invitation. In 1683, the first permanent Mennonite settlement was established at Germantown, Pennsylvania. The language of this song reflects the German of the 17th and 18th century Rhineland. In conversation, wonderful Pennsylvania Dutch phrases abound in what they call "ferhoodled English": The lady serving food at the church picnic announced, "The pie is all, but the cake is yet." Advice to a courting couple: "Kissin' wears out — cookin' don't."

138

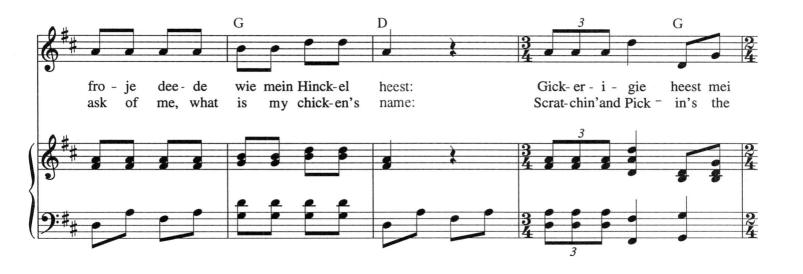

fro - je dee-de wie mein Hinck-el heest: Gick-er-i-gie heest mei
ask of me, what is my chick-en's name: Scrat-chin'and Pick - in's the

Insert each new animal here

glein- es Hinck-e - lie. 2. No kâf ich mir en [End] un
name of my chick - en. And so I bought a [duck] and

D.C. al 𝄋 ⊕

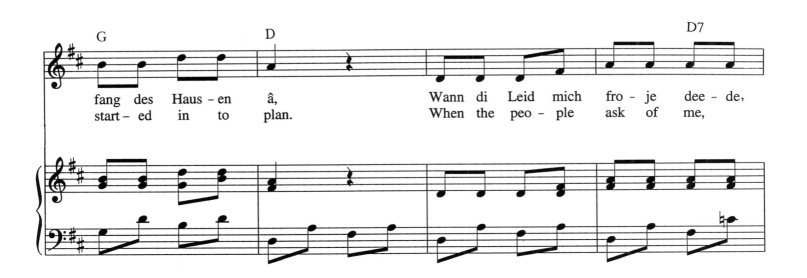

fang des Haus - en â, Wann di Leid mich fro - je dee - de,
start - ed in to plan. When the peo - ple ask of me,

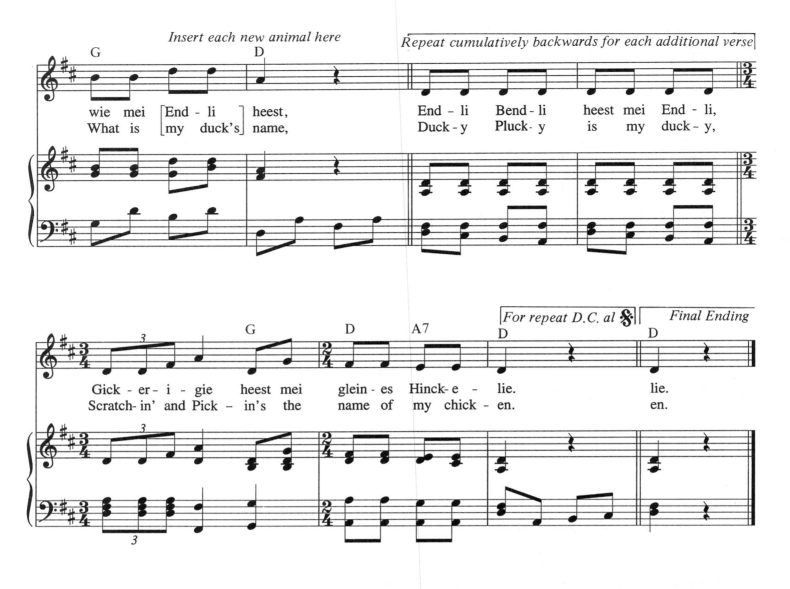

Each verse begins with measure 1. Each new animal (and, in the last verse, the wife) is inserted into the music as indicated. Measures 24 and 25 are repeated cumulatively, with the new animal sung first, followed by all the other animals in reverse order — back to "chicken." (Note the slight change of the text in the last verse.)

3. …Kuh…Uff und Zu heest mei Kuh…
4. …Genzel…Schtumm Schwenzel heest mei Genzel…
5. …Gaul…Hawwer Maul heest mei Gaul…
6. …Hund…Immer Gsund heest mei Hund…
7. …Haus…Rei un Naus heest mei Haus…
8. …No **grie** ich mir en Frâ…
   Hell Deiwel heest mei Weiwel…

3. …cow…Here-and-Now is my cow…
4. …goose…Fast-and-Loose is my goose…
5. …horse…No Racecourse is my horse…
6. …dog…Trot-and-Jog is my dog…
7. …house…Gripe-and-Grouse is my house…
8. …So **I got** myself a wife…
   Full-of-Strife is my wife…

Sherman Collection, National Park Service

Nun Ist Die Scheidestunde
Now Is The Parting Hour

Bremen was a major port of departure for German and other emigrants. This song, published in Berlin in 1855, is but one of many that takes a last look at Bremen before departing for the unknown.

And when we come to Bremen town,
Straight to an inn we sit us down.
And there we drink a flask of wine,
Leave Switzerland and Germany behind.

Germany

Ach, wie vie - le schön - e Sach - en Er - zählt man
Of A - me - ri - ca, they tell me Such pret - ty

aus ___ A - me - ri - ka. ____ Und dort - hin wol - len wir uns
things, __ with - out com - pare. ____ And we are go - ing, Oh so

mach - en, Das schön - ste Le - ben hat man da.
quick - ly, For life is sure - ly bet - ter there.

Hier hat man täglich seine Not	Every day we have what we need here,
Wohl um das liebe schwarze Brot.	All you want of tasty dark bread.
Wohlauf zu leben hat man da	And everything you'd want to succeed here —
Im schönen Land Amerika.	America, you're way ahead.
Komm, wir wollen auf die Reise gehn,	Come, we're ready to make the journey,
Der liebe Gott wird uns beistehn,	And God will surely lend a hand.
Er wird uns schützen mit seiner Hand	Yes, He'll protect us and stay with us,
Und wird uns führen ins gepriesene Land.	And lead us to that wondrous land.
Und als wir kommen in Bremen an,	And when we arrived in Bremen,
Da heißt es "Brüder tretet an	It was then, "Brothers get on board,
Fürchtet keinen Wasserfall,	And do not be afraid of the ocean —
Der liebe Gott ist überall."	Just put your faith all in the Lord."
Und als wir kommen nach Baltimore,	And when we come to Baltimore,
Da heben wir die Hand empor	We raise our hands and loudly roar.
Und rufen laut Viktoria,	And then cry out, *"Viktoria,*
Jetzt sind wir in Amerika.	Now we are in America."
In Amerika ist gut sein,	In America things are fine,
Da gibt's gutes Bier und roten Wein.	Here they have good beer and red wine.
Der rote Wein, der schmeckt uns gut	The red wine, it tastes so good,
Und macht uns allen frohen Mut.	And it puts us in a happy mood.

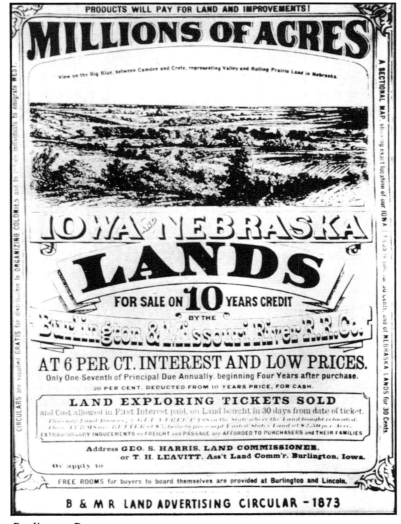

Burlington Route

Auf Der Cimbria
On Board The Cimbria

The *Cimbria,* an emigrant ship, collided with the British steamer *Sultan* in the fog near Borkum Island, off the German coast, on January 19, 1883. It sank rapidly, with a loss of life of 420 people. On board, and among the victims, were two brothers from the town of Espa in Hesse. The wife of the pastor of Espa, Frau Schmitborn, was so moved by the fate of her neighbor's two sons that she quickly composed the text, which was then set to a simple tune by the pastor's serving girl. This tragic tale captured the popular imagination and was soon widely sung.

Germany

Zwei Brü – der woll – ten wan- dern wohl nach A- me – ri – ka, Sie
Two bro - thers wished to wan- der all to A- me – ri – ca, They

zo – gen mit viel an – dern wohl auf der *Cim - bri - a.*
went with man – y oth – ers on board the *Cim - bri - a.*

Der erste Tag war helle,
Dann stieg ein Nebel auf;
Die schiffer fuhren langsam
Den vorgeschriebnen Lauf.

Doch plötzlich sah man's blinken
Zur Seit' ein helles Licht!
„Ihr Lieben, wir versinken,
Die *Cimbria,* sie bricht."

Der Bruder sprach zum andern:
„Wenn du gerettet wirst,
So ziehe in die Heimat
Und grüsse sie von mir!"

Der Bruder aber schweiget,
Sein Mund war schon verstummt,
Da zogen die Gewässer
Die beiden in den Grund.

Nun hat's ein End mit diesen,
Die hier versunken sind.
Lebe wohl, du mein Feinsliebchen,
Lebe wohl, auf Wiedersehen!

The first day it was sunny,
But then a cloud appeared.
The ships proceeded slowly,
As on their course they steered.

And then we saw a blinking,
A bright light in the gloom.
Dear friends, I fear we're sinking,
The *Cimbria* is doomed.

Then brother spoke to brother,
"When you will rescued be,
Return unto our homeland,
And greet them all for me."

The brother, he was silent,
His mouth, it spoke no more,
For soon beneath the waters
Both sank forevermore.

So there's an end to those two
That drowned beneath the main.
Live well, my dearest sweetheart,
Live well, *auf Wiedersehen.*

Greece

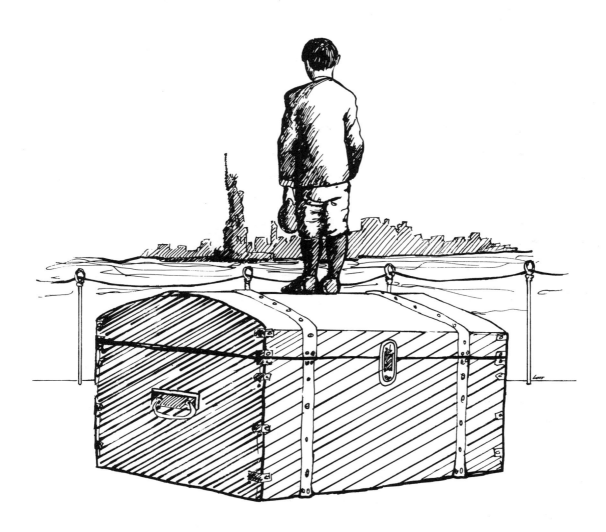

O Yero Amerikanos
The Old American

The "rich American" returning to his impoverished home town in search of a bride must have caused a mixture of awe and resentment. This song was recorded in Athens by D. Perdicopoulos sometime during the 1930s, but the reference to Castle Garden (which was the immigrant reception center in Battery Park at the southern tip of Manhattan between 1855 and 1890) indicates that the song dates from that period.

Greece

1.
Pou hi - lia 'na - the - ma_ o yios, Pou dhen er - ho - ta - ne pio neos.
A thou-sand times be cursed the son, Who did-n't come back look-ing young.

2.
Mon' il - the me psa - ra mal - lia, Yi - re - vi ke yi - ne - ka_ nea.
In - stead he came back with gray_ hair, A young bride seek- ing ev-'ry - where.

3.
Va - zi poun - dra_ ke ko - lo - nia, Ma dhen_ kri - voun_ de ta hro - nia.
U - ses pow - der_ and co - logne,_ But by _ his _ age he_ is un - done. ___

146

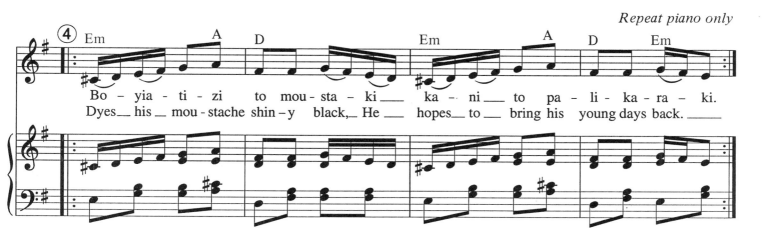

④ Bo - yia - ti - zi to mou - sta - ki___ ka - ni ___ to pa - li - ka - ra - ki.
Dyes___ his ___ mou - stache shin - y black,__ He ___ hopes__ to ___ bring his young days back. _____

Sung to melody 3:

Oti thelete na pite,	Anything you say about him,
Tipota dhe tha tou vrite.	We're much better off without him.

Sung to melody 4:

Mena to pouli mou kani,	The value of my little birdie:
Yia sarand' Amerikani.	Forty old *Amerikani*.

Sung to melody 3:

San tha pas sto Kastigari,	She'll leave you at Castle Garden,
Kapios allos tha sti pari.	And won't even beg your pardon.

Sung to melody 4:

Kapios allos tha sti pari,	You will lose her very quickly —
Yero eksindapendari.	Sixty-five years old and sickly.

Sung to melody 3:

Me dhollaria ke lires,	With your dollars and your promise,
Ti mikroula mas ti pires.	You took our young girl from us.

Sung to melody 4:

Vrase ta dhollaria sou,	Why don't you just boil your dollars
Yia na vapsis ta mallia sou.	To dye your hair a darker color?

Repeat verses 1 and 2

Sherman Collection, National Park Service

147

Fevgho Glikia
I'm Leaving Now

This song was sung by Greek steelworkers in Pittsburgh in the 1920s. The back-breaking toil in the mills represented a very different kind of reality from that which they had imagined America to be.

Greece

Ke ti ftohi,	And oh, you poor,
Ke ti ftohi,	And oh, you poor,
Ke ti ftohi kardhoula mou, Ah!	And oh, you poor sad heart of mine, Ah!
Ke ti ftohi kardhoula mou,	And oh, you poor sad heart of mine,
Mi mou ti kommatiasis.	Oh, please will you not break.
Tha pagho stin,	Now I will go,
Tha pagho stin,	Now I will go,
Tha pagho stin Ameriki, Ah!	Now I will go to America, Ah!
Tha pagho stin Ameriki,	Now I will go to America,
Grighora na ploutiso.	Soon to be a rich man.
Ta dhakria sou,	Those tears of yours,
Ta dhakria sou,	Those tears of yours,
Ta dhakria sou, mana mou, Ah!	Those tears of yours, sweet mother mine, Ah!
Ta dhakria sou, mana mou,	Those tears of yours, sweet mother mine,
Egho na ta sfonghiso.	Won't you wipe them away?
Ti m'ofeli,	Oh, what's the use,
Ti m'ofeli,	Oh, what's the use,
Ti m'ofeli Ameriki, Ah!	Oh, what's the use of America, Ah!
Ti m'ofeli Ameriki	Oh, what's the use of America,
Ke ola ta kala tis.	And of all her great riches?
Pou marane,	When I have crushed,
Pou marane,	When I have crushed,
Pou marane tis manas mou, Ah!	When I have crushed the sweet green leaves, Ah!
Pou marane tis manas mou	When I have crushed the sweet green leaves
Ta filla tis kardhias tis.	Of my dear mother's heart?

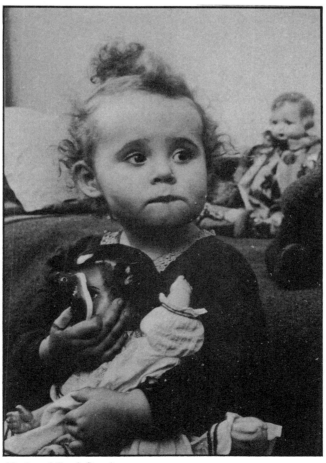

National Park Service

149

Tin Idha Ti Ksanthoula
I Saw My Dear Ksanthoula

Despina Disberakis of Watertown, Massachusetts, sang this song for her grandson, Michael Kaloyanides, in 1972. It is one of the many songs that she recalls being sung on the ship that brought her to America in 1920 from her village of Eressos on the island of Mytilene. "Ksanthoula" means a blonde girl.

Greece

Tin i - dha ti Ksan - thou - la, Tin i - dha hthes __ ar - gha. _____ Pou
I saw my dear Ksan - thou - la, I saw her yes - ter - day, _____ When

bi - ke sti - var - kou - la, Ke pai sti kse - ni - tia. _____
she got up on board __ ship, That would soon sail __ a - way. _____

Efis aghri ta aeri,
Lefkotata pania.
Ke san to peristeri,
T aploni ta ptera.

The winds, they blew so fiercely
Against the sails so white,
And then, just like a little dove,
The ship did take its flight.

Stekontan i fili,
Me lipi, me hara.
Ke kin ap to mandili,
Tis apohereta.

Old friends, they stand and wait about,
With sorrow and with joy;
And she, with her white handkerchief,
She waves a last good-bye.

Ke sto heretismo tis,
Estathika na dho.
Edhakrisan i fili,
Edhakrisa ke gho.

And as I stretched and craned my neck
To see her wave good-bye,
Her friends shed bitter, bitter tears,
And also so did I.

To West
The West

We Greeks who leave go everywhere. . . .
Some of us go to dark and ugly towns or bright modern towns
Where hungry factories give money for our souls.
We go to busy cities to vend ice cream, flowers and *souvlaki,*
Or to take some job that no one else will take. . . .

(*Let Us Be Greek* by Norman Weinstein, 1975)

Greece

Py – ga kai sto___ San Fran-cis- co, Py – ga kai sto___ SanFran-cis - co,
I tra-veled to___ San Fran-cis - co, I tra-veled to___ SanFran-cis - co,

Py – ga kai sto___ San Fran-cis- co, O – lo me- ra___ kli - des vris-ko.
I tra-veled to___ San Fran-cis- co, I took a ter – ri - ble risk-o.

Sacramento kai Vallejo,	(3)	Sacramento and Vallejo,	(3)
Ti eho pathi dea sto leyo.		What happened there I won't say-o.	
Sacramento kai Lodayi,	(3)	Sacramento and Lodi,	(3)
O Theos nasa filaei.		May God protect you from on high.	
Sto So Laki kai sto Butti,	(3)	And at Salt Lake and at Butte,	(3)
Mou tin skasan sto barbouti.		They beat me bad at a crapshoot.	
Pyga yia na paro tsengi,	(3)	I went there to change my money,	(3)
Kai m'afikan m'oute sentgi.		They left me there without any.	
Kai sto South oi sfoungarades,	(3)	And in the South the sponge divers,	(3)
Hasane poulous parades.		Lost all their tens and ones and fivers.	
Tous diliksane sta zaria,	(3)	For loaded dice they were rollin',	(3)
Kai tous fagan ta sfoungaria.		And then their sponges were stolen.	

Haiti

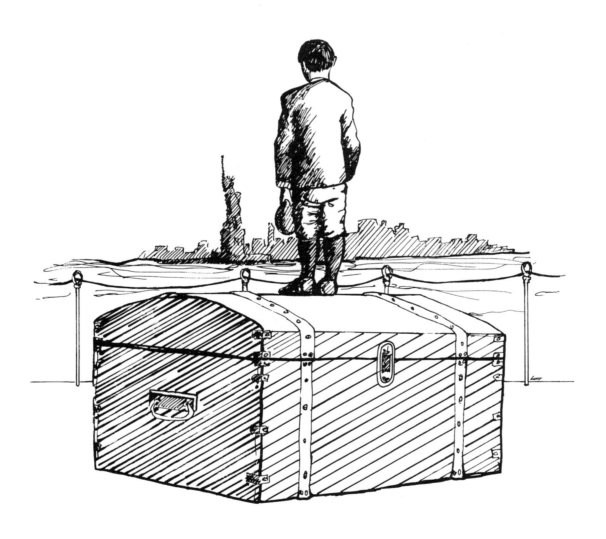

Les Émigrés
The Emigrants

When this song was recorded by Theophile Salnave in New York in early 1930, the full effect of the Wall Street crash of 1929 had yet to make itself felt to its fullest extent. He could still look around and see evidence of "the American dream" for all — except "we Ethiopian sons." The reference to another immigrant group (the Jews) who, according to the singer, have "made it," is relatively unusual in immigrant song literature.

Haiti

Yo ri – vé Nou Yòk, yo pa pale an – glé, yo pa gen la –
Yòk pa ka – pab kon – pram kot chans sa so –
They come to New York, they don't speak En – glish, they don't have a
zens can – not un – der – stand what good luck they

jan, yo pa jwenn bon djob. A – pré kèk a – né yo vin pale an –
ti pou le – vé pou yo. La – jan djob yon mwa, pe – yi yo ba
cent they can't get good jobs. A few years then pass, they learn to speak
have. The mon – ey they earned in one month back home in the old coun –

glé, yo kou – ri la bank, pran yon ti ka – nè.
yo, Nan Nou Yòk yo
well, they run to the bank to put in their cash.
try, they earn in New

Ki bou-ré la-jan,_____ Kon syel la bou-re zét-wal.
It has as much mon-ey____ As there are stars in the sky.

Nou Yòk se yon vil	*Chorus 2:*	New York is a town	*Chorus 2:*
Ki pa kab konté	Devan yon dousè parèy,	Which just cannot count	Because of such good luck,
Diferan peplad	Yo fe yo Ameriken,	The different groups	They become citizens,
Ki groupé ladan'l.	Pou yo siveyé	Of people here found.	In order to protect
Kanta bèl medam,	Leurs propres intérêts	Its women are beauties,	Their proper interests.
Ranpli detiket,	Se pa yon dezoné,	And have great charm.	It's not a dishonor,
Yo sanble ti zanj	Se pa yon lacheté,	They are just like angels	It is not cowardice.
Ki soti nan syel.	Se to simpman	Down from the skies.	It's simply a matter
Lòganizasyon	Yon devwa yo ranpli.	The way life is run	Of doing what must be done.
Vi Nou Yòk la		Right here in New York,	
Fe tout moun maché	*Chorus 3:*	Makes every man	*Chorus 3:*
Na dwa chemen.	Nou zòt pitit Etiopi,	Just stick to his work.	But we Ethiopian sons,
An deyò de sa,	Lè nou rivé bo la,	And what's even more,	When we come to these shores,
Nou jwenn tout bagay,	Sa rèd pou nou jwenn yon	There's so much around,	It's hard to find the path,
Mwen pa kwe Leròp	rout,	I don't think Europe	And so we often fail.
Kapab fè pou nou. *Chorus*	Nou tonbé an derout.	Could do more for us. *Chorus*	Though we wait nights and days,
	Nou mèt tann nwit kon jou,		The road is blocked for us.
Si w rivé Nou Yòk,	Chemen baré pou nou.	So when you get here,	A hopeless condition
Lo w fin pale anglé,	Se yon dezespwa	And English you learn,	For him who's born with black
Ou pa fè lanjan,	Pou nom ki gen po nwa.	If you don't do well,	skin.
S'on krim w ap peyé.		It would be a crime.	
Kar nenpòt nasyon		For any nation	
Ki rantre Nou Yòk,		That comes to New York,	
Apre kèk ané,		After a few years	
Li tounen Kresus.		Becomes like Croesus.	
Avan kek ané,		And then pretty soon	
Li gentan maryé.		They all get married,	
La pe banboché		Enjoy a good life	
Avek madanm li.		With their darling wife.	
Li vin gen oto,		Then they buy a car,	
Li vin gen bilding.		Then buy a building.	
Si nou kwè'm manti,		If you think I'm lying,	
Al mande Jwif yo.		Go ask the Jews.	

Sherman Collection, National Park Service

Holland

Though the Dutch presence in America dates back to the earliest years of the 17th century with the voyages of Henry Hudson and the founding of New Amsterdam through the settling of New Holland, Michigan, in the 1840s, there does not exist a body of songs relative to those experiences. The Dutch did sing psalms and hymns in church, but secular singing was against the strictures of the Calvinists in the New World.

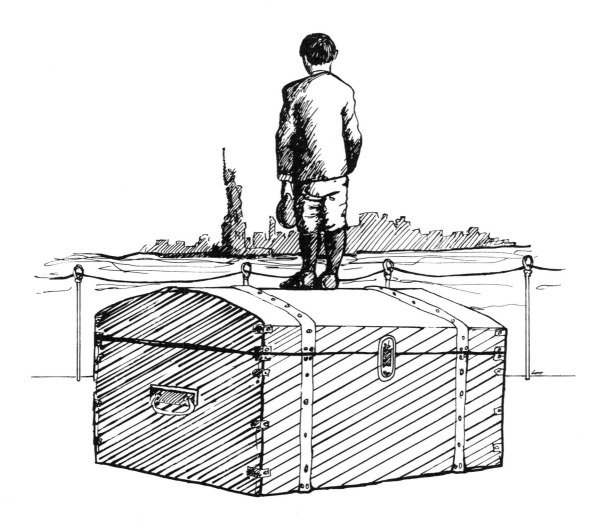

Song Of The Holland-Americans

In an attempt to fill the gap of Dutch songs about America, a collection of *Holland–American Songs* was published in Chicago in 1906.

> Herewith we publish a collection of Holland Songs, for which we believe there is a great need. . . . The condition of the mind may be such, that it cannot express itself through any other medium than Song. . . . We call attention especially to [Mr. Beets'] "Song of the Holland Americans.". . . [It] will fill a long felt want in Social gatherings of our people. Its wording has been praised highly by several able Critics and its well known tune will help it the more to secure a permanent place among our popular songs. Patriotic reasons have accorded it the place of honor in our collection. May this collection find its way everywhere into the homes of Hollanders in America.

Holland

Words by Henry Beets
Music: *Wien Neerlandsch Bloed,* **by J. M. Wilms**

4-part choral arrangement

Come ye who boast of Dutch de - scent, Sons of New Neth - er - land, __ And ye who reached our friend - ly shores with __ west - ern __ pil - grim band! U - nite with us in fes - tive song, song __ which the heart e - lates, __ And sing the prais - es __

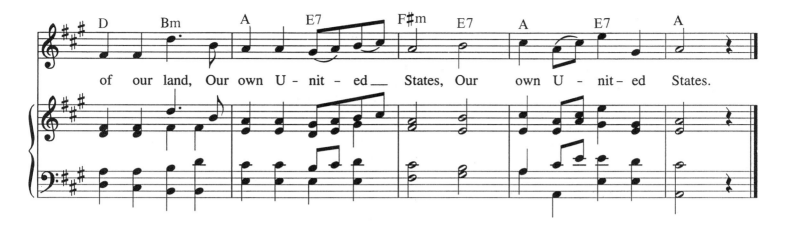

of our land, Our own U - nit - ed __ States, Our own U - nit - ed States.

We love the land across the sea
  We glory in its past;
We pray for its prosperity,
  May it forever last!
But tho' we love old Holland still,
  We love Columbia more,
The land our sons and brethren fill
  From east to western shore.

We praise the beauty of our land
  Displayed by rocks and rills.
Its fertile plains, its mighty streams,
  Its mountains, lakes and hills;
We praise its glory-laden past,
  Which made our country free,
Its institutions, grand and strong,
  Its opportunity.

O God of nations, bless our land,
  Its every place and state
From where the dark Atlantic rolls
  Unto the Golden Gate;
O bless our rulers and our flag,
  Uphold our liberty,
Make us a blessing to the world,
  A praise, Lord, unto Thee.

One special boon, our fathers' God,
  We crave from Thy right hand:
Make us a blessing more and more,
  To our beloved land;
Infuse the best of all our past,
  The noblest of our traits,
Into the life, into the deed
  Of our United States!

Sherman Collection, National Park Service

Hans And Katrina

Between 1920 and 1930 various members of the Vassar College (Poughkeepsie, New York) folklore classes gathered songs from old residents of the mid-Hudson Valley. This song was sung in 1925 by Miriam Wood of Poughkeepsie, who had the text from a pre-1859 copy written by her mother. The melody is the perennial British music-hall favorite, "Villikins And His Dinah" (known in another reincarnation as "Sweet Betsy From Pike"). The story of the demanding father and recalcitrant daughter and their tragi-comic dialogue was transposed from the original locale ("There was a rich merchant in London did dwell . . .") to the Dutch settlement somewhere in New York. The "comic Dutchman" (who may sometimes have been a "German") was a standard personage in 19th century American vaudeville — an era that saw each successive wave of immigrants lampooned (kindly or otherwise) by the previous wave. In this case, the humor is gentle and no harm was intended.

Holland

There was one fine Dutch-man in New York did live. He had one fine daugh-ter, you'd bet-ter be-lieve. Her name was Ka-tri-na, as fair as a rose, And she

162

had   a   large   for - tune   in   the   hands   of   old   Mose.

As Katrina was drawing a lager one day,
Her fader came to her and thus he did say,
"Hurry up, Katrina, the parlor go to,
Der's a customer wants to go ridin' mit you."

"Oh, Fader, why don't he some udder gal find?
To ride mit dese fellows I don't feel inclined.
For de way dey dribe de buggy it makes me feel weak,
For I wants to get married to Hans Dunder next week."

My fader got mad and he swore his goddam
That I nebber should marry wid any young man.
"If you love this Hans Dunder, so go take his pags
Mit his hooks and his packets and go gater rags."

So Katrina den back to de kitchen she ran,
Says, "I'll eat up mine preakfast so fast, vat I can
And trable all day if I can't be his wife!"
And dis was de way dat she los-ed her life.

For as she was eating a pig paloney sausage,
It sticked in her throat and stopped up a passage.
She tried for to preathe, but by grief overcome,
Her head it reeled 'round and she fell very dumb.

Hans Dunder he happened to walk in de door.
He spied his Katrina lying dead on de floor,
A pig paloney sausage was lain by her side.
Says Hans, "I'll be blamed 'twas mit tis ting she died."

Now all you young womans whatever you do,
Don't let tis Hans Dunder tink something of you.
And all ye men dat court in de passage,
Think of Hans and Katrina and de pig paloney sausage.

Sherman Collection, National Park Service

163

Wie Gaat Er Naar Amerika Varen?
Who Is Sailing Off to America?

As I write the translation, I feel how I would love to get back to the canals and meadows and moors and colorful villages and speak some good old Dutch. Funny — when I have never been homesick. . . . (Fried de Metz Herman)

Holland

By Fried de Metz Herman

Wie gaat er naar A- me- ri- ka va- ren, Va- ren, va- ren op de zee? 't Zal___ me heus geen zor- gen ba- ren, Weg- te gaan___ van huis en stee. Ver-

Who is off to A- me- ri- ca sail- ing, Sail- ing, sail- ing on the sea? Leav- ing hearth and home be- hind will sure- ly not___ be hard for me. To

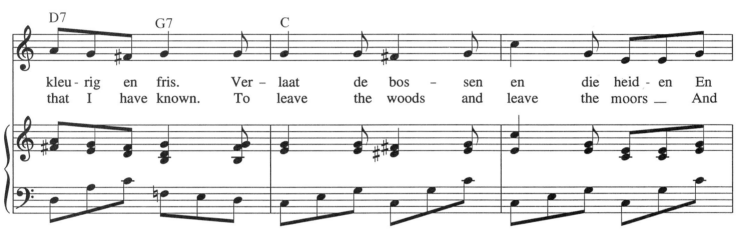

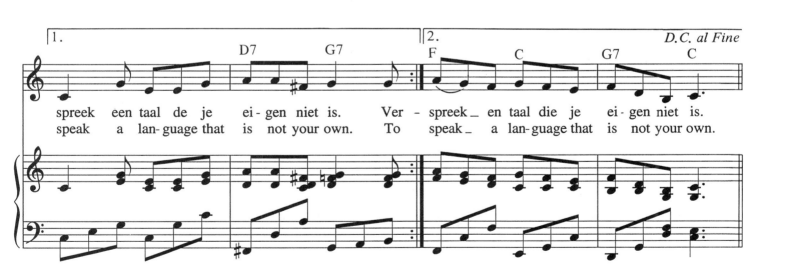

Curaçao

Dutch sailors did not feel inhibited about singing of their adventures, the feelings of their landlubber countrymen to the contrary notwithstanding. It's too bad we could not find a similar salty tale about New Amsterdam — but we may be permitted to imagine that they dropped anchor in those northern waters with similar songs on their lips.

Holland

Cu – ra – çao,   'k heb jou   zo   me – nig-maal be – ke – ken, En
Cu – ra – çao,   I have   so   of – ten looked up – on   you, And

al   jou lo – ze   stre – ken die   sta – ne mij niet aan.   Want
all   your cra – zy   man – ners just don't ap-peal to   me.   Since

al   jou lo – ze   stre – ken die   sta – ne mij met aan.   Daar-
all   your cra – zy   man – ners just don't ap-peal to   me,   I

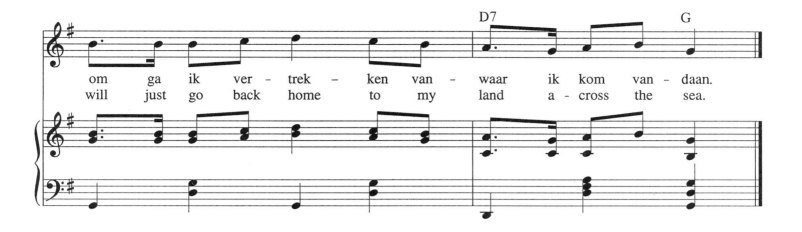

om ga ik ver- trek- ken van- waar ik kom van- daan.
will just go back home to my land a - cross the sea.

'k Kwam laatst met haast al door het Herenstraatje,
Men sprak: "Mijn lieve maatje, kom, zet u hier wat neer.
En drink dan eens een glaasje en rook een pijp tabak,"
Dan met die loze streken raakt het geld [wel] uit de zak.

Een zoen kan doen de hele nacht te blijven,
Dan hoort men niet het kijven van onze officier;
Zo raken wij aan 't dwalen zo dronken als een zwijn,
Het schip ligt voor de palen, aan boord moeten wij zijn.

Maak los de tros, de voor — en achtertouwen,
En wilt [het] maar aanschouwen; wij gaan naar Holland toe.
Waar is het beter leven dan bij een echte vrouw,
'k verzeg [er] al de vrouwtjes [voor] van 't land van Curaçao!

Well, the last time that I walked down Little Lord Street,
They said, "My darling sailor, come sit down over here,
And drink a little glassful and have a little smoke."
But with such crazy manners, you soon find that you're broke.

Now, a kiss can make the dark night last forever,
For then we do not hear our officers' complaints.
So we begin to wander as drunk as any lord,
The ship, she lies at anchor, and we must be on board.

Untie the ropes — the fore and after hawsers,
And everyone take notice — for Holland we are bound.
For life with a real woman is better, boys, and how!
Good-bye to all the women in the land of Curaçao.

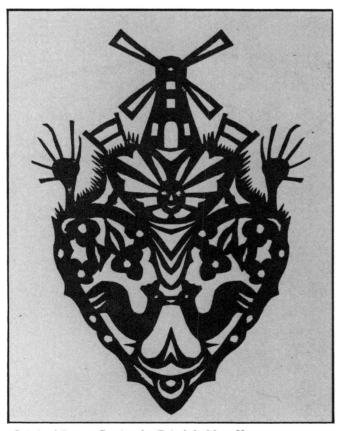

Original Paper Cutting by Fried de Metz Herman

Hungary

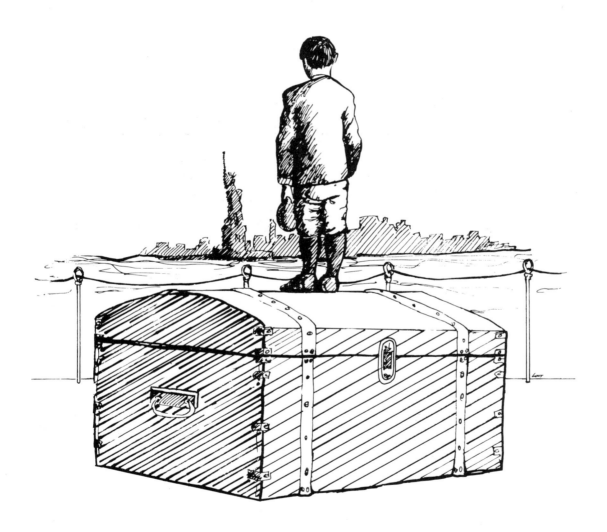

Elment A Rózsam Amerikába
My Love Has Gone To America

New York is the second largest Hungarian community in the world after Budapest. When this traditional song was published in Budapest in 1922, it is easy to imagine how many young men and women wept bitter tears and how many parents said, "I told you so!"

Hungary

El – ment a ró – zsám Á – me – ri – ká – ba, De én nem me – gyek u – tá – na.
Off to A – me – ri – ca has my love gone, But I can – not fol – low af – ter.

El – ment a ró – zsám Á – me – ri – ká – ba, De én nem me – gyek u – tá – na.
Off to A – me – ri – ca has my love gone, But I can – not fol – low af – ter.

A – nyám mond – ta há – za – sod – jam mog. De én mond tam an – yám, nem le – het.
Moth – er told me that I ought to wed. I said, "Moth – er, I will wait in – stead."

El – ment a ró – zsám Á – me – ri – ká – ba. Es én me- gha- lok u – tá – na.
Off to A- me- ri – ca has my love gone, And I am just dy –ing for her.

Elment a rózsám Ámerikába, (2)
És én elmegyek utána.
Egy nagy hajó visz át a vizen,
Édös a nyám oda mit izen?
Elment a rózsám Ámerikába,
És én elmegyek utána.

Elment a rózsam Ámerikába, (2)
Én is elmegyek utána.
Akármilyen messze van azér,
A nagy hajó hamar odaér.
Elment a rózsám Ámerikába,
És én elmegyek utána.

Elment a rózsám Ámerikába, (2)
Én is elmentem utána.
Irtam néki levelevelet,
Hogy szeressik kicsit engömet.
Páros csólkot adtam rája,
Mégis másnak lett a párja.

Off to America has my love gone, (2)
I've decided I will follow.
A great ship will take me 'cross the water.
Mother, do you have a message for her?
Off to America has my love gone,
I've decided I will follow.

Off to America has my love gone, (2)
I, too, will now follow after.
I don't care how long it takes to sail,
The great ship will get there without fail.
Off to America has my love gone,
I, too, will now follow after.

Off to America has my love gone, (2)
And I, too, have followed after.
Letters I sent to her 'cross the sea,
To make sure that she'd remember me.
I sent them off with hot, steaming kisses,
But she married with another.

Elindultam Szép Hazámból
I Left My Nice Country

The next three songs tell essentially the same story — one of homesickness and despair. Like all immigrants, when Hungarians arrived in America, they strove to maintain contact with their homeland as well as with each other. During the 1920s, there were three daily Hungarian newspapers in New York, as well as a number of less frequently published labor, sports, and literary journals. Still listed in the telephone directory are the *Hungarian Weekly Nepsava,* which used to be one of the dailies, *The Hungarian Word,* a number of Hungarian churches, and . . . a Hungarian Pastry Shop.

Hungary

Freely

El - in - dul - tam szép ha - zám - ból, Hí - res kis Ma - gyar - or - szág - ból.
I left my nice coun - try one day, From my Hun - ga - ry I did stray.

Visz - sza - néz - tem fél - u - tam - bol, Sze - mem - böl a könny ki - csor - dult.
When I had gone half the jour - ney, Then a tear rolled out of my eye.

Bu ebédem, bu vacsorám,	Sad my lunch and sad my dinner,
Boldogtalan minden órám,	I'm like some unhappy sinner,
Nézen a csillagos eget, (2)	Gazing at the stars and sighing, (2)
Sirok alatta eleget.	I can never cease my crying.
Jaj Istenem, rendelj szállást,	My God, a home won't you find me?
Mert meguntam a bujdosást,	Put all this hiding behind me.
Idegen földön a lakást, (2)	I cannot live in this strange place, (2)
Éjjel-nappa a sok sirást.	Night and day the tears wet my face. (2)

Elmegyek, Elmegyek
I Am Leaving

Hungary

El - me - gyek el - me - gyek, Hosz - szú út - ra me - gyek.
I am leav - ing, leav - ing, A long trip I'm tak - ing.

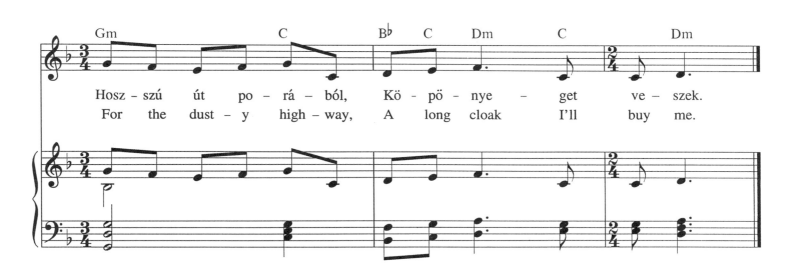

Hosz - szú út po - rá - ból, Kö - pö - nye - get ve - szek.
For the dust - y high - way, A long cloak I'll buy me.

Búval és bánattal
Kizsinóroztatom,
Sürü könnyeimmel
Kigomboztattatom.

Fúdd el jó szél, fúdd el
Hosszú útnak porát,
Hosszú útnak porát,
Az én szívem búját.

I will decorate it
With my melancholy.
Teardrops for its buttons —
I weep at my folly.

Blow, oh blow away, winds,
The dust of the long road,
The dust of the long road,
And my sad heart's great load.

Elindultam
Now I Leave

This song dates from the Hungarian revolution of 1848, in which the remnants of the feudal system were destroyed and Hungary's independence declared. Revolutionary leader Louis Kossuth, imprisoned and swiftly exiled by Austrian authorities who feared his influence, was invited to America in 1851. He toured the country, hoping to win support for Hungary's independence from Austria.

... I have seen America still a radiating sun, as it was of yore, but risen so high on mankind's sky as to spread its warming rays of elevated patriotism far over the waves. Gentlemen, I trust in God, I trust in the destinies of humanity, and I entrust the hopes of oppressed Europe to the consistent energy of America. (Louis Kossuth, speaking in Fanueil Hall, Boston, in 1852)

Hungary

El - in - dul - tam szép ha - zám - ból,___
Now I ___ leave my love - ly coun - try,___

Drá - ga szép Ma - gyar - or - szág - ból.
Yes, my dear, love - ly Hun - ga - ry.

Visz - sza - néz - tem fél - u - tam - bol,
As I look back while I jour - ney,

Sze - mem - ből a kön - ny ki - csor - dult.
From my eyes the tears are fall - ing free.

Bu ebédem, bu vacsorám,
Boldogtalan minden órám,
Nézen a csillagos eget,
Sirok alatta eleget.

Jaj Istenem, rendelj szállást,
Mert meguntam a bujdosást,
Idegen földön a lakást,
Éjjel-nappa a sok sirást.

Sorrow is my lunch and dinner,
How unhappy's this life of mine.
I gaze up at the heavens,
And I weep bitterly all the time.

Oh my God, please give me shelter,
I've gown tired, always on the run.
In strange lands my restless living,
Night and day my weeping's never done.

American Red Cross

Big Joe Magarac

The legendary Hungarian immigrant Joe Magarac was the Paul Bunyan of the Pennsylvania steel mills. Stories of his prowess abounded among the old-timers in the mills. I have simply taken some of these tall tales and set them to the traditional tune "Crawdad."

Hungary

By Jerry Silverman

I'll tell you a-bout a steel-mill man,___ hon-ey.___

___ I'll tell you a-bout a steel mill man,___ babe.___

___ I'll tell you a-bout a steel-mill man, The best steel mak-er in

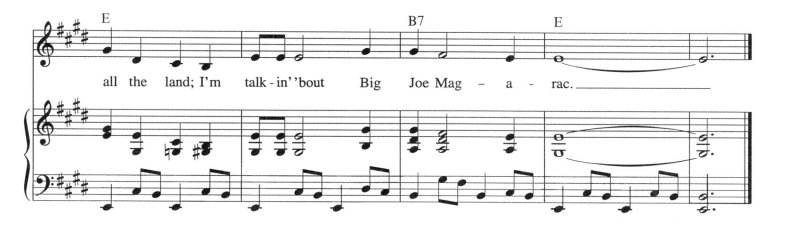

all the land; I'm talk-in' 'bout Big Joe Mag - a - rac. _____

He was born in a bucket of red-hot ore, honey,
He was born in a bucket of red-hot ore, babe.
He was born in a bucket of red-hot ore,
Raised in a furnace, soothed by its roar.
I'm talkin' 'bout Big Joe Magarac.

His shoulders are wide as the steel-mill door, honey,
His shoulders are wide as the steel-mill door, babe.
His shoulders are wide as the steel-mill door,
Head in the rafters, feet on the floor.
I'm talkin' 'bout Big Joe Magarac.

His muscles are strong as iron bands, honey,
His muscles are strong as iron bands, babe.
His muscles are strong as iron bands,
He can shape an ingot with his bare hands.
I'm talkin' 'bout Big Joe Magarac.

The boss came around with a great big roar, honey,
The boss came around with a great big roar, babe.
The boss came around with a great big roar,
Yelled, "Let's go, boys — let's cook this ore."
I'm talkin' 'bout Big Joe Magarac.

Joe checked to see if the soup was hot, honey,
Joe checked to see if the soup was hot, babe.
Joe checked to see if the soup was hot,
With a fifty-ton ladle he stirred the pot.
I'm talkin' 'bout Big Joe Magarac.

He grabbed the cooling steel in his hand, honey,
He grabbed the cooling steel in his hand, babe.
He grabbed the cooling steel in his hand,
Made thirty-foot rails as fast as he can.
I'm talkin' 'bout Big Joe Magarac.

Joe can work like a hundred men, honey,
Joe can work like a hundred men, babe.
Joe can work like a hundred men,
Work all day and start again.
I'm talkin' 'bout Big Joe Magarac.

For men who have come from the other side, honey,
For men who have come from the other side, babe,
For men who have come from the other side,
Joe Magarac is a source of pride.
I'm talkin' 'bout Big Joe Magarac.

New York Public Library Picture Collection

177

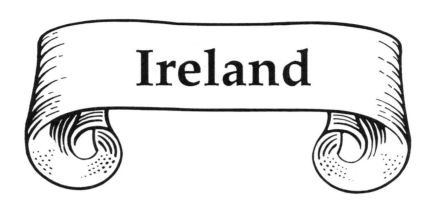

Ireland

Molly Durkin

Ireland

I'm a da-cint hon-est work-in' man, as you might un-der-stand, And I'll tell to you the rea-son why I left old I-re-land. 'Twas Mol-ly Dur-kin did it when she mar-ried Tim O'-Shea, And to keep my heart from break-in', I sailed to A-mer-i-cay. Ar-ragh, Good-bye, Mol-ly

Dur-kin, I'm sick and tired of work-in', And my heart is near-ly brok-en, but no

long-er I'll be fooled; And as sure as my name is Coon-ey, I'm bound for Cal-i-

foon-y, And in-stead of dig-gin' mor-tar I'll be dig-gin' lumps of gold.

Well, I landed in Castle Garden,* sure I met a man named Burke
And he told me remain in New York until he got me work.
But he hasn't got it for me, so tonight I'll tell him plain,
For San Francisco in the morn I'm goin' to take a train. *Chorus*

Well, I'm out in Cal-i-forn-i and my fortune it is made.
I'm a-loaded down with gold and I throw away my pick and spade,
Sail home to dear old Ireland with the Castle out of sight,
And I'll marry Miss O'Kelly, Molly Durkin for to spite. *Chorus*

*Castle Garden was the immigrant reception center in New York before Ellis Island was used.

Paddy Works On The Railway

The work that the Irish immigrants accomplished "upon the railway" in the 19th century did much to unite and enrich this country. One of the more memorable feats of construction that they engaged in (with others, as well) was the six-year ordeal of the linking of the two coasts by rail. The transcontinental railroad became a reality on May 10, 1869, when the eastern and western links were joined with a golden spike at Promontory, Utah.

Ireland

In eight - een hun - dred and for - ty one I put my cor - du - roy brit - ches on, I

put my cor - du - roy brit - ches on to work up - on the rail - way.

Chorus

Fil - i - mi - oo - ri - oo - ri - ay, Fil - i - mi - oo - ri - oo - ri - ay,

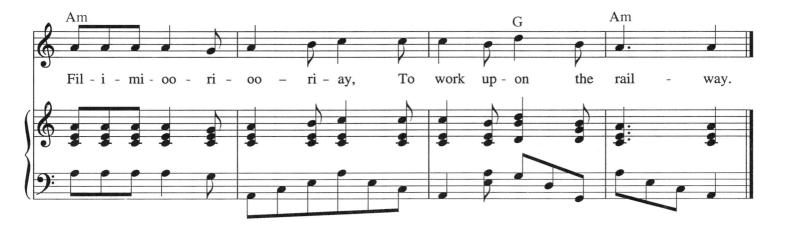

Fil - i - mi - oo - ri - oo - ri - ay,   To   work   up - on   the   rail - way.

In eighteen hundred and forty-two,
I left the old world for the new,
Bad cess to the luck that brought me through,
To work upon the railway. *Chorus*

In eighteen hundred and forty-three,
'Twas then I met sweet Biddy McGee,
An elegant wife she's been to me,
While working on the railway. *Chorus*

In eighteen hundred and forty-four,
I worked again, and worked some more,
It's "Bend your backs," the boss did roar,
While working on the railway. *Chorus*

It's "Pat, do this," and "Pat, do that,"
Without a stocking or cravat,
And nothing but an old straw hat,
While working on the railway. *Chorus*

In eighteen hundred and forty-five,
They worked us worse than bees in a hive,
I didn't know if I was dead or alive,
While working on the railway. *Chorus*

In eighteen hundred and forty-six,
They pelted me with stones and sticks,
Oh, I was in a terrible fix,
While working on the railway. *Chorus*

In eighteen hundred and forty-seven,
Sweet Biddy McGee, she went to heaven.
If she left one child, she left eleven,
To work upon the railway. *Chorus*

National Park Service

Pat Murphy Of The Irish Brigade

The Irish Brigade was, and is, the New York 69th — "The Fighting Irish."

When the Prince of Wales came over here and made a hubbaboo,
Oh everybody turned out, you know, in gold and tinsel too;
But then the good old Sixty-Ninth didn't like these lords or peers,
They wouldn't give a damn for kings, the Irish volunteers!
We love the land of Liberty, its laws we will revere,
"But the divil take the nobility!" says the Irish volunteer.

Ireland

U.S. Civil War Song

pipe in his mouth sat a dash-ing young blade, And a song he was sing-ing so gai-ly._____ It was hon-est Pat Mur-phy of the I-rish Bri-gade, And he sang of the sprig of shil-le-lagh._____

Says Pat to his comrades, "It's a shame for to see
Brothers fightin' in such a queer manner,
But I'll fight till I die — if I shouldn't get killed,
For America's bright starry banner."
Far away in the East there's a dashing young blade,
And a song he was singin' so gaily,
'Twas honest Pat Murphy of the Irish Brigade,
And the song of the splintered shillelagh.

The morning came soon and poor Paddy awoke,
On the rebels to have satisfaction.
The drummers were beatin' the devil's tattoo,
A-callin' the boys into action.
Then the Irish Brigade in the battle was seen,
And their blood for the cause shedding freely.
With their bayonet-charges they rushed on the foe,
With a shout for the Land of Shillelagh.

The battle was over, the dead lay in heaps,
Pat Murphy lay bleeding and gory,
A hole through his head from a rifleman's shot
Had ended his passion for glory.
No more in the camp shall his laughter be heard,
Or the songs he was singin' so gaily,
He died like a hero, in the Land of the Free,
Far away from the Land of Shillelagh.

Now surely Columbia will never forget,
While valor and fame hold communion,
How nobly the brave Irish volunteers fought
In defense of the flag of our Union.
And if ever Old Ireland for freedom should strike,
We'll a helping hand offer quite freely.
And the Stars and the Stripes will be seen alongside
Of the flag of the Land of Shillelagh.

185

The Seven Irishmen

The British army recruiter is a recurrent and much-despised figure in Irish song. The recruiting officer would offer a young prospect a drink and then slip a shilling into the glass. The minute he put the glass to his lips, the recruit was politely, but every so firmly, informed that he had just enlisted, having taken the "king's shilling." Imagine the surprise and indignation of the seven Irish immigrants upon finding that the same dirty trick had been played on them in "Americay." This is the other side of the coin (!) of the sentiments expressed by poor Pat Murphy of the Irish Brigade.

Ireland

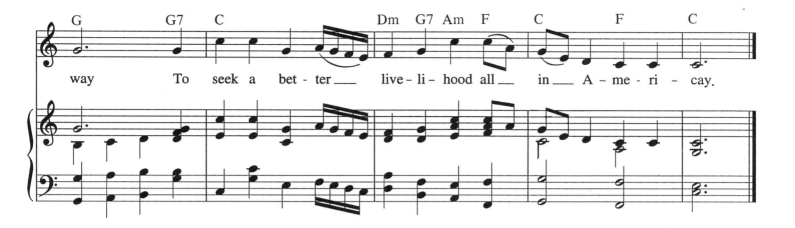

way To seek a bet-ter____ live-li-hood all____ in ____ A – me – ri – cay.

On the fourteenth day of April our noble ship did sail,
With fifty-five young Irishmen, true Sons of Grannuaille.*
They landed safely in New York on the nineteenth day of
 May,
To see their friends and relatives all in Americay.

Some of them had friends to meet as soon as they did land,
With flowing bumpers drank a health to poor old Paddy's
 land.
Those who had no friends to meet, their hearts were stout
 and bold,
And by the cursed Yankees they would not be controlled.

Seven of those young Irishmen were walking through
 George's Street,
When a Yankee officer they happened for to meet.
He promised them employment in a brick-yard near the
 town.
There he did conduct them; their names were taken down.

He took them to an ale-house; he called for drinks galore,
I'm sure such entertainment they never had before.
When he thought he had them drunk, these words to them
 did say,
"You are 'listed now as soldiers to defend Americay."

They looked at one another, these words they then did say,
"It's not to 'list that we did come into Americay,
But to labour for our livelihood as we often did before,
And we lately emigrated from the lovely shamrock shore."

Twelve Yankees dressed as soldiers came in without delay.
They said, "My lads, you must prepare, with us to come away.
You signed with one of our officers, so you cannot now refuse,
So prepare, my lads, to join our ranks, you've got to pay your
 dues."

The Irish blood began to rise, one of those heroes said,
"We have one only life to lose, therefore we're not afraid.
Although we are from Ireland, this day we'll let you see,
We'll die like Sons of Grannuaille, and keep our liberty."

The Irish boys got to their feet, it made the Yankees frown,
As fast as they could strike a blow, they knocked the soldiers
 down.
With bloody heads and broken bones, they left them in crimson gore,
And proved themselves St. Patrick's Day, throughout Columbus' shore.

You'd swear it was a slaughter-house where those Yankees
 lay,
The officer and all his men on cars were dragged away,
With bloody heads and broken bones, they'll mind it ever
 more,
With a drop of sweet shillelagh that came from Erin's shore.

A gentleman from Ohio had seen what they did do.
He said, "I will protect you from this crimson Yankee crew.
I'll bring you to Ohio where I have authority,
And you shall be in my service while you are in this country."

They thanked him very kindly for the offer that he made,
And said, "If we go with you, what wages will be paid?"
He said, "I'll pay a dollar a day if you will go."
So they shook his hand and went out west to the banks of the O-hi-o.

*i.e., Ireland

The Loss Of The Atlantic Steamship

Halifax, N.S. April 1. — One of the most terrible disasters that has ever occurred on this coast happened at an early hour this morning, when the White Star ocean steamship Atlantic went ashore at Mars Head . . . during a heavy gale. It is understood that over 700 of the unfortunate passengers were lost out of the thousand that were on board. All of the women and children were drowned. . . . (*The New York Times,* April 2, 1873)

For days after this disaster, the pages of the *Times* were filled with accounts of what happened off the storm-tossed, fog-shrouded coast of Nova Scotia. It is interesting to note the discrepancies between what actually took place and the romanticized version in the song. For example, the "gallant crew": "Statements are made that the crew of the ship indulged in the plunder of dead bodies, and one instance is related of a wretch who mutilated the hand of a lady to obtain possession of a diamond ring on her finger" (*Times,* April 4). The board of inquiry also turned up the fact that an inferior grade of coal had been used, which was incapable of raising a sufficient head of steam to propel the ship through the stormy North Atlantic to her intended destination, New York — which was the reason she had headed for Halifax instead. Finally, the date of departure from Liverpool, given in the song as April 6, is obviously wrong, since the accident took place on April 1.

Ireland

You — tend - er heart - ed Chris - tians of high and low de - gree, — I — hope you'll pay at - ten - tion and now lis - ten un - to me, — While — I re - late the aw - ful fate of coun - try - men so brave, — Who were

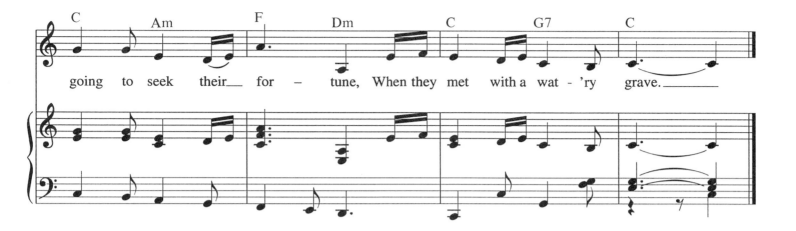

going to seek their for - tune, When they met with a wat -'ry grave.

The *Atlantic* was our good ship's name, as you may under-
  stand;
With sixty of a gallant grew, most nobly she was manned.
Besides nine hundred passengers with hearts both light and
  gay
Who little thought 'twould be their fate to sleep within the sea.

'Twas from the docks of Liverpool our gallant ship set sail,
'Twas on the sixth of April, with a sweet and pleasant gale.
She had some hundred Irishmen, who on her deck did flock,
And they gave three cheers for Ireland, as she moved out from
  the dock.

For eleven days she ploughed the seas, and all things went on
  well,
And before that sad twelfth morning what a dismal tale to
  tell —
We steered our course for Halifax, till just at two o'clock,
It was by a false ill-fated light our good ship struck the rock.

The night was dark and gloomy, and the seas rolled moun-
  tains high;
Our captain should have known right well the danger it was
  nigh.
He cared not for our safety as you may plainly see;
He went to bed and left the ship to prove our destiny.

And in a short time after, both passengers and crew,
All rushed on deck and screamed for help, not knowing
  what to do.
Now wasn't that an awful shock, that night and they in bed,
When our gallant ship she struck a rock at a place called
  Meagher's Head.

Oh had they landed in New York, their friends would happy
  be;
But alas, these sons of Erin sleep in the briny sea.
Our steamboat, the *Atlantic,* she sank to rise no more,
And many an aching heart is left around green Erin's shore.

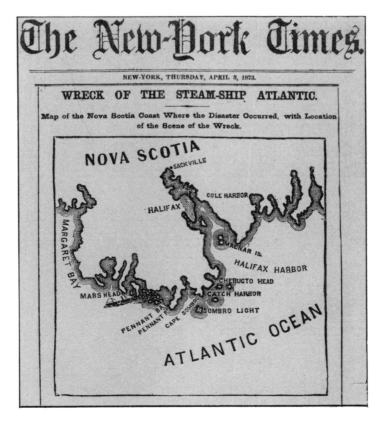

No Irish Need Apply

Irish immigrants were more often than not greeted by a less than royal reception when they landed in America. But they fought back in deeds as well as in song. "Meagher's men, and Corcoran's Brigade" refers to Irish–American regiments which distinguished themselves during the Civil War.

Ireland

By John F. Poole

I'm a de-cent boy, just land-ed from the town of Bal-ly-fad, _____ I want a sit-u-a-tion, yes, I want it ver-y bad. I have seen em-ploy-ment ad-ver-tised, "'Tis just the thing," says I, _____ But the dir-ty spal-peen end-ed with "No I-rish need ap-ply." _____ "Whoo," says

190

I started off to find the house, I got it mighty soon;
There I found the ould chap saited: He was reading the
 Tribune.
I tould him what I came for, whin he in a rage did fly:
No! says he, you are a Paddy, and no Irish need apply!
Thin I felt my dandher rising, and I'd like to black his eye —
To tell an Irish Gintleman: No Irish need apply! *Chorus*

I couldn't stand it longer: so, a hoult of him I took,
And I gave him such a welting as he'd get at Donnybrook.
He hollered: Millia murther! and to get away did try,
And swore he'd never write again: No Irish need apply.
He made a big apology: I bed him thin good-bye,
Saying: Whin next you want a bating, add: No Irish need
 apply! *Chorus*

Sure, I've heard that in America it always is the plan
That an Irishman is just as good as any other man;
A home and hospitality they never will deny
The stranger here, or ever say: No Irish need apply.
But some black sheep are in the flock: a dirty lot, say I;
A dacint man will never write: No Irish need apply! *Chorus*

Sure, Paddy's heart is in his hand, as all the world does
 know,
His praties and his whisky he will share with friend or foe;
His door is always open to the stranger passing by;
He never thinks of saying: None but Irish may apply.
And, in Columbia's history, his name is ranking high;
Thin, the Divil take the knaves that write: No Irish need
 apply! *Chorus*

Ould Ireland on the battle-field a lasting fame has made;
We all have heard of Meagher's men, and Corcoran's brigade.
Though fools may flout and bigots rave, and fanatics may cry,
Yet when they want good fighting-men, the Irish may apply.
And when for freedom and the right they raise the battle-cry,
Then the Rebel ranks begin to think: No Irish need apply. *Chorus*

Library of Congress

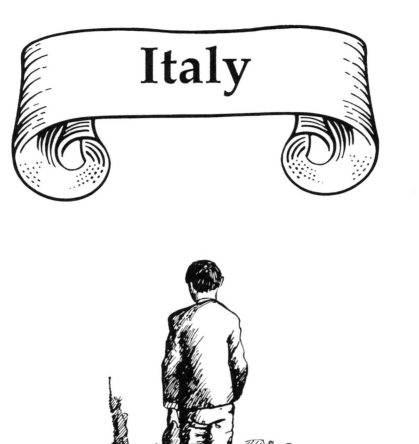

Italy

La Rondinella Dell' Emigrato
The Emigrant's Swallow

The music to this *romanza* was impossible to locate. Its polished literary tone sets it apart from most other songs of this genre, and it would have been a pity not to have included it in this collection. Accordingly, I set it to an original melody in the hope that the swallow might once again take wing.

Italy

Music by Jerry Silverman

Ron-din-el - la, pas - se - ge - ra_____ De - gli spa - zii_____ sen - za
O, you swal - low, in your pas-sage_____ O - ver spa - ces_____ with-out

fi - ne._____ Vo - la dol - ce mes - sag - ge - ra_____ Al ri –
end - ing,_____ Fly, my sweet and bring a mes - sage_____ Hear the

den___ te mi - o con - fi - ne._____ O - ve vi - ve a - ban - don
mes - sage that I am send - ing._____ From where now lives, all for –

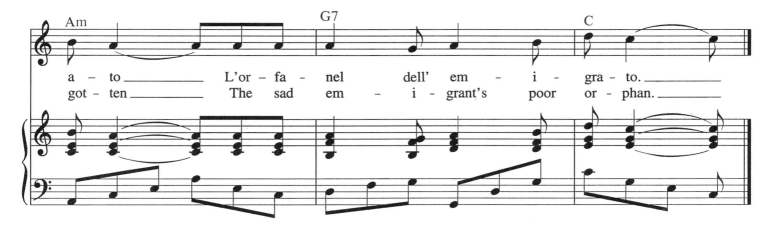

a – to _____ L'or – fa – nel dell' em – i – gra – to. _____

got – ten _____ The sad em – i – grant's poor or – phan. _____

Se dall' alte dell' empiro,
Tu ravvisi il tetto mio,
E odi il suono d'un
    sospiro,
O una prece alzata a Dio.
Ferma il volo e ti riposa,
Sopra il sen della mia
    sposa.

Nella soglia abbando-
    nata
Forma il nido o Rondi-
    nella;
Sulle penne equilibrata
Tu del profugo favella.
E col gemito natiò,
Addormenta il figlio
    mio.

Te beata ! almen potrai
Del mio mar veder le
    spume.
Del mio ciel goder i rai,
Bever l'onda del mio
    fiume.
E vagar sera e mattina
Sulla patria, mia collina.

Ti rammenta ch'io
    t'accolsi,
Traboccata fuor del nido;
Alla madre non ti tolsi,
Che ti chiese con un grido,
Ti rammenta che il mio
    tetto
Fu tua culla e tuo ricetto.

Repeat first verse

From the heights as you go fly-
    ing,
If you see my roof way down
    there,
And you hear my plaintive sigh-
    ing,
As to God I send a faint prayer—
Stop your flight and come to rest,
Pause a while on my wife's
    breast.

On the balcony so lonely
Is your nest, o little swallow;
And your feathers know the jour-
    ney
That a refugee must follow.
And with your plaintive cry,
Sing my son a lullaby.

Blessed are you beyond measure
To observe my sea's foam quiver.
My sky's sun rays give you plea-
    sure,
And you drink from my own river.
Morn and night you range so wide
O'er my country's green hillside.

You remember I did save you,
When down from your nest you
    tumbled.
To your mother then I gave you,
While she flew around and
    grumbled.
Just remember that you nested
On my roof — that's where you
    rested.

Repeat first verse

Dall'Italia Noi Siamo Partiti
When From Italy We Did Take Our Leave

Well, I came to America because I heard the streets were paved with gold. When I got here I found out three things: first, the streets weren't paved with gold; second, they weren't paved at all; and third, I was expected to pave them. (An Italian immigrant's recollections, Ellis Island Museum)

Italy

Dall' I - ta - lia___ noi sia - mo___ par - ti - ti,___
When from I - ta - ly we did___ take our___ leave,___

Siam par - ti - ti___ col nos - tro o - no - re.___
We de - part - ed with our hon - or on that o - cean trip.___

Tren - ta sei gior - ni di mac - chi - na a va - po - re,___
Thir - ty six days we did trav - el on___ that great steam - ship,___

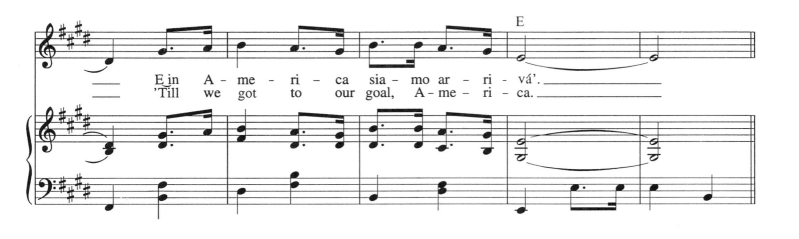

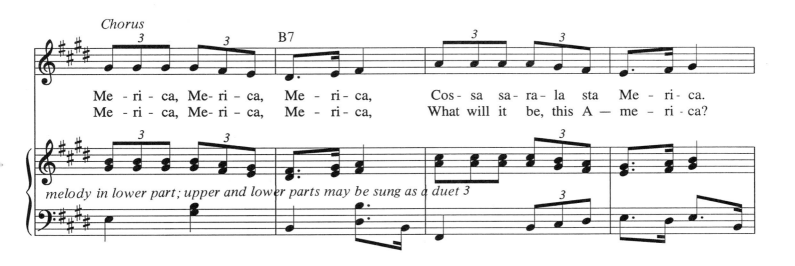

All'America noi siamo arrivati,
Non abbiam trovato né paglia né fieno.
Abbiam dormito sul nudo terreno;
Come le bestie abbiam riposá'. *Chorus*

L'America l'è lunga e l'è larga.
L'è formata di monti e di piani.
E con l'industria di noi altri italiani,
Abbiam fondato paesi e cittá. *Chorus*

But when we did arrive in America,
Neither hay nor straw was to be found.
We were forced to sleep upon the ground;
Just like animals we had to rest. *Chorus*

O, America is long and it is very wide.
It is made up of mountains and broad plains.
With the hard work of all of us Italians,
We have built up the city and the land. *Chorus*

Il Sirio
The Sirio

On August 4, 1906, the Italian steamship *Sirio,* out of Genoa, bound for Montivideo and Buenos Aires with 690 passengers, struck a reef near the Hormigas Islands off Cabo Palos on the Mediterranean coast of Spain. There was a chaotic struggle for the few lifeboats, and 422 people drowned.

Italy

Quan-do da Ge – no–va _____ Il *Si – rio* part – ti – va _____ per l'A-
When out from Ge – no–a _____ The *Si – ri – o* sailed a – way _____ for A-

me – ri–ca, _____ al su–o des–ti – no, Sen–za ti – mo – re _____ Il *Si–rio* cor-
me – ri–ca, _____ and to its mis–for – tune, With out the slight-est fear _____ The *Si – ri – o*

re – va, _____ leg–gier le – ge – ro _____ sul pla – ci–do mar. _____
sped a –long, _____ Ev – er so light – ly _____ it crossed the calm sea. _____

Sull' alto mare la nave s'infranse,	While on the high sea, the *Sirio* shattered
Incontrando lo scoglio fatale.	When it ran against the reef of misfortune.
Quattro barchette scorrevan sull'acque	Four little lifeboats sped over the water,
In soccorso dei nostri fratelli. *Chorus*	Hoping to rescue our brothers that day. *Chorus*
Tra quei naufraghi i Preti pregavano,	Among these shipwrecked ones the priests prayed to heaven,
E poi lor davano la benedizione.	And they gave them their last benediction.
Padri e madri baciavano i figli,	Fathers and mothers, they kissed their dear children,
Poi sparivano tra le onde del mare. *Chorus*	And then they sank beneath the waves of the sea. *Chorus*

Mamma Mia, Dammi Cento Lire
Mama, Please Give Me A Hundred Lire

Could this unfortunate young man have been a passenger aboard the ill-fated *Sirio?* This song dates from the early 1900s. . . .

Italy

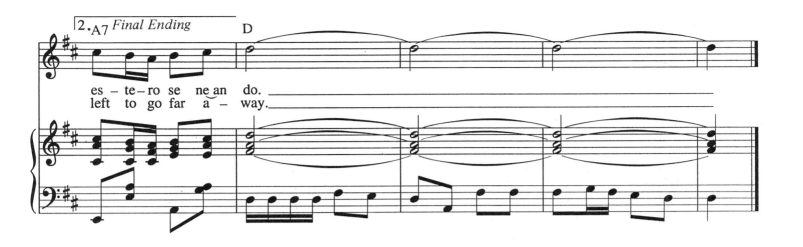

es – te–ro se ne an do. _____
left to go far a – way. _____

Cento lire, io te le dò,	(2)	A hundred *lire,* yes that is so,	(2)
Ma in America — no, no, no!		But in America — no, no, no!
Si tu parti, o figlio mio,	(2)	Oh, my son, if you should go,	(2)
Dal dolore io moriró.		Then I would die of sorrow.
Voglio andar' alla fortuna,	(2)	I would leave to seek my fortune,	(2)
Ma l'amore — no, no, no.		But a sweetheart — no, no, no!
I fratelli dalle finestra	(2)	All the brothers looked out of the window,	(2)
Gridan, "Mamma, lascialo andar'."		And cried, "Mama, just let him go."
Quando giunto in mezzo al mare,	(2)	And when out on the ocean wide,	(2)
Bastimento s'inabissò.		The great ship sank beneath the tide.
Le parole di ogni mamma	(2)	When a mother speaks to you,	(2)
Dicon sempre la verità.		Every word that she says is true.
Alla mamma ora rimane,	(2)	And now all that is left the mother,	(2)
Il ricordo del suo figlio.		Is the memory of her son.
Di quel bacio che le diede,	(2)	O, the kiss that she did give to him,	(2)
Quando all'estero se ne andò.		When he left to go far away.

Sacco E Vanzetti
Sacco And Vanzetti

Nicola Sacco, a shoemaker, and Bartolomeo Vanzetti, a fish peddler, were put to death by the State of Massachusetts on August 22, 1927, convicted of murder during the course of a robbery seven years earlier. They had been arrested in 1920 in the aftermath of the infamous Palmer Raids that were designed to deport as many immigrants as possible, especially the radical ones. Despite proof of the federal government's awareness of their innocence and worldwide protests against this frame-up, Governor Fuller of Massachusetts (identified in the song as "President Fuller") refused to commute their sentences. In 1977, on the 50th anniversary of their execution, Governor Michael Dukakis of Massachusetts declared August 23 Sacco and Vanzetti Day.

Italy

Il ven – ti – tre   a – gos – to,_____   a Bos – ton in A –
The twen – ty third   of   Au – gust,_____   in Bos – ton in A –

me – ri – ca,_____   Sac – co e Van – zet – ti_____   so – pra la sed – ia e –
me – ri – ca,_____   Sac – co and Van – zet – ti_____   were sent off to the e –

let – tri – ca._____   E con un col — po   di   e – let – tri – ci – tà,_____
lec – tric chair._____   And with a great   charge   of   e – lec – tri – ci – ty,_____

All' al – tro mon – do li vol – ler – o man – dar.
Straight to the oth – er world both their souls were set free.

Circa le undici e mezzo guidice e la gran corte
Entrano poi tutti quanti nella cella della morte.
"Sacco e Vanzetti, state a sentir
Dite se avete da raccontar."

Sacco e Vanzetti, tranquilli e sereni:
"Noi siamo innocenti. Aprite le galere."
Ma lor risposero, "Non c'è pietà
Voi alla morte dovete andar."

Entra poi nella cella il bravo confessore.
Domanda a tutti e due la santa religion.
Sacco e Vanzetti, con grande espression:
"Noi moriremo senza religion!"

E tutto il mondo intero reclama la loro innocenza.
Il presidente Fuller non evve più clemenza.
"Siano pure di qualunque nazion,
Noi li uccidiamo con grande ragion."

"Addio moglie e figlio, e te sorella cara.
E noi per tutti e due c'è pronta già la bara.
Addio amici, in cuor la fé.
Viva l'Italia e abbasso il re!"

About eleven thirty the judge and his attendants
Came for a final visit to the death cell of the defendants.
"Sacco and Vanzetti, now you listen to us,
And tell us finally if you want to confess."

Sacco and Vanzetti: "Calmly and serenely you see us.
We say that we're not guilty. Open your cell and free us."
Then came the answer: "No, that cannot be so.
There is no mercy — and to death you must go."

Then into the dark death cell came the father confessor,
Offering to hear their prayers, as with any transgressor.
Sacco and Vanzetti with feeling spoke then:
"We are prepared to die — but without religion."

People the whole world over say that they are not guilty.
But President Fuller he did not show them mercy.
"I could not care less what country they're from.
We're going to kill them — our duty be done!"

"Good-bye, dear wife and son, and to you, sister dear.
The coffins are prepared, yet we have no fear.
Farewell, dear friends — faith in our hearts does ring.
Viva l'Italia and down with the king!"

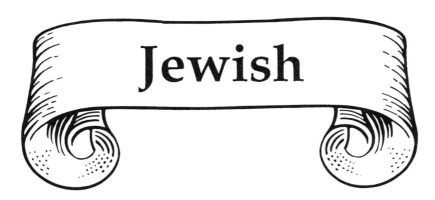

Jewish

Unlike the songs of the other immigrant people, who came to America from their homelands, the songs of the Jewish immigrants — like the Jews themselves — do not represent one specific country. The Yiddish-speaking Jewish population was spread out over vast areas of Eastern Europe; and, as borders shifted and new capitals replaced old ones, the hapless Jewish population (as well as non-Jews) would find themselves now subjects of a tsar, now subjects of a king, now subjects of an emperor. It is, therefore, difficult to pin down specific locales for the creation of many Jewish folk songs, all the more so since the Yiddish language crossed and re-crossed all political boundaries. Add to this the fact that a great many Jewish songs — immigrant and otherwise — also crossed and re-crossed the Atlantic in both directions, and one is faced with a labyrinthine trail that often cannot be tracked down.

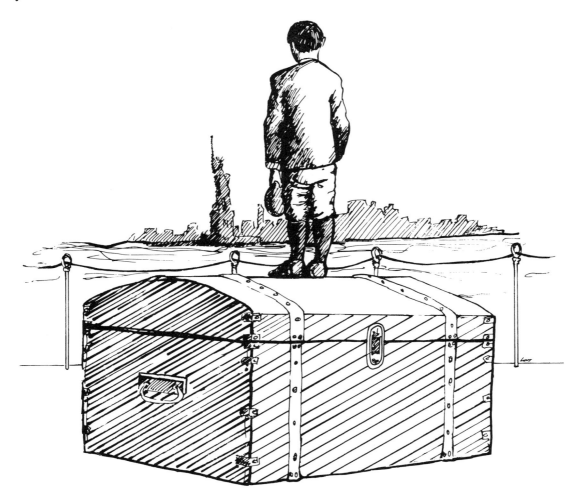

Shikt A Tiket
Send A Ticket

This poignant appeal for passage to America ends with a realistic warning about the difficulties of passing through U.S. immigration inspection at Castle Garden. Immigrants had begun to be processed in 1855 in this fort, which was built in 1807 on a small island near the west side of the Battery. By the 1880s the outdated structure clearly could not accommodate the thousands of immigrants who arrived each week. In 1892 Ellis Island was dedicated as the main immigration center. Castle Garden was joined to the Battery by a landfill — but the memories remained.

Jewish

In Rus – land gants vayt, dort vart a – za tsayt, Ayn
In Rus – sia, so far, the land of the tsar, A

or – e – me fa – mil – ye on shir._____ Zey der –
fam – i – ly that's poor with – out end._____ In great

var – tn a – tsind, fun A – me – ri – ke ge – shvind, Dem
an – guish they wait, and be – fore it's too____ late, The

206

ant – vort dos shti – ke – le pa – pir. _____ Zey
an – swer A – me – ri – ca will send. _____ They're

shray–bn tsu a fraynt "Es iz di tsayt shlecht haynt, Po –
writ – ing to a friend "Our trou–bles nev – er end, Po –

gro – men un tso – res on tsol; _____ Da –
groms and af – flic – tions per – sist; _____ So

rum be – tn mir aych, shikt a ti – ket glaych; Far –
we will make this vow, send a tick – et now, We

ge — sn ve — ln mir aych keyn mol."_____ Ba —
nev — er will for – get you keyn for this."_____ Just —

tracht nor a – tsind in Ke – sl Gar – dn ge – shvind, Vi – fil
think, my dear friend of that place, Cas – tle Gar – den. All the

tre — rn gi – sn zich dort._____ Un
tears that peo – ple shed there. _____ And

ver es hot keyn glik, dem shikt men tsu – rik, Tsu —
he who has no luck dem they send him right back, Right

rik — oyf — dem — um – glik – le – chn — ort._____
back — to — that — land — of — great — des – pair._____

Jewish Refugees from Russia   *Sherman Collection, National Park Service*

209

Elis Ayland
Ellis Island

All passenger vessels are boarded at Quarantine by inspectors from the Immigration Bureau . . . and if any passenger is thought to be a person who comes within the restrictive clauses of the law he is compelled to go to Ellis Island and await investigation. . . . As an instance of the care that is exercised to prevent improper persons from landing, statistics show that as many as 800 immigrants have been detained and returned to their homes in Italy in one month. (*The New York Times,* January 31, 1897)

Jewish

O Elis Ayland, Du grenets fun frayland, Vi groys un vi shreklech du bist!_____ A zelche r'tsiches Dos kenen nor ruches. Du plagst di geplagte um-

O Ellis Island, You border of free land, How big and how fearful you are!_____ You visit such crimes without reason or rhyme on the people who come from a-

A Briv Fun Amerike
A Letter From America

I am a greenhorn, being only five months out of Odessa, and I cannot forgive myself for being in America now. My head and heart ache when I read in your paper that thousands of workers stand on the barricades in Russia and fight like lions . . . oh, how I would like to be there in the midst of battle, to stand shoulder to shoulder with my comrades that my blood, too, may make our flag red. But the great ocean does not permit one to flee without a ticket, and the boat and railroad do not want to know of my thoughts, and they say that without the dollars they will not take me. Money to pay I have not. What shall I do? (from a letter to the editor of the *Jewish Forward* by Joseph Thest, January 20, 1906)

Jewish

Tay – e – re ma – me, tay – e – re mut – ter,
Dear – est ma – ma, dear – est moth – er,

Du___ mayn tay – er ko___ sher___ harts, Tsu
My___ dear heart, let me___ ex – plain. Do

veys – tu vi ich veyn a – zoy bi – ter, Un___ vi___ tif iz
you___ know why I cry___ so bit – ter, And___ the___ depth of

do mayn shmerts? Vos___ volt ich___ nit a – vek___ ge – ge – bn,
all my pain? I'd___ be all___ my___ rich___ es giv – ing,

Ich___ zol tun oyf dir a blik, Ich volt___ far dir ge –
If___ I could see you a – new, For you___ I'd glad — ly

shrekt___ dos le – bn, Ich___ zol___ ku – men tsu dir tsu – rik.
give___ up liv — ing, If___ I___ could but come back to you.

National Park Service

213

Eyn Zach Vel Ich
Only One Thing I Ask

When Tsar Alexander II was assassinated by revolutionary terrorists on March 1, 1881, the modest attempts at liberalism *vis-à-vis* the Russian Jews came to an abrupt end. With the accession of Alexander III came a wave of bloody pogroms and persecutions that set into motion a monumental exodus.

The first Jewish immigrants had arrived in the Dutch colony of New Amsterdam as early as 1654. Over the intervening two centuries, a slow trickle of Jews (some 7,500 between 1820 and 1850, for example) had made their way to the New World. By the 1870s that trickle had grown substantially, as over 40,000 new arrivals were counted. Emigration up to that point was, however, a decision prompted by individual desire. The reign of terror of Alexander III changed all that. Now it became literally a question of collective survival.

From the text of this song we know that the singer is a Russian Jew, with an imperfect awareness of American society (believing that slavery still existed), but so desperate to leave Russia that he would even sell himself into bondage.

Jewish

Eyn zach vel ich Got bay dir be - tn, az di
On - ly one thing I ask of you God, and I

zach zol mir zayn ba - shert; Fun Rus - land muz ich op
hope it be my fate; From Rus - sia I must de -

tre - tn, Keyn A - me - ri - ke vet zayn mayn pa - chod. Fun
part now, To A - me - ri - ca I now turn my gait. I

214

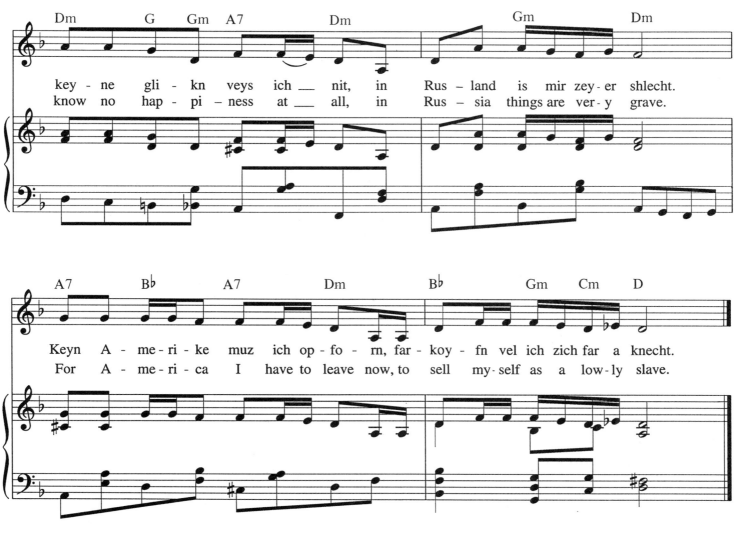

key - ne gli - kn veys ich __ nit, in Rus - land is mir zey - er shlecht.
know no hap - pi - ness at __ all, in Rus - sia things are ver - y grave.

Keyn A - me - ri - ke muz ich op - fo - rn, far - koy - fn vel ich zich far a knecht.
For A - me - ri - ca I have to leave now, to sell my - self as a low - ly slave.

Registry Room at Ellis Island
National Park Service

215

Kolumbus, Ich Hob Tsu Dir Gornit
Columbus, I Give You The First Prize

Jewish

Al Jolson, Famous Ellis Island Immigrant   *National Park Service*

Lebn Zoll Kolumbus
Long Life To Columbus

In many Jewish immigrant songs, one gets the impression that Christopher Columbus is being held personally responsible for all that America represents — both good and bad. This rambunctious number comes to us from the Jewish music hall of the early 1900s.

Jewish

A – shte – tl iz A – me – ri – ke, A me – chay – e chle – bn; Es
A – mer – i – ca's a hap – py place, Real – ly, what a treas – ure. You'll

rut oyf ir di shchi – ne – le, Mir zo – ln a – zoy le – bn. Mil –
see it plain an ev – 'ry face, There's noth – ing here but pleas – ure. For

cho – mes, bik – sn, men – tshn blut, Dar – fn mir oyf tso – res, A
wars and guns and shed – ding blood, No – bo – dy does need them, A

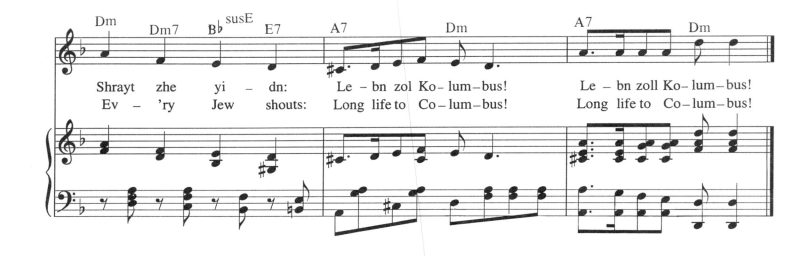

Di Grine Kuzine
The Greenhorn Cousin

This is arguably the most famous of all Jewish immigration songs. My mother sang it to the rhythm of the sewing machines along with other young Jewish and Italian working women in New York's garment district. It was often sung lightly or hummed without paying too much attention to the words, which recount one of the recurring tragedies of immigrant life. Here again we find Columbus involved in the fate of the new arrival.

Jewish

Words by Hyman Prizant
Music by Abe Schwartz

be - ke - lekh vi roy - te po - me - ran — tsn,
ros - y cheeks we all found so en - tranc — ing,

Fi - se - lekh vos be - tn zikh tsum tan — tsn, tan - tsn.
Lit - tle feet that nev - er could stop danc — ing, danc - ing.

Nit gegangen iz zi — nor geshprungen,
Nit geredt hot zi, nor gezungen;
Freylekh, lustik iz geven ir mine.
Ot aza geven iz mayn kuzine. (2)

Ikh bin arayn tsu mayn "nekst-dorke"
Vos zi hot a "milineri-storke,"
A "dzhab" gekrogn hob ikh far mayn kuzine — (2)
Az lebn zol di goldene medine!

Avek zaynen fun demolt on shoyn yorn,
Fun mayn kuzine iz a tel gevorn;
"Peydes" yorn lang hot zi geklibn, (2)
Biz fun ir aleyn iz nisht geblibn.

Unter ire bloye sheyne oygn
Shvartse pasn hobn zikh fartsoygn;
Di bekelekh, di royte pomerantsn, (2)
Hobn zikh shoyn oysgegrint in gantsn.

Haynt, as ikh bagegn mayn kuzine
Un ikh freg zi: Vos zhe makhstu, grine?
Entfert zi mir mit a krumer mine: (2)
— Az brenen zol Kolombuses medine!

Never walking — always lightly springing,
Never talking — always brightly singing,
Full of joy — and smiles a dime a dozen;
That's the way she carried on, my cousin. (2)

I dropped in to visit my "next-doorkeh,"[1]
The one who has a millinery "storkeh."[2]
For my cousin I found some employment, (2)
And that was the end of her enjoyment.

Since that fateful day my cousin blew in,
The poor girl has just become a ruin;
Years of paydays — working, slaving, straining, (2)
'Til of her there was nothing more remaining.

Underneath her once blue, pretty eyes now
Dark black lines of sorrow do arise now,
And her rosy cheeks, so full of color — (2)
All you see now is a sickly pallor.

Nowadays, if I should meet my cousin,
And I ask her, "Greeny, so what's buzzin'?"
Bitterly she answers, "Understand now — (2)
Devil take Columbus's new land now!"

1. Yiddish–English for "female next-door neighbor."
2. Yiddish–English diminutive for "store."

Latvia

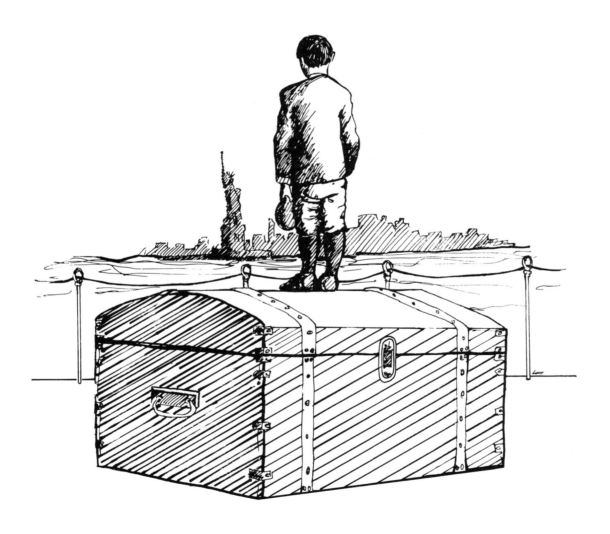

223

Tikai Viena Dziesma
Only One Song

This song was collected in Ottawa, Ontario, in 1976. It was originally performed by choirs, but has now passed into the oral tradition — always a good sign when it comes to assuring the survival of a song.

Latvia

Ti - kai vie - na dzies - ma mī - lą man, _____ Cau - ri
On - ly one song is so dear to me, _____ And it

vi - sām vēt - rām vi - ņa skan, _____ Viļ - ņi vi - nu rit - mā aiz - šu
car - ries o'er the storm - y sea, _____ On the waves it's heard at ev - 'ry

po, _____ Sa - vai dzim - tai zem - ei dzie - du to. Tie, kas
hand, _____ And I sing it for my fa - ther - land. They who

Lithuania

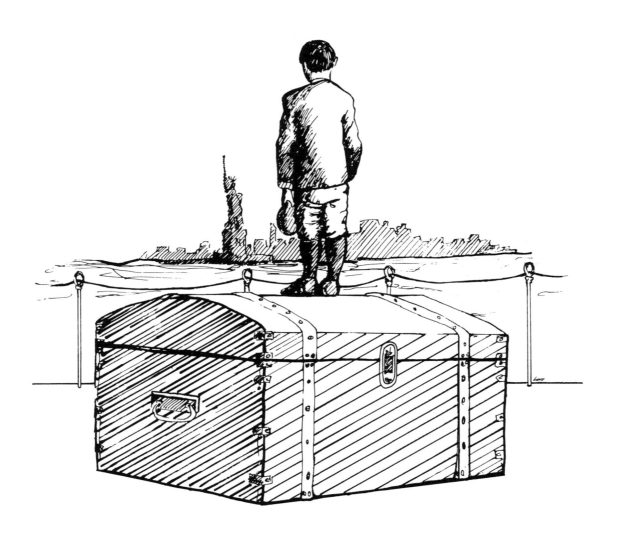

Už Atlanto Jūros Valstybė Yra
On The Other Side Of The Atlantic

Regina Kutka of Ottawa, Ontario, learned this song from her mother, who had composed it while living in Brazil. The Kutka family was originally from Lithuania. Many European immigrants lived in South America before moving on to Canada or the United States.

Lithuania

Už At - lan - to jū - ros vals - ty - bė yra,
Far a - cross the sea from A - me - ri - ca,

O ji pa - vа - din - ta gra - ži Lie - tu - va.
There is found a land called Lith - u - an - i - a.

Ten gi - miau, ten au - gau ten ma - ža bu - vau,
That is where I'm from, that's where I spent my youth,

228

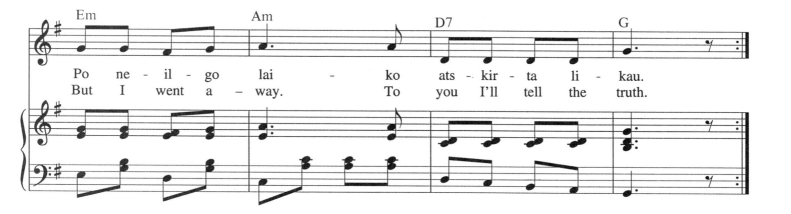

Po ne - il - go lai - ko ats - kir - ta li - kau.
But I went a - way. To you I'll tell the truth.

Kai mes atvažiavom šalin svetimon,
Tai čia aš neradau nieko iš savų.
Neradau tėvelių, sesių, nei brolių,
Anei kaimynėlių, nei pažįstamų. (2)

Čia nėra tų draugių, kur aš vaikščiojau,
Nei rūtų darželio, kur rūtas sėjau.
Nėr nei tu takelių, kur aš vaikščiojau,
Anei to bėrnelio, katrą mylėjau. (2)

Čia nėr man draugių, kur aš draugavau,
Negirdžiu, dainelių, kurias dainavau,
O jei ir dainuočiau, kas gi jas supras?
Kai man širdį skauda, kas mane atjaus? (2)

But when we arrived in this strange country,
There was no one here that was known to me.
Couldn't find my parents, sisters or my brothers,
Neighbors or my friends or any of the others. (2)

Gone, the friends of mine whom I used to talk with,
Through the flower garden, that I used to walk with.
I can see it all in my mind so clearly.
But where is the lad whom I loved so dearly? (2)

Here I have no friends. Where do I belong?
I don't ever hear a familiar song.
Even if I sang songs, who would understand?
When my heart is aching, who would hold my hand? (2)

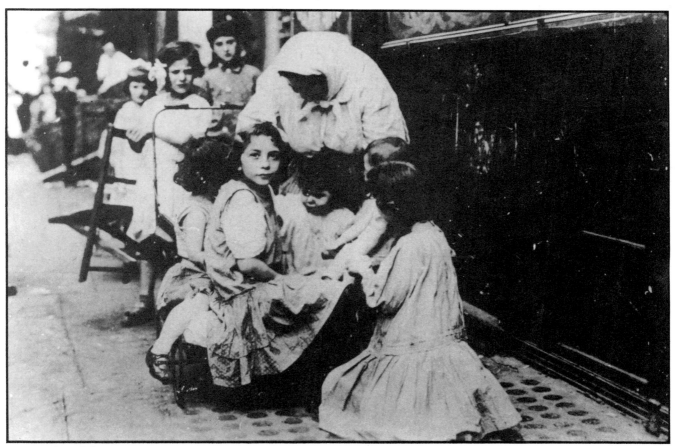

National Park Service

Einu, Stoviu, Guliu, Keliu
Walking, Standing, Lying, Rising

There are many reasons for emigrating — leaving one's homeland for the unknown. Political, economic and religious reasons have driven millions to these shores. Then there are the romantic reasons. . . .

Lithuania

Einu, sto-viu, gu-liu, ke-liu, mis-lis ma-ne i-ma A-pie Lie-tu-vos mer-ga-čiu var-gin-gą bu-vi-mą, A-pie Lie-tu-vos mer-gai-čiu var-gin-gą bu-vi-mą

Walk-ing, stand-ing, ly-ing, ris-ing I've got just one man-ia, All a-bout the prob-lems of the girls of Lith-u-an-ia, All a-bout the prob-lems of the girls of Lith-u-an-ia.

Koks jų yra padėjimas Lietuvos šalelėj,
Kiek daug vargo tur nukęsti neviena panelė. (2)

Apjuokimų ir apkalbų daug tur atlaikyti,
Bemergaujant — žiuri sensta, ir nėr ka daryti. (2)

Vienos perka didžias knygas, žada davatkauti,
O ir nėra ką daryti — vyrą sunku gauti. (2)

Ten už jūriu, šaly svieto, daug yra vaikinų,
Kurie laimėje gyvena ir apie mus žino. (2)

Tai tarkimės mes sesytės, pas juos nukeliauti,
Nukeliavę gal kiekviena po vaikiną gauti. (2)

Oh, the girls of Lithuania, they are in a panic.
With the troubles they do suffer they are getting manic. (2)

They must stand a lot of gossip from getting the cold shoulder.
Still unmarried, then they notice they are getting older. (2)

One buys big books, starts to study, wants to join a convent.
She can't do a thing about it — wonders where the men went. (2)

There are bach-e-lors aplenty far across the ocean,
Living there contentedly — they'd show us devotion. (2)

So let's talk it over, sisters — what's the use of waiting?
Let's go over, get a husband, and start celebrating. (2)

Sherman Collection, National Park Service

231

Pamenu Tą Rytą
I Recall That Morning

Love, and even worship, of nature plays a strong role in Lithuanian culture. The young girl in the song who bids a tearful farewell to fields and garden is instinctively following the ancient tradition of the veneration of great oaks, a widely spread custom in Lithuanian villages.

Lithuania

Pa - me - nu tą ry - tą, Kai sau - lė te kė - jo,
I re - call that morn - ing when the sun was ris - ing,

Pa - ža - di - nai, mo - ti - nė - le, ke - lio - nė - lei kel - tis,
Then you woke me up, dear moth - er, to pre - pare the jour - ney,

Pa - ža - di - nai, mo - ti - nė - le, ke - lio - nė - lei kel - tis.
Then you woke me up, dear moth - er, to pre - pare the jour - ney.

Kelkis, dukruže, kelkis, mylimoji,	Get up, my dear daughter, we will soon be leaving.
Sakyk sudiev tėviškėlei — Iš jos išvažiuoji. (2)	Say good-bye to our homeland, there's no time for grieving. (2)
Iš lovelės kėliau, į kiemelį ėjau,	I got up from my bed, went outside so early,
Daugel akių ašarotų i mane ziūrėjo. (2)	Many were the tear-filled eyes that were looking at me. (2)
Gegutė kukavo, lakštutė čiulbėjo,	The cuckoo called out to me, and the nightingale.
O ten toliau rugių laukas taip gražiai bangavo. (2)	Over there the field of rye was waving in the vale. (2)
Ėjau pro kiemelį, pro rūtelių darželi.	I gazed at the rue, my courage for to harden,
Girdžiu verkia sesserėlė rūtelių daržely. (2)	Then I heard my sister crying sadly in the garden. (2)
Cit, neverk, sesute, cit, neverk, jaunoji,	Shush, don't cry, my sister — don't be so downhearted,
Paklausyki, ką mums sako močiutė senoji. (2)	Listen to what mother says — it's time that we got started. (2)
Tenai už jūrelių, yr' šalis aukselio,	Overseas there is a land of gold, so hurry.
Nieks nežino, nieks nemato ten sunkaus vargelio. (2)	It's a land that knows no hardships, no one has to worry. (2)
Kai mes atvažiavom į svetimą šalį,	But when we arrived there after weeks on board ship,
Tai pažinom, tai pamatėm mes tikrą vargelį. (2)	Only then we learned to know the meaning of true hardship. (2)
Pasakyk, močiute, pasakyk, senoji,	Tell us, mother, tell us what that old wives' tale meant,
Kur yr' aukso kalnužėliai, kur laimužė toji? (2)	Where are all the hills of gold and where is true contentment? (2)
Dukružėle mano, mylimoji mano,	Listen, my beloved — oh, my darling daughter,
Kur Lietuva, kur tėvynė, ten laimužė toji. (2)	We knew happiness in Lithuania 'cross the water. (2)

233

Photo by Maury Englander

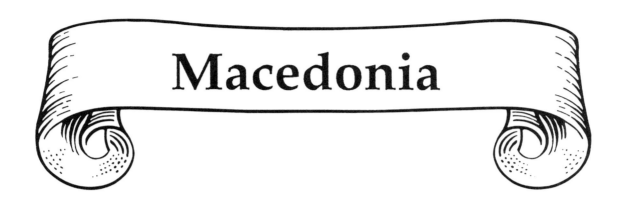

Macedonia

The second half of the 19th century witnessed a mass exodus of the Macedonian people from their homeland. They were driven out by the excesses of the occupation by the Turks of the Ottoman Empire. In search of employment and freedom from ethnic persecution, many Macedonians found their way to such industrialized cities in America as Cincinnati, St. Louis, Madison, Chicago, Toledo, and New York.

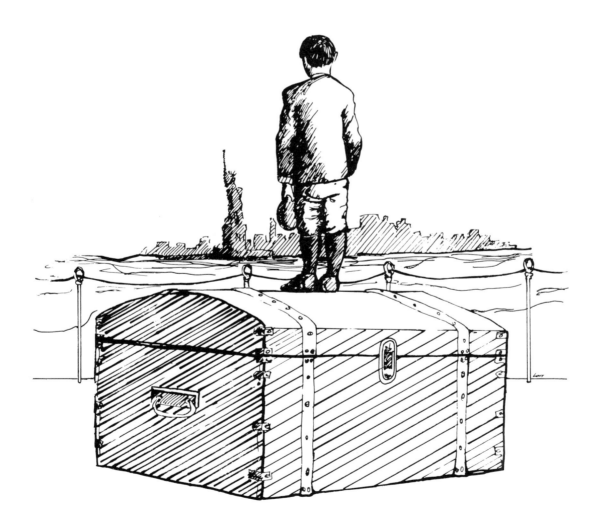

Bog Da Bie Kaj Prv Pojde
God Punishes Him Who Goes First

Despite the many compelling reasons to leave Macedonia, feelings of guilt and regret for having left were hard to overcome. This song dates from 1903 and was recorded by Alexander Sarievsky in the village of Galicinik in Western Macedonia.

Macedonia

Bog da bi e koj prv poj de.
God pun - ish - es him who goes first.

Koj prv poj - de, mi - lo li - be, na pe - chal - ba. ba.
Him who goes first, oh, my dear love, seek - ing for gain. gain.

Na tugina na pechalba,	To a foreign land seeking for gain,
Na pechalba, milo libe, Amerika. (2)	Seeking for gain, oh, my dear love, to America. (2)
Tri godini bez rabota,	Three great long years without any work,
Bez rabota, milo libe, bez pet pari. (2)	Without any work, oh, my dear love, without a cent. (2)
Prodaj si go elecheto,	Now you may sell your dowry coat,
Prodaj si go, milo libe, elecheto. (2)	Now you may sell, oh, my dear love, your dowry coat. (2)
Ako ne stiga elecheto,	If your dowry coat be not enough,
Prodaj si go, milo libe, gerdancheto. (2)	Then you must sell, oh, my dear love, your fine necklace. (2)
Prati pari da si dojdam,	Then send to me money for my return,
Da si dojdam, milo libe, kade tebe. (2)	For my return, oh, my dear love, back home to you. (2)

Mexico

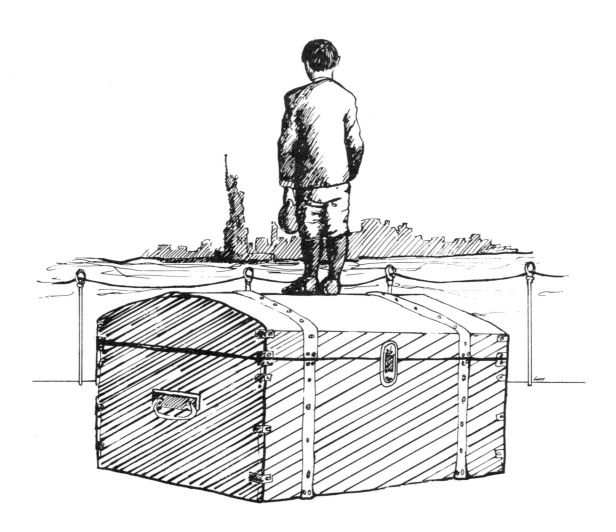

Corrido De Joaquín Murieta
Corrido About Joaquín Murieta

A *corrido* is a typical Mexican narrative ballad, a perfect vehicle for recounting the exploits of Joaquín Murieta, California's most notorious bandit. Murieta came to the Gold Rush country in 1849 from his native Mexico to seek his fortune as a miner. One disaster followed another: His land was stolen from him, his wife was raped, his brother was hanged, and he himself was flogged. In his grief and in desperation he turned outlaw, organizing a band which terrorized the countryside for three years. A Robin Hood legend grew up around him and his exploits as he hunted down and killed those who had raped his wife, lynched his brother, and driven him from his claim. Eventually he was betrayed, and in a running gun battle he was killed. As proof of his death, his head was put on display (admission: one dollar) in San Francisco in 1853.

Mexico

Yo no soy a-me-ri-ca-no, pe-ro com-pren-do el in-
I'm not an *a-me-ri-ca-no,* but En- glish I un-der-

glés. _____ Yo lo a-pren-dí de mi her-ma-no al
stand. _____ I learned it all from my broth-er, I

de-re-cho y al re-vés,___ Ya cual-quier a-me-ri-ca-no lo ha-
write it with eith-er hand,___ And I can cause an-y Yank-ee to

238

	F#7	Bm	D	G Gm	D	

go _____ tem - blar a mis pies. _____
trem _____ — _____ ble at my com-mand. _____

Cuando apenas era niño,
Huérfano a mí me dejaron
Sin quien me hiciera un cariño;
A mi hermano lo mataron,
Y a mi esposa Carmelita
¡Cuanto la martirizaron!

Yo me vine de Hermosillo,
En busca de oro y riqueza;
Al indio bueno y sencillo,
Lo defendí con fiereza,
A buen precio los Sherifes,
Pagaban por mi cabeza.

Me he paseado en California
Por el año del cincuenta;
Con mi pistola fajada,
Y mi canana repleta,
Yo soy aquel mexicano,
De nombre Joaquín Murieta.

Ya nos vamos de estampida,
Todos vamos a tropel,
Con bastante caballada,
Y cien mil pesos en papel,
También les traigo a Tres Dedos;
Que ha sido un amigo fiel.

Por cantinas he venido,
Castigando americanos;
Tú serás el capitán
El que mataste a mi hermano,
Lo agarraste indefenso,
Orgulloso americano.

When I was just a young fellow,
I lost my father and mother.
I had nobody to love me —
And then they killed my brother.
My poor wife, Carmelita,
Was tortured by another.

I came in from Hermosillo,
In search of riches and gold.
The good Indian I defended —
The story has often been told.
The sheriffs, they were all hoping
My head could be bought and sold.

In eighteen hundred and fifty,
I was in California,
With cartridges and with pistols —
And I was riding afar.
For I am that *mexicano*
Whose name is Joaquín Murieta.

We're going to stage a hold-up,
It will be a bloody clash,
With plenty of our fast horses,
And one hundred thousand in cash.
With my true friend, "Three Fingers,"
We will be gone in a flash.

I've been in every cantina,
Americanos I've fought:
"You are my brother's killer.
Captain, it's you that I've sought.
An unarmed man you did murder,
And now, proud man, you are caught."

Corrido De Kansas
Kansas Corrido

In the 1880s, a group of Mexican cowboys drove a herd of cattle up the trail from Texas to Kansas. In true *corrido* style, a ballad grew out of this adventure. These cowboys were the descendants of the original Mexican cowboys of the west Texas plains. Mexican cowboys were doing their roping and riding several decades before their American counterparts came on the scene. They have left us a rich legacy of words of Spanish origin — "lariat," "rodeo," "pinto," "corral," "stampede," "buckaroo" (which comes from *vaquero,* the Spanish word for "cowboy"), and many others.

Mexico

Cuan - do sa - li - mos pa' Kan - sas _____ con u -
na gran - de par - ti da, _____ Nos de - cí a el ca - po -
ral: _____ "No cuen - to ni con mi vi - da." _____

It was when we left for Kan - sas _____ With a
man - y a brave ran - ger, _____ That the fore - man, he said
to us, "Ev - en my life is in dan - ger." _____

Quinientos novillos eran Pero todos muy livianos, No los podíamos reparar Siendo treinta mexicanos.	There were fifteen hundred longhorns, And we had to keep on our toes, They were wild — we could not herd them, Just us thirty *mexicanos*.
Cuando dimos vista a Kansas Era puritita correr, Eran los caminos largos, Y pensaba yo en volver.	When we caught sight of Kansas, It was nothing but pure running. The roads were long and endless, And I thought about returning.
Cuando llegamos a Kansas Un torito se peló, Fue a tajarle un mozo joven Y el caballo se volteó.	And when we arrived in Kansas, A young steer started thrashing. A young boy went to head him, And his pony, it went crashing.
La madre de un aventurero Le pregunta al caporal: — Oiga, déme razón de mi hijo, Que no lo he visto llegar.	The mother of a cowboy — Her son has gone off to roam — Asks the foreman, has he seen him, He has not yet come back home.
— Señora, le voy a decir Pero no se vaya a llorar, A su hijo lo mató un novillo En la puerta de un corral.	"Lady, I am going to tell you, But don't cry as I relate How a longhorn steer did kill him, On a wooden corral gate.
Treinta pesos alcanzó Pero todo limitado, Y trescientos puse yo Pa' haberlo sepultado.	"All he had was thirty pesos, But he owed it on his pay, And I put in three hundred For his burial that day.
Todos los aventureros Lo fueron a acompañar, Con sus sombreros en las manos, A verlo sepultar.	"All of his fellow drivers, From the company around, They followed him bareheaded, When we laid him in the ground."

Deportados
Deportees

The line between a *bracero* (see next song) and a *deportado* was often finely drawn and, in many instances, did not exist at all. This song dates from the early 1900s but is still being sung, and not merely for historical reasons. The conditions that created the song still exist.

Mexico

Voy a con — tar — les, se — ño — res, voy a con —
I'm going to tell you, good peo — ple, I'm going to

tar — les, se — ño — res, to — do lo que ___ yo su — frí,
tell you, good peo — ple, of all that I ___ had to bear,

Cuan — do de — je yo a mi pa — tria, cuan — do de —
When I de — part — ed my coun — try, When I de —

242

je yo_a mi pa – tria, Por ve – nir a_e – se pa – ís. _____
part – ed my coun–try, To come all the way up here. _____

Serían las diez de la noche,
Serían las diez de la noche,
Comenzó un tren a silbar;
Ay, que dijo mi madre,
Hay viene ese tren ingrato
Que a mi hijo se va a llevar.

It was about ten in the evening,
It was about ten in the evening,
A train whistle pierced the dark night.
"Ay," then cried out my mother,
"The cruel train is arriving
To carry my son out of sight."

Llegamos por fin a Juárez,
Llegamos por fin a Juárez,
Ahí fué mi apuración
Que donde va, que donde viene,
Cuanto dinero tiene
Para entrar a esta nación.

We finally got to Juárez,
We finally got to Juárez,
And there my troubles began.
Whether you're coming or going,
It's money you must be showing,
If you want to enter this land.

Señores, traigo dinero
Señores, traigo dinero
Para poder emigrar
Su dinero nada vale,
Su dinero nada vale,
Te tenemos que bañar.

But sirs, I'm carrying money,
But sirs, I'm carrying money,
In order to emigrate.
"Your money, it is worth nothing,
Your money, it is worth nothing.
We have to send you away."

Hoy traen la gran polvadera
Hoy traen la gran polvadera
Y sin consideración,
Mujeres, niños y ancianos,
Los llevan a la frontera,
Los echan de esa nación.

Today comes the great disorder,
Today comes the great disorder,
And without consideration,
Women and children and old men,
They take them to the border.
They kick them out of this nation.

Adiós, paisanos queridos,
Adiós, paisanos queridos,
Ya nos van a deportar
Pero no somos bandidos
Pero no somos bandidos
Venimos a camellar.

Farewell, my dear companions,
Farewell, my dear companions,
They've come to deport us today.
Although we are not bandits,
Although we are not bandits —
We've come to work for our pay.

Los espero alla en mi tierra,
Los espero alla en mi tierra,
Ya no hay mas revolución;
Vamonos cuates queridos
Seremos bien recibidos
En nuestra bella nación.

So wait for them there in my country,
So wait for them there in my country.
There is no more revolution.
Let's all go back to our farms now,
They'll greet us with open arms now,
In our beautiful nation.

Los Braceros
The Migratory Workers

Braceros — those who walk "arm in arm" — are the migratory Mexican agricultural workers of the Southwest who have been encouraged to come to this country during the harvesting season. Their legal rights are at an absolute minimum, and they are often the victims of both employers and local law-enforcement officials. This song originated in New Mexico.

By Benito Amador and
Justino Alarcon

Mexico

Ya son mu - chos los pai - sa - nos ___ que se van al ___ ex - tran -
Man - y of my coun - try - men now ___ at the bor - der ___ are all

je - ro, ___
lined up, ___

Y pa - ra po - der sa - lir ___ se con -
And to be a - ble to cross it, ___ as "bra -

tra - tan ___ de "bra - ce - ros," ___
ce - ros" ___ they have signed up. ___

Des - pués de lar - gos seis me - ses ___ les re - co - gen___ los pa -
Af - ter six months have gone by and ___ when the beets have ___ all been

pe - les _____
crat - ed, _____

Cuan do a - ca - ban de "ta -
Their pa - pers are tak - en

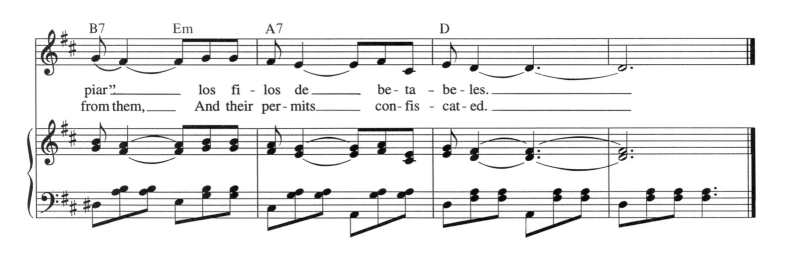

piar" _____ los fi - los de _____ be - ta - be - les. _____
from them, ____ And their per - mits _____ con - fis - cat - ed. _____

Se desiertan de los campos
Y se hacen los inocentes,
Se van buscando trabajo
Durmiendo bajo las puentes.
Y después de tantas penas
Si es que ellos tuvieron suerte,
Caminan por los desiertos
Enfrentándose a la muerte.

Se los llevan los rancheros
A la pizca de algodón.
Para no pargarles nada
Les echan la inmigración.
De ahí van a las prisiones
Y graves penas les dan,
Luego los mandan pelones
Al puerto de Mazatlán.

Cuentan cien mil mexicanos
Los que no están inmigrados,
Entre ellos hay desertores,
"Alambristas" y "mojados."
Ya con esta me despido
Y los vuelvo a amonestar;
Que no salgan del terruño
Que después les va a pesar.

Leaving the bare fields behind them,
For employment they go seeking.
Hoping the police don't find them,
Under bridges they are sleeping.
And after all of their sorrows,
If they're lucky and not hunted,
They travel over the deserts,
Where by death they are confronted.

Then they are taken by ranchers
To pick cotton on plantations.
Then in order not to pay them,
They call up the Immigration.
Now they have nothing but trouble,
As to prison they're transported.
Then with their heads freshly shaven,
To Mazatlán they're deported.

A hundred thousand *mexicanos*
Tell those who've not immigrated,
And who have passed through the fences,
And as wetbacks, who have waded —
With this I will now say so long,
And remember that I said it:
Don't ever part from your country —
If you do, you will regret it.

New York Public Library Picture Collection

Norway

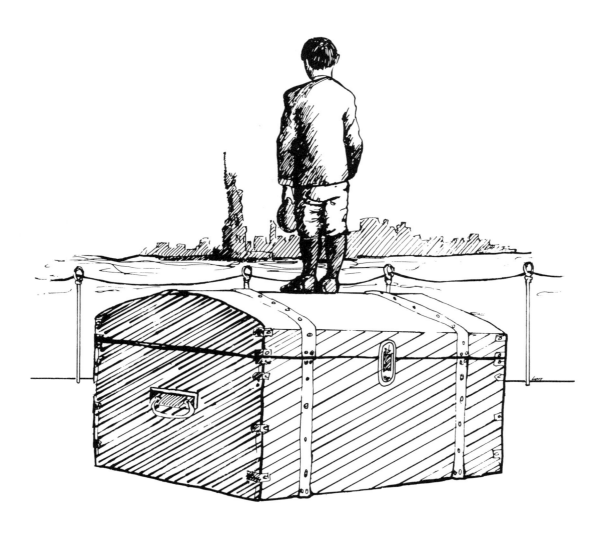

Oleana

Ole Bull (1810–1880) was a famous Norwegian violinist. He was touched by the poverty of many Norwegian farmers and, after touring the United States a number of times, decided to do something for his countrymen. In 1852 he bought 125,000 acres of land in Pennsylvania, hoping to set up a model farm.

Unfortunately, his dream — to be called Oleana — did not quite work out the way he had planned. He was cheated by land swindlers. The people who sold him the land never owned it. Things became so complicated that he had to give up the project altogether — much to the disappointment of many poor Norwegian families that had already emigrated to Pennsylvania, or were getting ready to leave their homes for a new life in the New World. Many people thought the whole thing was a big joke — at poor Ole Bull's expense. In 1853, Ditmar Meidell wrote this song poking fun at Ole and his dream.

Norway

By Ditmar Meidell

I O – le – a – na der er det godt at _____ væ – re, i
In O – le – an – na, that is the place where _____ I would stay, In –

Nor – ge vil jeg in – te Sla – ve – laen – ken _____ bae – re.
stead of bear – ing sla – v'ry's chains and suf – fer – ing in Nor – way.

Chorus

O – le O – le – a – na, O – le O – le – a – na,

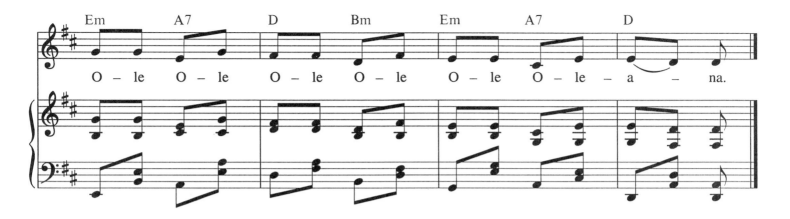

I Oleana der faar Jeg Jord for Intet, Af Jorden voxer Kornet, Og det gaar gesvindet det. *Chorus*	In Oleana, land they'll give you, And it won't cost you a thing. Grain, it will grow by itself, While you just sit around and sing. *Chorus*
Aa Kornet det tærsker sig Selv oppaa Laaven, Imens ligger jeg aa Hviler mig i Koven. *Chorus*	And then the grain will thresh itself After the harvest, While all I do is lie around. That's the part that I like best. *Chorus*
Hej Markedsgang! Poteterne skulde Du se, Du. Der brændes mindst en Pot Af hvereneste en Du. *Chorus*	At the market are for sale The biggest spuds you e'er did see. Each one yields a quart of whisky At the distillery. *Chorus*
Ja Bayerøl saa godt, Som han Ytteborg kan brygge, Det risler i Bækkene Til Fattigmandens Hygge. *Chorus*	Fine Bavarian beer is here, As good as you have tasted. It runs through all the streams in town, And not a drop is wasted. *Chorus*
Aa Laxene dem springer Saa lysting i Bække, Dem hopper selve i Gryden aa roper: Dem ska' dække! *Chorus*	The salmon leap into the kettle Fast as they are able. Then they wiggle from the pot Right onto the table. *Chorus*
Aa brunstegte Griser De løber om saa flinke Aa forespør sig høfligt, Om Nogen vil ha' Skinke. *Chorus*	Rushing 'round the streets, Roasted piggies cause a traffic jam, Inquring so politely if Perchance you'd like a slice of ham. *Chorus*
Aa Kjørene dem melker Aa kjærner aa yster Liksaa naturlig Som Else, mi Syster. *Chorus*	And the cows, they milk themselves. Please believe me, mister. Then they churn out cheese as good As does Else, my sister. *Chorus*
Aa Kalvene de slagter sig Hurtig og flaar sig, Aa stejker sig fortere End man tar en Taar sig! *Chorus*	And the calves, they kill themselves Right before your very eyes. Then roast veal is served to all, Quicker than you realize. *Chorus*
Aa Høna værper Æg Saa svære som Stabur, Mens Hanen angir Tiden Som et ottedags Slaguhr. *Chorus*	The hens lay eggs so big, Their size surely would give you a shock. And the roosters strike the hour As well as an eight-day clock. *Chorus*

Aa Maanen hver Aften er fuld —
Det er sikkert.
Jeg ligger just aa ser paa'n
Med Flaska tel Kjikkert. *Chorus*

Ja to Daler Dagen
Det faar Du for at svire,
Aa er Du rektig doven,
Saa kanske Du faar fire. *Chorus*

Fra Skyerne det regner
Med Kolerakaker.
Aa Gubervare Dere vel
For dejlige Saker! *Chorus*

Kronarbejde findes ej —
Nej det var saa ligt da!
Jeg sad nok ikke ellersen
Saa frisk her aa digta. *Chorus*

Vi gaar i Fløjelsklæder
Besat med Sølverknapper,
Aa ryker af Merskum,
Som Kjærringa stapper. *Chorus*

Aa Kjærringa maa brase
Aa styre aa stelle —
Aa blir hu sint, saa banker hu sig selv —
Skal jeg fortælle. *Chorus*

Aa Fiolin det speller
Vi Allesammen — hejsan!
Aa Danser en Polskdans,
Aa den er'nte lejsan. *Chorus*

Ja rejs til Oleana,
Saa skal Du vel leve,
Den fattigste Stymper
Herover er Greve! *Chorus*

Repeat first verse

There is a full moon every night,
So there is no need to grope.
I am observing it right now —
My bottle for a telescope. *Chorus*

When you go carousing,
You'll get two dollars, and what's more,
If you do it very well,
They will surely give you four. *Chorus*

Cakes and cookies rain down
From the heavens day and night.
Good Lord, they are so delicious,
They're a source of great delight. *Chorus*

No need to support your kids,
And to fill their purses.
If I had to work, I couldn't
Sit here spinning verses. *Chorus*

Velvet suits with silver buttons,
We all wear without a fuss.
And we smoke our meerschaum pipes,
Which the old woman fills for us. *Chorus*

And she has to sweat and toil,
All her work completing.
If she doesn't finish it,
She gives herself a beating. *Chorus*

Everyone plays violin,
And dances polkas daily.
Life is very pleasant here,
We pass the time so gaily. *Chorus*

So just you go to Oleana,
And you'll never have a care.
The poorest wretch in Norway
Becomes a count once over there. *Chorus*

Repeat first verse

250

Amerikasangen
America Song

The population of Norway in 1800 was less than one million, but from 1815 there was a marked increase, much of it absorbed by emigration to the United States. The "America Song" was a true siren's song: In the hundred-year period between 1836 and 1936 some 860,000 Norwegians left for the New World.

Norway

Far – vel du mo – der Nor – ge, nu rei – ser jeg fra dig. Jeg
Fare – well, you moth – er Nor – way, I'm trav – 'ling far from you. You

si – ger dig så man – ge takk for du opp –fost – ret mig. Du
did your best to bring me up, but it would nev – er do. I

blev for knapp i kos – ten i – mod din ar – beids – stokk, men
nev – er had e – nough food, the times were al – ways rough; But

di – ne "lær – de" søn – ner du giv – er mer enn nok.
ed – u – cat – ed peo – ple, they al – ways had e – nough.

Så reiser vi som gøvla,
fra dig til fremmed land,
alt over verdenshavet,
det store brede vann,
der kan vi tjene brødet,
om vi vil bruge flid,
jeg takke må Columbus;
som viste veien hid.

Dog elsker jeg dig Norge
med dine fjeld og vann
og vil dig nødig bytte,
med vestens fjerne land;
men når det gjelder brødet,
er det så strengt et bud,
at vi som skovens fugler,
straks må av reden ud.

I en av disse dale,
min vugge stod engang,
der vandret jeg som barn,
og gjætet fæ og sang.
Der har jeg velvet stene,
der har jeg sanket bær,
ei nogen plett på jorden,
kan blive mig så kjær.

Og da jeg skulde reise,
fra fedreland og hjem,
da faldt der mangen tåre,
og hjertet var beklemt,
jeg vendte mig på veien,
for engang til å se,
de gamle kjære tomter,
og gamle birketre.

Min broder var min følge,
til hovedstaden frem,
da var jeg tung om hjertet
thi jeg var uten hjem.
Der traff vi emigranter,
både store og små,
vi skulle bli i følge,
henover bølgen blå.

Jeg stod med hjertets vemod,
på skibets dekk og så,
det gamle kjære Norge,
forsvinde i det blå,
og jeg kan rent ud tilstå
mitt jherte var i brand,
da jeg så Norge dukke,
bag horisontens rand.

Jeg tenkte på min fader,
jeg tenkte på min mor;
som vandret der tilbage,
igjen på Norges jord,
jeg med min broder sendte,
en kjærlig hilsen hjem,
jeg vender ei tilbage,
for jeg må lengre frem.

Og om det skulde hende sig,
udi min levetid,
at jeg kom der tilbage,
da går jeg lige did,
der er mitt kjære hjemme,
der så jeg solen først,
jeg kan det ikke glemme,
for lengsel i mitt brøst.

I travel 'cross the ocean
Unto an unknown land.
There life it will be better,
As I do understand.
If we work hard once we get there,
We're sure to earn our pay,
So thanks to you, Columbus,
For showing us the way.

Although I live in Norway,
Her fields and streams are best,
And I would not exchange her
For that land way out west —
Still I cannot survive here,
And even though I grieve,
I must pack my belongings,
And sadly take my leave.

'Twas in this very valley
Where I did first explore,
I sang and picked its berries —
Did I need any more?
I never could imagine
That I would go away.
And never could I love
Another land than my Norway.

And when from fatherland and home
My leave I had to take,
I shed many a bitter tear,
I thought my heart would break.
I gazed back sadly one last time
At the land that I loved most.
The trees, they seemed to wave good-bye,
Along old Norway's coast.

My brother he came with me,
To take me to the ship.
I felt that I was homeless
As I began the trip.
The emigrants were many,
We met upon the quay.
They would be my companions,
When we would sail away.

As I stood on the ship's deck,
I shed a mournful tear,
As far off in the blue mist,
My Norway disappeared.
I'm not ashamed to say it,
How I did feel that day,
When over the horizon
My Norway slipped away.

I thought about my father,
And of my mother, too,
Who stayed behind in Norway,
And how they felt, I knew.
And so I told my brother
To take this message home:
My life was just beginning,
And I was bound to roam.

If ever it should happen,
When many years have passed,
That I could cross the ocean,
And come back home at last,
I'd go back to the village,
The place that gave me birth —
For I cannot forget my home
On Norway's sacred earth.

Kjistå Hev Eg Pakka
I Have Finished Packing

Many Norwegian immigrant farmers, driven by crop failures in the last decades of the 19th century and the early years of the 20th, chose the open spaces of Minnesota and the Dakotas to begin their new lives. The young lady in question here knew that full well. If, on the other hand, she would have fancied a sailor, she could have settled in Brooklyn, where the Norwegian Seaman's Church was founded in 1878.

Norway

Words by Per Bolstad

Kjis – tå hev eg pak – ka, og al – le hev eg tak – ka. No
I have fin – ished pack – ing, and there is noth – ing lack – ing, So

skal eg rei – se o – ver til A – mer' – ka, jes ål – reit! For
thank you, friends, I'm off now for A – mer' – ca, yes al – right! For

kven kan le – ve hei – me, der al – le er så slei – me til å
who can live in Nor – way, ex – ist in such a poor way here, Where

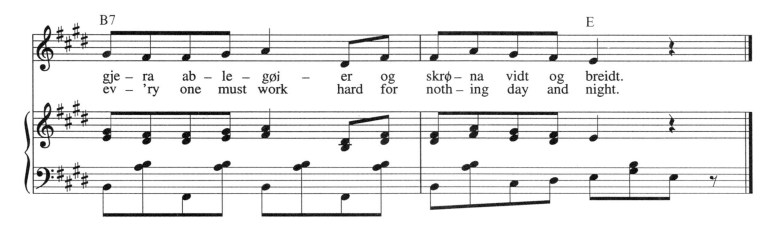

gje — ra ab — le — gøi — er og skrø — na vidt og breidt.
ev — 'ry one must work hard for noth — ing day and night.

Sjølvsagt er her fagert,
men altfor mykje magert.
Nei, over i Junaiten der er alt so gildt og feitt.
Her lyt ein gå og slite
for mykje mindr' enn lite,
men der dei verte miljonærar før ein ordet veit.

Heime vil dei nekte
ein ungdom plent å sjekte,
men burte i Amerika er der sjekting, jes, ju nå!
Der fer kvar taus og renner
og byks med adelsmenner,
ein storkar, slik som prest og lensmann berre blæs ho på.

Greivar og baronar
gjeng der som lassaronar,
og dollarprinsesser heng som eple på ei grein,
og gullet ligg klumpar
for foten så du stumpar
og slær deg naseblod på diamant og edelstein.

Straks du kjem på brygga
så byrjar også «hygga»,
der kjem ein jænki flott og sei: «Gu morning, miss, mei dir.
Mitt hjarta stend i lue,
og vil du bli mi frue,
so skal ditt liv heretter verte berre dans og flir.»

Ja, eg vil ut or landa!
Eg blæs på heimestranda,
hjer heime fins'kje lukke kor ein vender eller snur,
men burt i Minnesota
der er der plenty guta,
og burt i Utah veit me at mormonarane bur.

Ven' min, spring og fli de',
og kom so straks og bli med'.
Kvi vil du traska her, når lukka ventar på deg der?
Her lyt du gå i møka
tess du vert sur og krøka,
men i Junaiten er kvar fattigfante miljonær.

Over here it's pretty,
But so poor, it's a pity.
While in the States it's beautiful and gold is to be found.
For here one has to settle
For so much less than little,
While there you become a millionaire before you turn around.

Your youth is denied here,
You're never satisfied here,
But over in America you're petted, "yes, you know!"*
For there a girl's respected,
She never is rejected,
Priests and governors do court her wherever she does go.

Counts and knights hang 'round her,
Like bums they do surround her,
And dollar princesses hang just like apples on each tree.
The gold it lies in clumps there,
You really get your lumps there,
As you bump your nose on diamonds and precious jewelry.

As soon as you arrive there,
The place just comes alive there,
A handsome Yankee comes and says, "Good morning, miss, my dear.*
My heart is pounding madly,
I'll marry you most gladly,
And your life from now on will only be merriment and cheer."

I would leave tomorrow,
And end all of my sorrow,
For happiness here runs right through your fingers like a sieve.
But out in Minnesota,
Each girl can find her quota,
And I know that out in Utah, that's where the Mormons live.

My friend, won't you hurry,
You really make me worry.
Why do you tramp around here when true happiness waits there?
Here you will walk in darkness,
Be soured by the starkness,
While out there in the "United"* each one's a millionaire.

---

*In Norwegian–English in the original.

255

Amerikafeber
America Fever

At the height of the "America fever" in the late 19th and early 20th centuries, there were more than 100 Norwegian-language newspapers in America. The Brooklyn-based *Norway Times,* which was founded in 1891, and the Seattle-based *Western Viking* are the only survivors. The only way these papers have been able to hang on is to publish most of their articles in English.

Norway

Words by Ivar Kårdal

No vil eg skri – va og pen – nen min gri – pa,
Now I will write with my pen in my fin – gers,

dik – ta ei vi – sa so best som eg kan;
And make a bal – lad as good as can.

dik – ta um stri – len, hans
We sim – ple folk have al –

båt og hans ki – pa, syng – ja um meg um mi bygd og mitt land.
ways been good sing – ers, Sail – ing our sail – boats and work – ing our land.

Syng – ja um dei som av lan – det burt – dra – ga,
So I will sing of my friends and my neigh – bors.

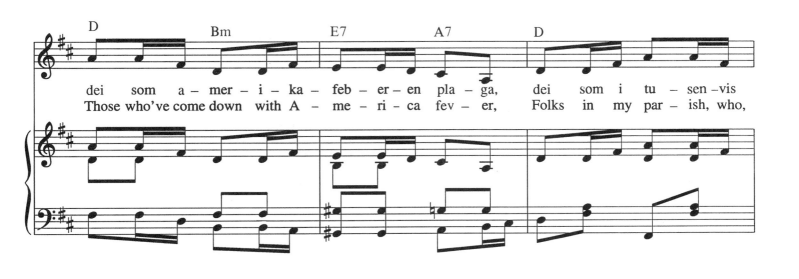

dei som a – mer – i – ka – feb – er – en pla – ga, dei som i tu – sen –vis
Those who've come down with A – me – ri – ca fev – er, Folks in my par – ish, who,

i des – se da – ga' rei – ser fra heim og frå fe – dre – ne – land.
tired of the la – bors pick up and leave our – dear fath–er – land.

Tidleg um vinteren, straks etter julen
er det feber som ytrar seg smått,
og der går mange so vantre og mutte,
inkje i landet kan smaka dei godt.
Sume går alltid å klaga og kyta,
andre kan bert um Amerika skryta,
so vil dei selja sin gard og si gryta
og reisa burt frå sitt fedreneland.

Seier ein at dei i landet bør bliva,
står dei og fniser og hev deg til narr,
skryta kva den eller hin monne skriva
um kor det godt i Amerika er.
Gutane deira vart futar og prestar,
og der er griser so store som hestar,
men til slikt prat me ei tillit vil festa
her i vår heim og vårt fedreneland.

Tida er komen dei avskjed skal take
kvar med sitt folk, med si bygd, og sitt land,
derpå til sjøen skal toget framdrage,
skipene bringer deim vidare fram,
unge og gamle og brafolk og fantar,
alle med meir eller mindre kontantar,
samlast i Bergen frå alle slags kantar,
alle vi burt frå sitt fedreneland.

Som eg sat stussa, so fekk eg ein tanke —
vore vel moro å sjå kor det gjekk,
tok mi blåtrøya og hatten den blanke,
kipo og båten snart ferdig eg fekk.
Ola og Sjur, mine grannar, vil fylgja,
me er'kje redd for ein nordveste-bylgja,
men til Amerika vil me'kje fylgja,
men vera her i vårt fedreneland.

Som me kom roande innover vågen
der som dei prektige skipane lå,
mastrar av rakaste tre uti skogen,
snart skulde dei til Amerika gå.
Det var eit underlegt syn til å skue,
dekket det vrimla som maur i ei tue.
Mangeslags hovudplagg, mangeslags lue,
alt skulde ut frå sitt fedreneland.

Me gjekk umbord, og der låg det i dungar
kister og sekkjer og folk kvar me såg,
der var eit skrik og eit skrål utav ungar,
sume var sjuk so dei knapt kunde gå.
Men me fekk mjølkost og lefsa og kaka
like eins fekk me og reisølet smaka,
men me var glad me fekk venda tilbaka,
heim til vår bygd og vårt fedreneland.

Hundravis gjekk dei på gata og vanka,
selde sin klædnad og kjøpte seg ny,
gjekk der med frakkar som storfolk og spanka,
røykte sigar og gjekk med paraply.
Gjentene kjøpte seg kjola' og duka',
slik som madammer og jomfruer bruka',
men desse gjentene var visst litt sjuka.
Dei skulde burt frå sitt fedreneland.

After the winter they all catch the fever,
It comes on strong in the spring of the year.
People are ready to pack up and leave here.
Grumbling and mumbling — that's all you hear.
Life in America must be a pleasure,
They'll sell their farms and gather their treasure.
They dream of wealth beyond any measure,
And say good-bye to our dear fatherland.

If you should say that they all should remain here,
They'll look at you and they'll call you absurd.
Then they'll recount with a kind of a pained sneer,
All of America's wonders they've heard.
All of the their children have first-rate positions:
Parsons and sheriffs and even physicians.
Hogs big as horses — how's that for conditions?
We don't believe it in the fatherland.

Now is the time for the mighty migration.
Now is the time to bid Norway farewell.
See how they come from all over the nation.
Will they succeed — who can say? Time will tell.
Gathered at Bergen, the young and the old there,
Decent folk, riff-raff, the brave and the bold there.
Each one with his little sack-full of gold there,
Ready at last to leave the fatherland.

As I sat thinking, I got an idea,
I'd like to see how such things they were done.
So before everyone put out to sea,
I got all dressed up, took my boat just for fun.
Ola and Sjur came along to help rowing,
We do not fear any nor'westers' blowing,
For to America we are not going.
We'll stay right here in our dear fatherland.

So we rowed up the bay over the waters.
There all the tall ships at anchor did ride,
Carrying Norway's brave sons and fair daughters,
Ready to sail at the turn of the tide.
What a remarkable sight we did see there.
Decks were aswarm with folks happy to be there,
Dressed in their finery, ready for sea there —
With but one thought: To leave the fatherland.

We went on board, and then what did we see there?
Duffels and sea chests and people in heaps.
It was a madhouse, I tell you, to be there.
And the sick children, it gave me the creeps.
They made us welcome on board of the big ship,
Shared bread and cake they had stocked for the big trip.
We drank their beer — I took many a big sip,
But we were glad to stay here, fatherland.

They knocked about in the streets by the hundred,
In their new clothes, just like so many tsars.
If you'd have seen them, you too would have wondered,
With their umbrellas and big fat cigars.
All the young girls bought themselves shawls and dresses,
Then strolled around like a bunch of princesses.
If our farm girls had seen them, my guess is
They would have wished to leave the fatherland.

Sidan so traff eg so mangein eg kjende,
nokre frå Hallingdal, andre frå Voss,
slike som gjekk med kramhandel og rende
gard ifrå gard med ei skreppa hjå oss.
No skulde dei til Amerika seila,
og på traktering det ikkje mon feila,
baierølflasker og brennevinspeila
tømtes til avskjed for fedreneland.

Kor det vil gå når dei koma på havet,
det kan eg slett ikkje skjøna meg på,
når dei vert sjøsjuke, går der å rave,
eg trur dei ynskjer seg heime dei låg.
Då er det fulla for seint til å vende,
då får dei venta til turen tek ende,
då vil dei tenkja på vener og frende
som er igjen i sitt fedreneland.

Nei, eg i Norge vil byggja og leva,
enn um innkomsten er ikkje so stor,
flittig for meg og for mine vil streva.
Dø vil eg her som min far og mi mor,
Eg vil arbeida og dyrka og grave,
sanka mi næring frå jord og frå havet,
takka min Gud for hans hjelp og hans gave,
og vera glad i mitt fedreneland.

No er eg heime, og no er til ende
dette mit korte, einfoldige dikt.
Visa er simpel, det må eg bekjenne,
strilen kun lite forstår seg på slikt.
Me er for tunghendt te pussa og fila,
men me er folk om ennskjønt me er strila',
og på vår truskap du aldri treng tvila,
helst mot vår konge og fedreneland.

I met a good many there that I did know,
Some came from Hallingdal, some came from Voss.
Some had been peddlers, to the farms did go,
Earning the money to get them across.
Off to America — it seemed so risky.
There were refreshments — it made them frisky,
Emptying bottles of beer and of whisky,
In fond farewell to their old fatherland.

How they will manage when they're on the ocean,
That I can't tell you — I'm sure I don't know.
When they get seasick by the rocking motion,
Then they will wish that they never did go.
But turning back will be out of the question.
Don't even make such a foolish suggestion.
They'll have to put up with their indigestion,
Thinking of friends in the dear fatherland.

As for myself, here in Norway I'm staying,
Though as a poor man, by cares I am worn.
I'll work and toil, though little it's paying,
I'll live and die where my fathers were born.
Here I'll remain with my friends and my neighbors,
Work in my fields and redouble my labors.
Give thanks to God for all of his favors,
And love and cherish my own fatherland.

Now I am home and my song is completed.
This little poem's gone on long enough.
It is so simple, I have to admit it —
We peasant folk are not good at this stuff.
Our hands are calloused — we may not be clever,
But we are men whom you may trust forever.
Loyal and faithful, we never will sever
Ties to our king and our dear fatherland.

Library of Congress

Philippines

Filipino immigrants in the 1920s were enticed to come to California by the glowing stories of labor contractors, who exalted America as the golden land of opportunity. Most of these new arrivals found themselves relegated to the position of stoop laborers, picking the crops wherever work could be found. In the 1960s, a new wave of Filipino immigration began, with California still the region of choice.

Staten Island, New York, is the site of a Philippine–American Civic and Cultural Community Organization. Professor Belen Manuel is a leading member of this organization. She and her lyricist, Dr. Gary Villanueva, composed these modern songs, which describe the feelings and sentiments of Filipino immigrants in the 1990s.

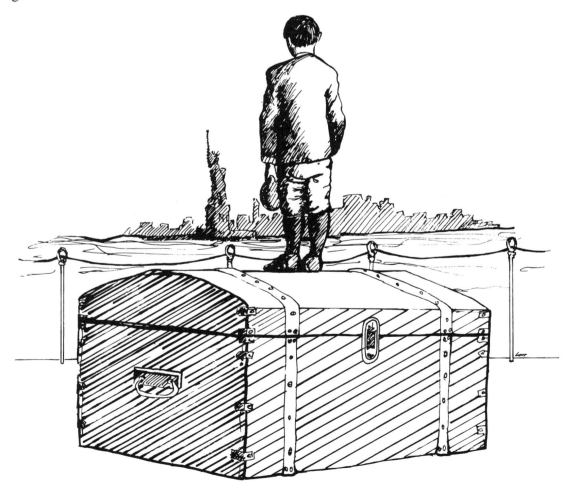

Kay Lungkot Ng Hating Gabi
It Is Very Sad At Midnight

Philippines

Words by Dr. E. G. Villanueva and
Belen Manuel
Music by Belen Manuel

Kay lung–kot ng ha–ting ga – bi,
Kung___ wa–lang nag–ma–ma–
At mid–night it is ve–ry sad,
When there is no one here to

hal.
Wa–lang bi–tuin wa–lang bu – wan na–ngu–ngu – li – lang pu–so
love.
There are no stars, there is no moon, And lone-some, lone-some is my

ko. Hi–na–ha–nap ki–ta sin–ta.
Ang a – mi–han ay lu–mi–
heart. I'm search-ing ev–'ry–where for you.
The au–tumn of the year has

Philippine Indepence Day Festival

Ako Ay Pilipino
I Am A Filipino

Philippines

Words by Dr. E. G. Villanueva
Music by Belen Manuel

A – ko ay Pi – li – pi – no di – to sa A – me – ri –
I am a Fi – li – pi – no, I'm here in A – me – ri –

ca, Bu – hat sa New York hang – gang sa Ha – waii, Pi – li –
ca, And wheth – er in New York or in Ha – waii, Fi – li –

pi – no a – kong tu – nay. Wi – kang Ta – ga – log ang gi –
pi – no is what I am. Our lan – guage is Ta – ga – log,

na – ga – mit na – min sa mga___ pag – ti – ti – pon. A –
and we do use it when we___ get – to – geth – er. I

Pilipinas Ang Bayan Ko
Philippines, My Native Land

Philippines

Words by Dr. E. G. Villanueva
Music by Belen Manuel

Kay Hirap Mabuhay
It's Hard To Live

Philippines

By Belen Manuel

Kay hi – rap ma – bu – hay di – to sa A-
It's ve – ry hard to be here in this A-

me – ri – ca, Ang a – ka la ko'y gin – to,
me – ri – ca, I thought it would be all gold,

Ang ya – ya pa – kan sa a – raw a – raw.
That I would walk up – on each and ev – 'ry day.

Sa ha – nap bu – hay Kai – lang – ang mag – a –
But in your dai – ly job you need to stu – dy

271

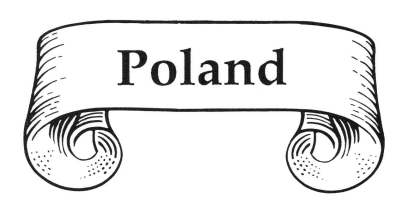

Poland

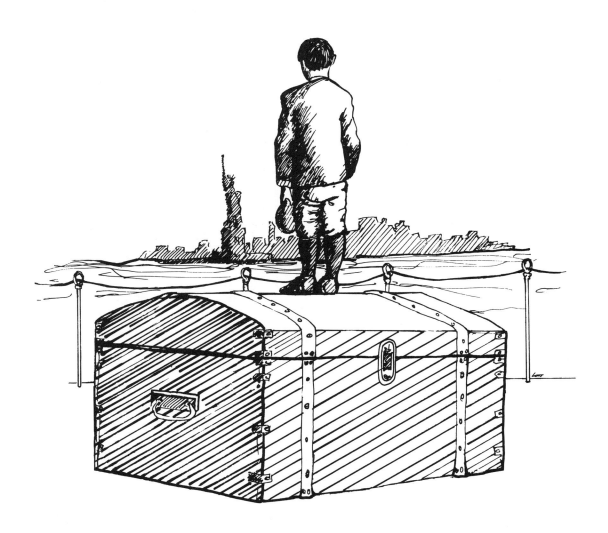

Jechał Jeden Polak
A Pole Was Traveling

Passaic, New Jersey, attracted a large Polish immigrant population. In 1940, Mrs. Sophia Dziob learned this song from friends living there. Its reference to landing at Castle Garden, which was the immigration reception center in New York from 1855 to 1890, gives us some idea of the period of the song.

Poland

Je – chał   je – den   Po – lak   ze   sta – re – go   kra –
A   Pole   was trav – el – ing   from   his   an – ces – tral

ju _____   Sta – ry   kraj   o – pusz – cza,   O –
home. _____   He   left   the   old   coun – try,   The

pusz – cza sta – ry   kraj;   we   świat   się   u –   da –   je. _____
old   coun – try   left   he   The   great   wide   world   to   roam. _____

Opuszcza stary kraj
I kawałek chleba,
I bierze na pomoc,
I bierze na pomoc
Matkę Boską z nieba.

Opuszcza stary kraj
I rodzonych ojców.
W świat się udaje,
W świat się udaje
I sam nie wie poco.

Jak jedzie tak jedzie,
Nigdy nie stopuje.
Przyjdzie wielka burza,
Przyjdzie wielka burza,
Szyfem powiewuje.

Szyfem powiewuje,
Mało co wywróci.
Co jednych odwiezie,
Co jednych odwiezie,
Po drugich się wróci.

Jak my przyjechali
Do tej Kasengardy,
Zaraz-ci to poznać,
Zaraz-ci to poznać
Który Polak każdy.

Pobogłosław Boże
Naszego cesarza
Że nas porozsyłał
Że nas porozsyłał
Po tych cudzych krajach.

Po tych cudzych krajach,
I to po Anglikach.
Bieda nie jednemu,
Bieda nie jednemu
Co niezna języka.

W Ameryce dobrze
Jak idzie robota.
Piwka się napije,
Piwka się napije
Przyjdzie sobota.

W Ameryce dobrze
Czy mały czy duży.
Piwka się napije,
Piwka się napije,
Cygara zakurzy.

W Ameryce dobrze
I śmiało i śmiało.
Ale w Ameryce,
Ale w Ameryce
Poczciwości mało.

Poczciwości mało,
Wesolości dużo.
Każda panna chodzi,
Każda panna chodzi
Jak kwiateczek róży.

He left the old country,
The bread that nourished him.
For aid and for comfort,
For aid and for comfort,
He chose the Virgin Queen.

He left the old country,
Bid family good-bye.
The world to discover,
The world to discover,
Not understanding why.

He traveled on and on,
And did not stop en route.
A powerful storm rose,
A powerful storm rose,
And tossed the ship about.

It tossed the ship about,
Which almost sank that day.
When one load was landed,
When one load was landed,
For more it sailed away.

And when at last we docked
At Castle Garden — whole,
We recognized quickly,
We recognized quickly,
The face of every Pole.

Oh, God Almighty bless
Our emperor so grand.
He's scattered us over,
He's scattered us over
These lonely foreign lands.

These lonely foreign lands
Where English is the tongue,
If only I'd studied,
If only I'd studied
English when I was young.

America is fine,
You work and earn your pay.
The beer is abundant,
The beer is abundant,
To drink on Saturday.

America is fine,
No matter who you are.
The beer is abundant,
The beer is abundant,
As you smoke your cigar.

America is fine,
To live in liberty.
But here in America,
But here in America
Life can be quite lonely.

Yes, lonely is our life,
Though joy is everywhere.
And every girl walks by,
And every girl walks by
With her nose in the air.

Registry Desk Inspection at Ellis Island

Jak Jechałem Z Ameryki
America I Was Leaving

Another song learned in the Passaic, New Jersey, Polish community. This time it is a detailed chronicle of an immigrant's return to Poland. The same return trip is described in a Ukrainian song. The melody is different, but all the other circumstances are virtually identical.

Poland

Jak je – cha – łem z A – me – ry – ki, Jak
A – me – ri – ca I was leav – ing. A –

je – cha – łem z A – me – ry – ki, I z tej że – laz –
me – ri – ca I was leav – ing, And the plant where

nej fab – ry – ki, I z tej że – laz – nej fab – ry – ki.
I was work – ing, And the plant where I was work – ing.

276

Ręce moje dziękowały;
Do roboty zawsze stały.

Przyjechałem do Nef Jorka
Po szyfkartę do agenta.

Agenci się mnie pytali
Czy wiozę trzysta dolary.

"Nie pytajcie się mnie o to,
Bo ja wiozę srebro, złoto."

Wyjechałem w środek morza;
Nic nie widzę, Matko Boża.

Szyf kapitan się nie nudził.
Tylko chodził, cieszył ludzi.

Jakżem ujżał miasto Hamburg,
To myślałem że sam Pan Bóg.

A jakżem już wylądował,
Panu Bogu podziękował.

"Dziękuje Ci, wielki Boże,
Żem przepłynął wielkie morze."

A z Hamburga do Berlina.
"Szynkareczko, daj mi wina."

A z Berlina do Krakowa,
Bo tam była żona moja.

I dzieci mnie nie poznały,
Bo odemnie uciekały.

"Dzieci moje, ja wasz tata;
Nie był u was przez trzy lata."

Each line is sung twice:

I clasped my hands in a brief prayer,
Hands that always did their share.

Arriving in New York's station,
To pick up my reservation.

The travel agent was funny.
Asked me if I had the money.

At that I nearly exploded.
I told him that I was loaded.

Midway across the ocean,
I prayed then with great emotion.

The captain kept himself busy,
Helping us when we got dizzy.

And when I saw Hamburg city,
I thought I saw God Almighty.

When at last I landed safely,
"Lord," I prayed, "I thank Thee greatly."

I thanked God with great emotion
That I'd safely crossed the ocean.

From Hamburg I went to Berlin,
I drank wine — my head was swirlin'.

From Berlin I went to Krakow,
My wife said, "You're really home now!"

My children did not remember,
They thought their father was a stranger.

Oh, I'm your father, don't you know me?
Three years I've been 'cross the wide sea.

Library of Congress

Zrobił Góral Krzyż Na Czole
The Mountaineer Crossed Himself

The Tatra Mountains are in the Podhale region of southern Poland. It is a region of small farmers and sheep herders. For several generations there has been a steady migration from Podhale to Chicago, as well as to parts of the East Coast. This song was recorded in Poland by a group of Podhale musicians in 1974.

Poland

Zro — bił gó — ral krzyż na czo — le, wy — ru — szył do dro — gi.
The moun-tain-eer crossed him— self when he pre – pared to leave home.

Żeg — nal oj – ca, żeg — nal mat – kę, I ro – dzin — ne pro – gi.
Good — bye, fa – ther, good–bye, moth — er, From this land I must roam.

Zeg — nal oj – ca, żeg — nal mat – kę, I ro – dzin–ne pro – gi.
Good — bye, fa – ther, good–bye, moth — er, From this land I must roam.

278

Żegnal braci, żegnal siostry —
Z wielkim w sercu żalem
Za swym domkiem urodzinnym; (2)
Za miłyn Podhalem.

Żegnal Tatry, góry, lasy,
Zieloną polanę
I potoku czyste wody (2)
Wioskę ukochaną.

I pojechał w świat daleki,
Od Tater kochanych.
Między ludzi mu nieznanych (2)
W Stanach Zjednoczonych.

Good-bye brothers, good-bye sisters —
And with a heavy heart
He left the home where he was born; (2)
From Podhale did part.

Farewell to the Tatra Mountains,
Where the waters run down,
And the clearing in the forest, (2)
And to his dear home town.

He left his home for the wide world.
Who can say what awaits,
Far from Tatra — among strangers (2)
In the United States.

Sherman Collection, National Park Service

Wilno Boys

The first Polish settlement in Canada was established in Wilno, Ontario, in the 1860s. The style of this song — both words and music — reflects the "Anglo" tradition rather than the Polish.

Poland

I'm a jol – ly old fel – la, you all know my name, I live _____ at Wil – no, the vil – lage of fame; For sing – ing and danc – ing and all kinds of fun, Sure the boys from Wil – no, they can't be out – done.

Now when on your patience I beg to intrude,
We hired with Fitzgerald, he was agent for Booth,
To go up the Black River, that's far, far away,
On the old Causewell farm to harvest the hay.

We packed up our turkeys on first of July,
Bronas Raczowski, Joe Shalla, and I;
On the straightway to Pembroke our luggage we take,
There we boarded the *Empress* and sailed up the lake.

We arrived in Fort Collins, a place you all know,
We tuned our fiddle, we rosined the bow,
The warming strings rang out in a clear, tuning voice,
And the Oslo Rocks echoed "Well done, Wilno boys."

But we left the next morning amid wishes and smiles,
From there to Causewell was forty-six miles.
On the north side of the mountain it was Joe led the route,
But when we got there we were nearly done out.

The board at the Causewell, the truth for to tell,
Cannot be surpassed in Russell's Hotel.
We had beefsteak, and mutton, now tea sweet and strong,
And the good, early carrots were six inches long.

We had custard, rice puddings, and sweet apple pie,
Good bread and fresh butter, that's much a surprise.
We had cabbage, cucumbers, both pickling and raw,
And the leg of a beaver we stole from the squaw.

When haying was over, we packed up our goods.
We shouldered our turkeys, we went to the woods.
There we felled the tall pines with our axes and saws,
Sure we're terrified by animals, both Indians and squaws.

Us boys we were merry, we dance and we sing.
We lived just as happy as Emperor or King.
We had seven good fiddlers, and none of them drones,
And I was the one I can rattle my bones.

When the drive will be over, I wish it was soon,
So we'd intend to go home on the first week of June;
And if God spares our lives to get home in the spring,
And we'll make our hall at Wilno to ring.

So now I conclude and I finish my song,
For I really believe I have kept you too long;
I am getting sleepy and nodding my head,
So I think I'll say my prayers and roll into bed.

Library of Congress

Portugal

O Emigrante
The Emigrant

Three-fourths of all Portuguese–Americans live in only four states: Massachusetts and Rhode Island on the East Coast, and California and Hawaii on the West Coast and beyond. "O Emigrante" is the classic lament of a person far from his or her native land. It is widely known in these coastal Portuguese–American communities, where the sea is a way of life. (No point in Portugal is further than about 100 miles from the Atlantic Ocean.)

Portugal

Lon – ge da ter – ra dis – tan — te, Lon – ge do
Far – from a dis – tant dear coun — try, Far from his

seu Por – tu – gal, _____ Vem lem – bran – do'o em – i –
Por – tu – guese earth, _____ The em – i – grant well re –

gran — te, A su – a ter – ra na – tal. _____
mem — bers The land that he knew at birth. _____

Na su – a grande an – sie–da — de, É tris – te vi – vir a –
He feels great an–guish and sor — row, How sad is liv – ing that

ssim, _____ Mas quan – do vem a sau–da — de,
way, _____ And when he starts to feel home — sick,

chó – ra sau – da – des sem fim. _____ Lon – ge dos
weeps with–out end night and day. _____ Far ge from his

seus, _____ Lon – ge do seu Por – tu – gal, _____
home, _____ Far from his own Por – tu – gal, _____

Ó, quantas saudades tem
Da sua pequena aldeia,
Do rosto de sua mãe
Trás noite e dia na ideia.
Baixinho sua alma reza,
Pra esquecer desaventuras.
Vai desafiando tristezas,
Num rosário de amarguras. *Chorus*

Oh, how much longing he feels
For his small town far away,
And for his mother's dear face,
Which he can see night and day.
Softly his soul breathes a prayer,
Longing for brighter tomorrows,
Challenging misfortune's fate
With a rosary of his deep sorrows. *Chorus*

National Park Service

Triste Vide É Do Marujo
How Sad Is The Life Of A Sailor

Portuguese fishermen sang this song in the water off three coasts: Portugal, Brazil, and New England.
Their hard life did not change in the New World — still at the mercy of the weather and the captain.

Portugal

Andar à chuva e aos ventos,
Quer de verão quer de inverno;
Parecem o próprio inferno
    As tempestades!
    As tempestades, bom, bom.

As nossas necessidades
Nos obrigam a navegar,
A passar tempos no mar,
    E aguaceiros.
    E aguaceiros, bom, bom.

O mestre logo se estriba,
Bradando desta maneira:
Moços ferra a cavadeira
    E o joanete!
    E o joanete, bom, bom.

Mais me valera ser visto
A porta de um botequim,
Do que ver agora o fim
    Da minha vida.
    Da minha vida, bom, bom.

Lembram-me certas senhoras
Com quem eu tratei em terra,
Que me estão fazendo guerra
    Ao meu dinheiro.
    Ao meu dinheiro, bom, bom.

Foi um velho marinheiro
Que inventou esta cantiga,
Embarcado tôda a vida
    Sem ter dinheiro.
    Sem ter dinheiro, bom, bom.

Out in the wind and the weather,
In summer and winter returning,
He suffers hell-fires burning —
    And oh, those tempests,
    And oh, those tempests, bom, bom.

Necessity drives us to it.
It sends us out on the ocean
To toil in endless motion —
    And oh, those rainstorms,
    And oh, those rainstorms, bom, bom.

The captain, he is excited,
Shouting at us to work faster:
"What a crew — what a disaster!
    Haul the topgallant,
    Haul the topgallant," bom, bom.

Well now, I'd rather be seeing
A tavern door — how much dearer —
Than to see getting nearer and nearer
    My life's sad ending,
    My life's sad ending, bom, bom.

I remember certain young ladies,
Whom I have met in the city,
Who did wage war, war without pity,
    All for my money,
    All for my money, bom, bom.

It was a tired old sailor
Who made up this little song.
All his life he sailed along —
    And made no money,
    And made no money, bom, bom.

Library of Congress

Sherman Collection, National Park Service

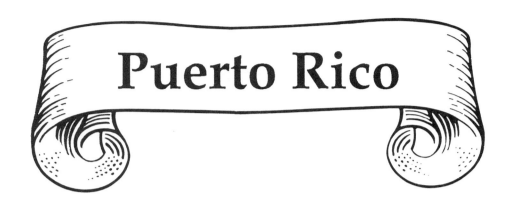

Puerto Rico

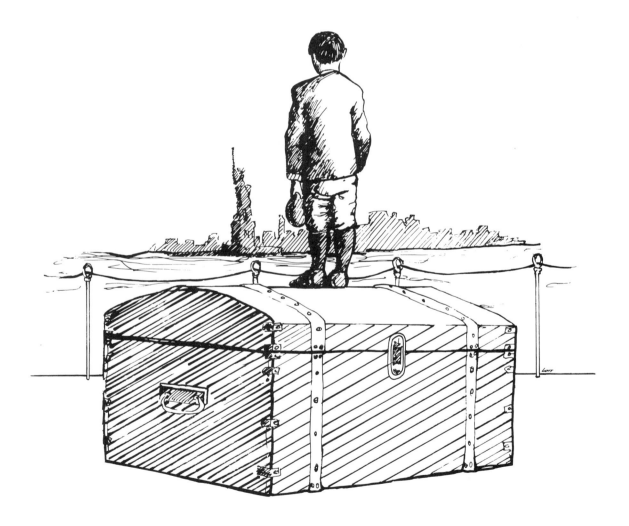

Un Jíbaro En Nueva York
A Peasant In New York

This ten-line verse form is called a *décima*. A typical *décima* is frequently improvised by the singer, who may be challenged to create clever, humorous rhymes on the spot.

Puerto Rico

292

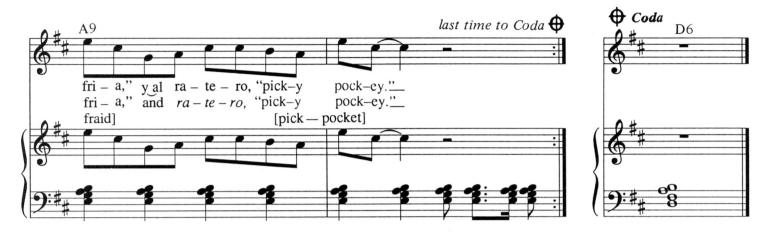

last time to Coda ⊕

⊕ **Coda**

fri – a," y al ra – te – ro, "pick–y pock–ey."
fri – a," and *ra – te – ro*, "pick–y pock–ey."
fraid]   [pick — pocket]

Woman
Hay alguna analogía
En lo que me has contestado,
Pero aun no has terminado,
Falta mucho todavía.
La vida me apostaría,
Que aunque tomes interés,
Si te diera todo el mes
El chance para pensar,
Tú no podrás hirvanar
Otra décima en inglés.

Man
Al beso le dicen "kiss,"
Para decir la hora le dicen "o'clock,"
Y a la señorita, "miss."
Al queso le dicen "cheese,"
Al te amo, "I love you,"
Al orgullo, "ballyhoo."
Le dicen "house" a la casa,
Y para decir "¿Qué pasa?,"
"What's the matter with you?"

Woman
Aunque de todas las redes
Saliste con facultad,
Tengo la seguridad,
Que finalizar no puedes.
Lo van a escuchar ustedes,
Qué por su derrota brindo.
Porque sólo cuando eres gringo,
Como aquel guerrero fuerte,
Que dijo al pie de la muerte,
"Muero, pero no me rindo."

Man
Y dicen al día, "day,"
Al pobre le dicen "poor."
Al tan bello, "so beautiful,"
Y a lo que está bien, "okay."
Y como cosa de ley,
A la luna dicen "moon."
Al tono le dicen "tune,"
Y en vez de fin dicen "end."
Venga un aplauso, *my friend,*
Que venga, *very soon.*

Woman
There are some words you do know.
But though you think you are winning,
This is just the very beginning,
You've still a long way to go.
I'd bet my life on it now,
That even if you would wish
To spend another month there,
To rack your brains for a rhyme,
You couldn't make up in time
Another *décima* in English.

Man
They call *beso* "kiss,"
To tell time they say "o'clock,"
And *señorita* they call "miss."
Queso becomes "cheese,"
For *te amo* they say "I love you,"
Orgullo is "ballyhoo."
They say "house" for *casa,*
And for "¿*Qué pasa?*" they say,
"What's the matter with you?"

Woman
Though you have made no mistakes,
With all the traps I have set you,
I am willing to bet you,
You don't have what it takes.
I celebrate your defeat.
For you will only speak the lingo
When you have become a *gringo.*
Like that warrior of old,
Who, when facing death, I'm told,
Said "I die, but don't surrender."

Man
They call *día* "day,"
For *pobre,* they say "poor."
Tan bello is "so beautiful,"
And what's *bien* is "okay."
And, as the law goes,
Luna is called "moon."
A *tono* is a "tune,"
Instead of *fin* they'll say "end."
Let's hear some applause, my friend,
Let's hear it very soon.

295

Problema Social
Social Problem

I decided to write a lyric that would make people happy and let them dance more because of the music and rhythm — but which also brings home a message about the very great truths in people's lives. (Eduardo Reyes, *People's Songs,* Vol. III, No. 11, December 1948)

Puerto Rico

By Eduardo Reyes

De_un — a is — li — ta del Ca — ri — be
From a Car — ib — be — an is — land,

En bus — ca de tra — ba — jo ven — go yo. A —
Look — ing for a job I ar — rived in town. But

som — bra — do me que — dé con lo que en — con — tré A —
what was my big sur — prise! I can't be — lieve my eyes! Sur —

Quie – ro_____ so – lo ga – nar un – os_____ bo – los_____ Pa' la de –
I want_____ to earn some mon – ey here_____ so that_____ I can sup –

fen – sa_____ del hu – mil – de ho – gar. Yo no ven – go a pe –
port my_____ hum – ble fam – i – ly. I don't come ask – ing_____

– dir li – mos – na. Lo que quier – o es so – lo tra – ba – jar.
____ cha – ri – ty.____ What I want now is job se – cu – ri – ty.

Yo, que peleaba en la guerra,
Americano al fin, como nací.
Aunque sirvo pa' pelear,
Yo no puedo votar
Pa' el presidente de la patria,
Y al venir a trabajar. *Chorus*

I, who soldiered in the army,
An American, as good as anyone.
The gun I had to tote
Did not get me the vote
For President, and when I look
For a job, I get their goat. *Chorus*

298

Rumania

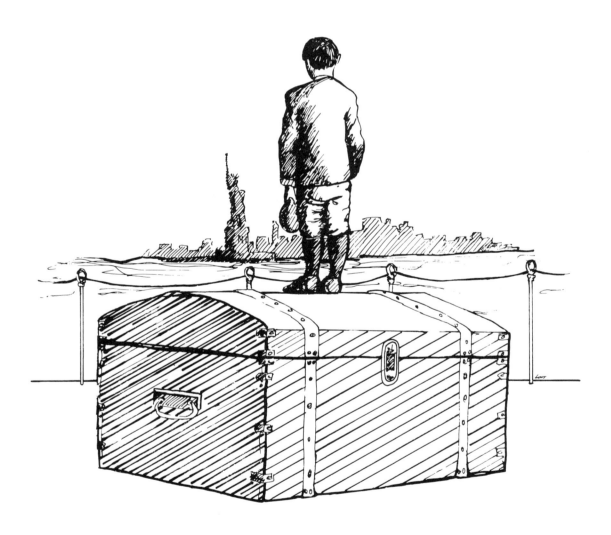

Plecat-am, Doamne, De-acasă
Lord, I Left My Home

Walk eastward toward the river, and between Second and First Avenues there is a restaurant to which all Rumanians flock. Within it the owner is playing the cymbalom, that curious old instrument so dear to the Rumanian Gipsies. He is as good on it as anybody has ever been; indeed, he is the Kreisler of the cymbalom. No matter what hour of the night you might drop in there, you will have to struggle to find a chair to sit upon. For although the noise of the waiters and the guests is deafening, the neighborhood comes there more to listen to the man's playing than to eat. And his playing has been heard of in other quarters than the Rumanian one. Most of the journalists on American papers come down when they can spare the time and can afford it. Eugene O'Neill, the playwright, drops in from time to time. John Dos Passos, Heifetz, the violinist, and Toscha Seidel and Mischa Elman, and others of the musical and literary professions. (*Around The World In New York*, Konrad Berkovici, 1924)

Rumania

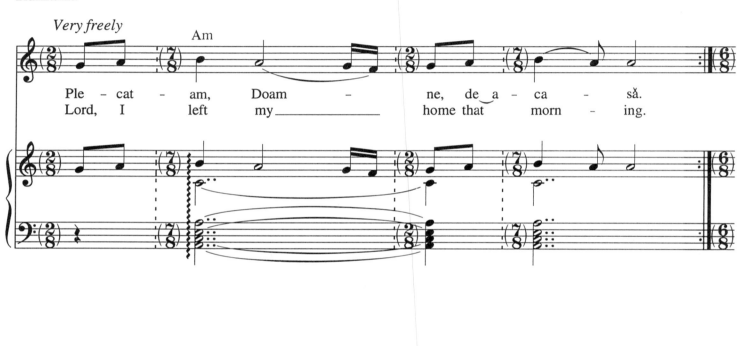

Ple - cat - am, Doam - ne, de - a - ca - să.
Lord, I left my _____ home that morn - ing.

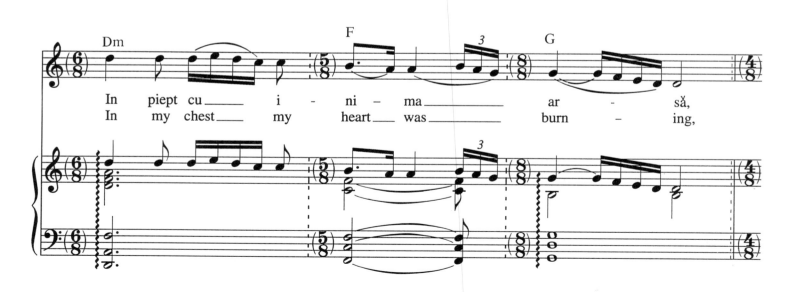

In piept cu _____ i - ni - ma _____ ar - să,
In my chest _____ my heart _____ was _____ burn - ing,

The first line of each verse is sung twice. In the two-line verses, the second line is repeated as well.

Ziua bună mi-am luat De la fir de iarbă lată, De la mamă, de la tată.	Then I bid them all good-bye, To the grass that grows nearby, And my parents, who did cry.
Si-am pornit apoi ca vîntu, Trei zile, trei nopţi de-arîndu.	Like the wind then, I was gone, For three days I travelled on.
Le Bremen a fost sfirşitu, Acol' trenu s-a oprit, Căci drumu s-a terminat.	Bremen was my destination, And the train stopped at the station. Journey's end — the explanation.
Şiacolo trei zile-am stat, Pîn vaporu ne-au luat.	Three days after my train trip, I got on board the steamship.
Ş-am plecat cu el pe mare; Şi plîngeam cu dor şi jale, C-am vazut apa cea mare.	Then there was a great commotion. Gazing on that mighty ocean, I did feel a strange emotion.
Şi mersăm v-o do-trei zîle, Şi vaporu merge bine.	By the second or third night, Things seemed to be going right.
Dar cînd am dat pre jumătate, A-nceput un vînt a bate, Şi-a-nceput un vînt a bate.	At the point of no returning, A huge storm began a-churning. Yes, a huge storm began churning.
Si-m curgeau lacrimi fierbinti, Că m-am dus de la părinti.	Weeping, I thought we were sinking. Of my parents I was thinking.
Dumnezeu ne-a ajutat Şi-am scăpat la uscat.	But the Lord's almighty hand Helped the ship to safely land.
Cu străinii mîn-am dat Şi străinii-au întrebat: Noi la iei ce-am căutat?	Strangers then did come to meet us, I shook hands as they did greet us. How, we wondered, would they treat us?
Dară noi am lăcrămat Prin semne lucru-am întrebat.	We just cried and showed by hand: "We want work — please understand."
Lucru nouă pine-au dat, Pentr-un dolar si cinzeci Lucram nopţi şi zîle-ntragi.	So they hired us right away. A dollar fifty was my pay, And I worked hard night and day.
Pentr-un dol' şi jumătate Rădicam la fier pe spate.	Then I earned two dollars fifty. Heavy iron I was lifting.
Zece dolari dam pe mîncare, Dacă vream să fiu mai tare.	Food cost ten dollars a week, For a workingman must eat.

Cîntecul Americii
Song Of America

Several versions of this song exist in North America. This one was collected by Dr. Emilia Comisel in Windsor, Ontario, in 1974. It was written around 1925 by a Rumanian immigrant named Radu George. The last two lines of the last verse were missing and were supplied by Lily Marcus of Hastings on Hudson, New York.

Rumania

Cînd e - ram _____ în sat _____ la mi - ne,
When in ___ my _____ vil - lage _____ I did dwell,

A- mă ţi ___ nea _____ măi - cu - ţa bi - ne.
There my ___ moth - er kept _____ me quite well.

Cu _____ to - ţi fra - ţii ___ lîn - gă mi - ne,
To _____ me and my broth - ers no - harm be - fell,

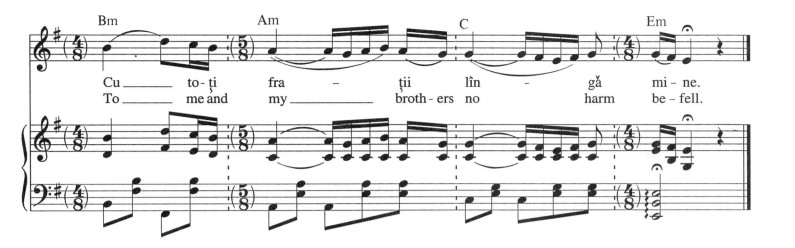

Dar de cînd am crescut mare,	When I grew to manhood, finally,
Am trecut o apă tare,	I crossed over the blue sea.
M-am înstrăinat prea tare,	I became so very lonely,
M-am înstrăinat prea tare,	I became so very lonely.
Acasă n-aveam dolaru,	Dollars, at home, we did not know,
Dar aveam boii şi caru,	Oxen pulled to make the cart go.
Aşa petreceam, sărmanu,	There my life did seem so empty,
Aşa îmi duceam amaru.	And I felt it, oh, so bitterly.
Vai, Doamne mare-i dolaru	Oh, Lord, how big is the dollar,
Că-i muncit, bată-l amaru.	But you have to wear the collar.
Şi de mici şi de voinici, mă	No matter if you're small or sturdy —
Oase rupte prin fabrici, mă.	Work 'til you drop — always dirty.
Auzit-am o minciună,	What's that lie that I've been told?
America-i ţară bună,	America's as good as gold.
Ţara bună şi bogată,	A good and a wealthy country,
Şi de bani e-ndestulată.	Where the people all have money.
Banul e cu număr mare,	Yes, there is big money there,
Lăcomeşte fie care,	With greedy people everywhere.
Cum am lăcomit şi eu	Greedy, too, I have become,
Ş-am plecat din satu meu.	Since I left my village home.
Am plecat pe-un, pe doi	I left for a year or so,
Să fac bani, să plec 'napoi.	To make money — then to go.
Anii or trecut la rind,	But the years passed one by one —
Lucrînd şi dolari răcînd.	Work and dollars — never done.
Dacă-am strîns v-o doi dolari,	Some two dollars, when I made it,
I-am cheltuit prin spital.	To the hospital I paid it.
Anii frumosí au plecat,	Now my youthful years have vanished,
Şi dorul m-'a terminat.	And in longing I am banished.

National Park Service

Russia

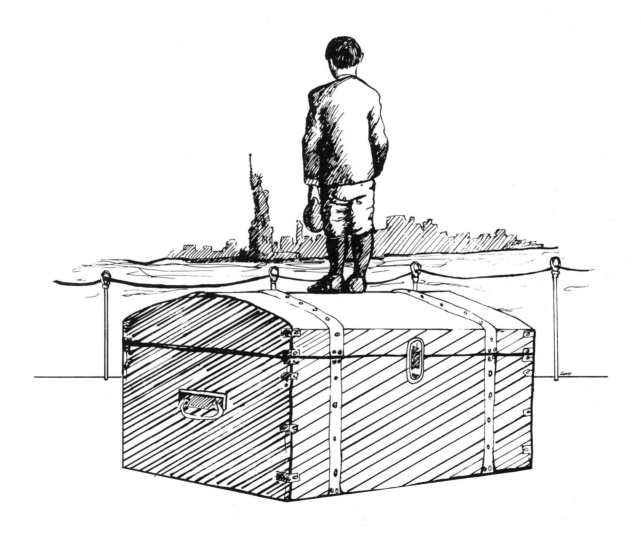

Proshchai, Rossiya
Farewell, Russia

The Brighton Beach section of Brooklyn, New York, is heavily populated by Russian Jews who have arrived here beginning in the 1970s. There are so many Russian stores, restaurants, and nightclubs that the residents call their neighborhood "Odessa by the sea." Anatoly Mogilevsky, himself a recent arrival, sings his witty and nostalgic songs in these clubs.

Russia

By Anatoly Mogilevsky

Vo Vnu - ko - vo raz - dal' - sya go - los v mik - ro - fon,
At Vnu - ko - vo re - sound - ed the long - a - wait - ed news, "We're

"Grazh - dan - ye Yev - re - i, vash vy - lyot za kor - don. Vsye vesh - chi na to - mozh - nye, na -
read - y now for board - ing, all you ci - ti - zen Jews. All lug - gage to the cus - toms, now

dyezh - di v pe - re - di," I my u - zhe pro - sty - e so - vyet - ski - e vra - gi.
hur - ry, if you please." And we are now al - read - y just So - viet en - e - mies.

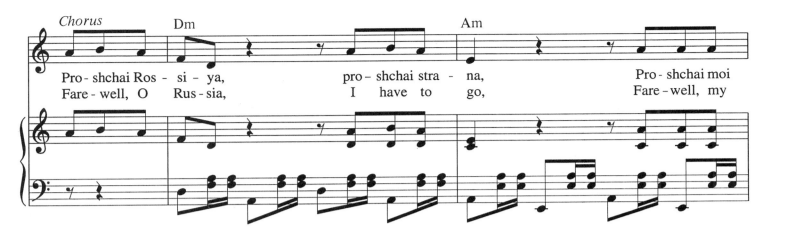

Pro - shchai Ros - si – ya,   pro – shchai stra - na,   Pro - shchai moi
Fare - well, O   Rus - sia,   I   have   to   go,   Fare - well, my

Pi - ter,   pro - shchai Mos - kva.   Pri - vyet O - dyes - sa,   "Gud – bai" Il' –
Pet - er,[1]   fare - well Mos - cow.   Re - gards, O - des - sa,   Good- bye Il' –

itch,___   Ya ot – by – va – yu   na Brai - ton   Bich .
yitch,[2]___   For I am   go - ing   to Brigh- ton   Beach.

V tamozhennoi proverka poslyednii chemodan,	And at customs inspection my last suitcase did pass.
A ya uzhe ne pomnyu, gdye ryumka, gdye stakan.	I really don't remember — I drank more than one glass.
Bez ogurtsa, bez khleba — sanyukhal yantaryom,	No pickles and no black bread — my hunger pangs they grew;
Proshchai narod velikii, poklon Vam nizkii shlyom.	Farewell "heroic people," my hat is off to you.

---

1. St. Petersburg
2. Vladimir Ilyitch Lenin

Choruses:
Proshchai Rossiya, proshchai strana,
Proshchaitye Sochi, Alma-Ata.
Privyet moi Kiev, "gudbai" Il'itch,
Ya otbyvayu na Braiton Bich.

Proshchai Tbilisi i Yerevan,
Proshchai Tashkent moi i Kazakhstan.
Privyet Bakintsi, "gudbai" Il'itch,
Ya otbyvayu na Braiton Bich.

Proshchai Rossiya, proshchai strana,
Proshchai moi Piter, proshchai Moskva
Privyet Rizhanye, "gudbai" Il'itch,
Ya otbyvayu na Braiton Bich.

Choruses:
Farewell, oh Russia — I'm off, ta-ta,
Farewell, oh Sochi, Alma-Ata.
Regards to Kiev, good-bye Ilyitch,
For I am going to Brighton Beach.

Farewell Tbilisi and Yerevan,
Farewell my Tashkent and Kazakhstan.
Regards to Baku, good-bye Ilyitch,
For I am going to Brighton Beach.

Farewell, oh Russia — I have to go,
Farewell my Peter, farewell Moscow.
Regards to Riga, good-bye Ilyitch,
For I am going to Brighton Beach.

Amerika-Rossiya
America-Russia

All immigrants retain an undying feeling for their homeland, no matter how hard life was there. This sentimental Russian waltz says it all.

Russia

By Anatoly Mogilevsky

Takiye zhe reki, ozyora i roshchi,
I lyudi pokhozhe na russkikh lyudyei.
No russkaya pesnya skromneye i proshche,
I shirye dushoyu i serdtsem dobryei.

I pust' Mississippi kak Volga krasiva,
I pust' po Baikal'ski shirok Michigan.
No vsyo-taki noch'yu mne snitsya Rossiya,
I russkoye polye i moi mal'chugan.

The very same rivers and lakes and green woodlands,
And just like the Russians are the people here.
But Russian songs are so more modest and simple,
And broader in feelings and ever more dear.

The broad Mississippi the Volga resembles,
And just like Lake Baikal is Lake Michigan.
But still in the nighttime I dream of my Russia,
The Russian fields and my son — my little man.

Sherman Collection, National Park Service

310

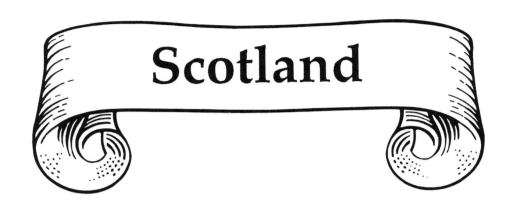

Scotland

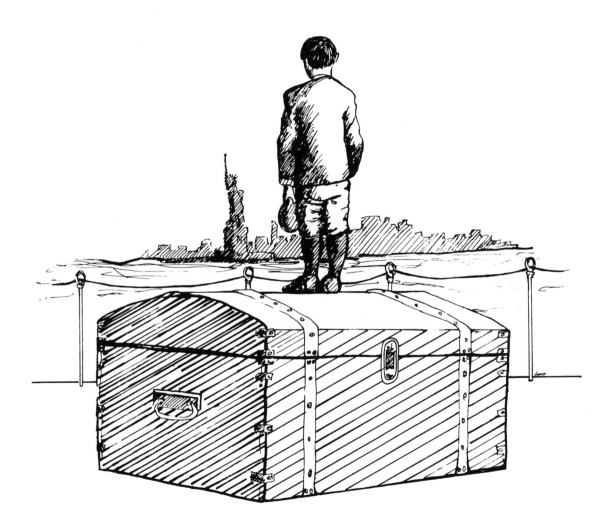

A Ballad Of New Scotland

Nova Scotia may well have been the Markland of the early Norse and Icelandic voyages, and Cape Breton was visited by the Cabots in 1497 and 1498. It was not until 1784, however, that a large Scottish immigration took shape which lasted until 1824. This song predates those years, having been published in England in 1750. While that technically makes it an English immigrants' song, the later Scottish immigrants must surely have known and sung it.

Scotland

Let's a - way to New Scot - land where Plen - ty sits queen O'er as hap - py a coun - try as e - ver was seen; She ___ bles - ses her sub - jects, both lit - tle and great, With each a good house and a

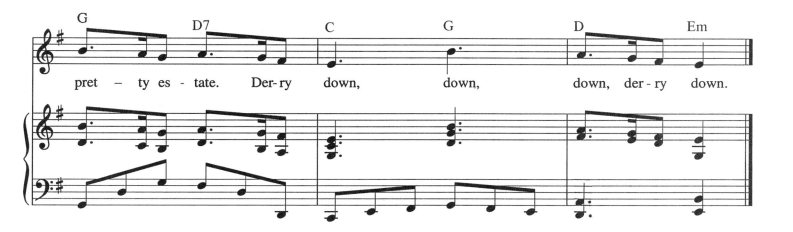

pret – ty es - tate. Der-ry down, down, down, der-ry down.

There's wool, and there's water, there's wild fowl and tame;
In the forest good ven'son, good fish in the stream,
Good grass for our cattle, good land for our plough,
Good wheat to be reap'd, and good barley to mow.
    Derry down, down, down, derry down.

No landlords are there the poor tenants to tease,
No lawyers to bully, nor stewards to seize;
But each honest fellow's a landlord, and dares
To spend on himself the whole fruit of his cares.
    Derry down, down, down, derry down.

They've no duties on candles, no taxes on malt,
Nor do they, as we do, pay sauce for their salt;
But all is as free as in those times of old
When poets assure us the age was of gold.
    Derry down, down, down, derry down.

Sherman Collection, National Park Service

Gu Ma Slan Do Na Fearaibh
Here's Good Health To The Heroes

Martinmas (November 11) was the time of the year when annual farm rental payments were due. The inability to meet these high payments because of poor crops forced many people off the land and over the water to America.

Scotland

Gu ma slan do na fear - aibh Chaidh thair - is an cuan, Gu
Here's good health to the he - roes Who've sailed o'er the sea, To

tal - amh a' gheall - aidh Far nach fair - ich iad fuachd; Gu man
the land of prom - ise, Where con - tent - ed they'll be; Here's good

slan do na fear - aibh Chaidh thair — is an cuan.
health to the he — roes Who've sailed o'er the sea.

Chorus

Sinn a' faig - ail na tir so, Oir cha chinn - ich ann ni dhuinn; Tha 'm bun-
We are leav - ing this coun - try, Since there's noth - ing that grows here; Our po-

tat' air dol dhi oirnn is cha chinn____ iad le
ta - toes have failed us In the cold____ wind that

fuachd; Gu ma slan do na fear - aibh Chaidh thair - is an cuan.
blows here; Here's good health to the he - roes Who've sailed o'er the sea.

Sinn a' fagail an ait' so,
Bho 'n a chuir iad mor mhal oirnn;
Nuair a thig an Fheill Martuinn
Cha bhi nair' air ar gruaidh;
Gu ma slan do na fearaibh
Chaidh thairis an cuan. *Chorus*

Gheibh sinn crodh ann is caoraich,
Gheibh sinn cruithneachd air raoin ann,
'S cha bhi 'm fearann cho daor dhuinn
'S a tha fraoch an taoibh tuath;
Gu ma slan do na fearaibh
Chaidh thairis an cuan. *Chorus*

We are leaving this region,
Since they've raised our rent;
And when Martinmas comes 'round,
We shall all be content.
Here's good health to the heroes
Who've sailed o'er the sea. *Chorus*

We'll raise sheep there and cattle,
Grow wheat on the loam;
For the land's not as dear there
As the heather back home.
Here's good health to the heroes
Who've sailed o'er the sea. *Chorus*

315

Dutaich Nan Craobh
Land Of The Trees

Eighteenth-century North America was, indeed, "the land of the trees" when Scottish immigration began. There were settlements in the Carolinas and in Cape Breton, Nova Scotia. During the Revolutionary War, Scotsmen were found among the Loyalists as well as the Continentals.

Scotland

A bhi fag – ail na __ duth – cha 'S a bhi to – gail a siuil rith', 'S a bhi
We are leav – ing our __ home – land, And our sails catch the breez – es, We are

stiui – readh a __ cur – sa __ Gu duth – aich nan craobh. Gur e
steer – ing our __ course to __ The land __ of the trees. It is

mi – se tha fo smuair – ein, 'S mi a' seo – ladh thar chuan – tan, Is mi'g
I who am a – griev – ing As I sail o'er the wide sea, While I

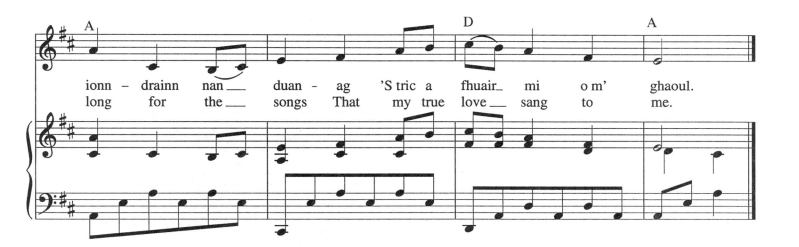

ionn – drainn nan ___ duan – ag 'S tric a fhuair___ mi o m' ghaoul.
long for the ___ songs That my true love ___ sang to me.

'N uair a bha mi le m' ghradh-sa
Ann an duthaich nan ard-bheann,
'S tric a dh' eisd mi ri manran
Fo sgaile nan craobh. *Chorus*

Di-domhnuich m' an d' fhag mi,
Is mi coiseachd na sraide,
Thachair orm-sa mo mhaldag,
Le blath-shuilean caoin. *Chorus*

Their iad riut gu bheil mi olar,
Gu bheil mi tric 's an tigh-osda;
'S mi gu'n gleidheadh an lon thu,
Ri m' bheo, 's cha b' ann faoin. *Chorus*

Faiceam long a' dol dachaidh,
Gu Albainn no Sasunn,
Sgriobhaidh mise gu m' leannan
Gur maireann mo ghaol. *Chorus*

Ach ma bhitheas mi maireann,
'S tighinn sabhailte dhachaidh,
Cha teid mi tuilleadh gu marachd;
Ni mi fanachd 's na caoil. *Chorus*

Thoir mo shoraidh thar saile,
Ceud soraidh gu brath uam,
Dh'ionnsaidh ribhinn nam blath-shuil,
Te 's fearr leam 's an t-saogh'l. *Chorus*

Ma ni thu 'm posadh m' an tig mi,
Feuch gur fearr e na mise;
Na gabh poitear no misgear,
'S na gabh idir fear faoin. *Chorus*

When I lived with my darling
'Midst the mountains and leas,
How she sang to me often,
In the shade of the trees. *Chorus*

Well, the Sunday I left home,
As I walked down the highway,
There I met with my true love,
And her soft eyes turned my way. *Chorus*

They will tell you that I'm drinking,
In the tavern you'll find me.
But in comfort I'd keep you,
Put all drinking behind me. *Chorus*

If to Scotland or England
A ship crossed the ocean,
I would write to my true love,
Tell her of my devotion. *Chorus*

But if I am still living,
And do safely return home,
It's good-bye to the ocean —
Through the kyles I will roam. *Chorus*

Take my greetings across there,
My greetings forever,
To my warm-eyed true love;
I'll forget her never. *Chorus*

If you should marry another,
You'd deserve someone better;
Not a drunkard or tippler,
Not an idler or debtor. *Chorus*

Sherman Collection, National Park Service

Serbia

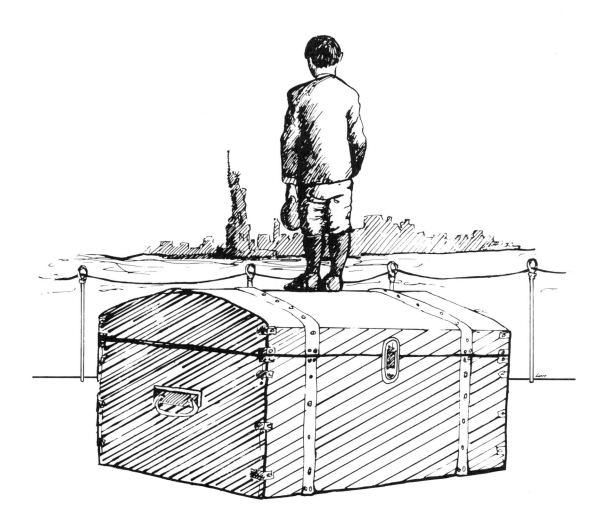

Tamo Daleko
So Far Away

During World War I, Serbs fought on the side of the Allies. Young Serbian–Americans joined with their countrymen in the conflict. This song dates from that period.

Serbia

Al' zar je mo - ra - la doć, _____ Tuz - na i
It had to come to this plight, _____ On this sad

ne - sret - na noć, _____ Da ti dra - ga - ne
un - luck - y night, _____ When my true love goes

moj, _____ O - de u kra - va - vi boj. _____
far, _____ Off to a great blood - y war. _____

Ta - mo da le - ko, da - le - ko
So far a - way now, A - way a -

kraj mo - ra, Ta - mo je se - lo
cross the sea, There in my dear old

mo - je, Ta - mo je lju - bav mo - ja.
vill - lage, My love is call - ing to me.

A još koji sat,
Bitče nam rastanak,
Ode moja ljubavi,
A mene ostavi.
    Tamo daleko,
    Gde cveće nema kraj,
    Tamo selo moje, (2)
    Tamo je zavičaj.

A sad ja odlazim,
U ratni krvavi boj,
Kad ču se vratiti ziv,
Andjeli moj mili.
    Tamo daleko,
    Kraj Save, Dunave,
    Tamo je varoš moja, (2)
    Tamo je Beograd.

There's still some time, my sweetheart,
Until the two of us part.
And then my love will be gone,
Leaving me here all alone.
    So far away,
    Away where bright flowers grow,
    There in my beautiful village, (2)
    Is the life that I did know.

Now I am going away,
Entering the bloody fray.
Will I return to your side,
Darling, my angel, my bride?
    So far away,
    By the Sava and Danube,
    There is my beautiful homeland, (2)
    And my beloved Belgrade.

Kad Ja Pođem U Ameriku
When I Go To America

From "leafy mountain, rushing water" to the fetid tenements of New York's Lower East Side: "Neither the Bulgars nor the Serbs nor the Macedonians nor the Montenegrins are permanently here. Some have been so minded when they first arrived, but have later changed their minds, waiting only until they have enough money, with perhaps a little over travelling expenses, to return to their plains and mountains. . . . All of these houses on Third, Fourth, Fifth and Sixth Streets, in which the Balkan people live, are the oldest in this part of the city, with no fire escapes and no conveniences of any kind, with walls almost falling by themselves and dark hallways and dark bedrooms. And the little light that would come in is obstructed by the rear houses — sun leeches." (*Around The World In New York* by Konrad Berkovici, 1924)

Serbia

Kad ja po - đem u A - me - ri - ku,
Po - slat ću ti mo - ju sli - ku.

From A - me - ri - ca when I go,
I will send to you my pho - to.

Chorus

Lis - taj go - ro, te - ci vo - do, Zbog - om dra - ga i - dem ja.
Leaf - y moun - tain, rush - ing wa - ter, Good - bye dar - ling, I'll be gone.

Kad sam bio na po puta,	When I'd travelled halfway o'er then,
Sjetio se tvoga skuta. *Chorus*	I recalled the dress you wore then. *Chorus*
Ako tebe snađu jadi,	If you are beset by sorrow,
Sliku moju ti izvadi. *Chorus*	From your purse then take my photo. *Chorus*
Slika neće govoriti,	But the picture speaks to no one;
To će tvoji jadi biti. *Chorus*	With your sorrows you must go on. *Chorus*
Ti ćeš piak nać' pokoja,	Soon there'll be an end to sadness,
Kad me vidiš dušo moja. *Chorus*	When together we'll know gladness. *Chorus*

Slovakia

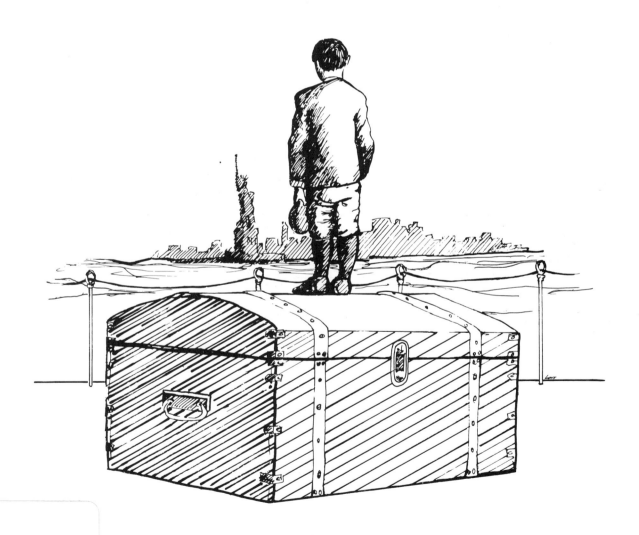

Opusceny Banik Z Wilks Barroch
The Lonely Miner Of Wilkes Barre

By the 1890s, Slovak miners began crowding out an earlier generation of Irish and Welsh miners in the Pennsylvania coal fields. At first isolated by the language barrier and willing to accept virtually any task imposed upon them, the Slovak miners were a coal operator's dream labor force. With the learning of mining skills and an increased awareness of the economic facts of life, some eventually became "contract miners," who themselves employed more recent immigrants to help them meet their tonnage requirements. "My miner," in verse 3, is just such a helper.

Slovakia

Mo – ja že – na v star – im kra – ju a ja_____ tu, Hle – dam
While my wife is left be – hind in the old_____ land, In A –

se – be v A – me – ri – ce ro – bo – tu, Na – šol ja ju u Wilks Bar – roch, u maj –
me – ri – ca I'm work – ing the coal_____ land. Here I am down in Wilkes-Bar – re's deep coal –

——noch, Lem ke bi mi mi – li Pan Boh do – po – moh.
——mine And may God keep me from harm just one more_____ time.

Každe rano ja še mušim hajsovac,
Štiri kari na šichtunaladovac.
Ohlednem še tristo razi v hodzine,
Či me uhle abi rak nezabije.

A jak prišla jedenasta hodzina,
Už moj majner še do domu odbira
Už ja ňemam vov tej majne nikoho,
Lem mileho Pana Boha sameho.

Ach Bože moj dopomož mi dorobic,
A ščešlivo še do domu navracic
Ku tej mojej milej žene i dzecom.
Višliš žadosc v mojim šercu žalosnom.

Every morning I descend down the deep hole.
In my shift I must load four cars of hard coal.
I am always looking over my shoulder,
Lest I be killed by a great falling boulder.

And when finally eleven o'clock sounds,
And my miner leaves to go home above ground,
Now there's no one left in this mine but me, Lord.
I'm alone, my God, in the mine with Thee, Lord.

Lord, I ask of you this one thing to grant me,
When I'm finished working let me leave safely,
To my home, my dear wife and to my children,
How my heart is sad here living without them.

GOING TO WORK.

AT WORK AT THE FACE.

Odpočívam V Americkej Pôde
I Lie In The American Land

I was a young foreman in a Bessemer mill here in McKeesport. A very good friend of mine, a member of my crew, had saved enough money to send to Slovakia for his family. While they were on the way to America, he was killed before my eyes under an ingot buggy. I tried to grab him but it was too late. It was terrible. I felt so bad that when I met his wife and little children at the railroad station I hardly knew how to break the sad news to them. Then I made this song. My friend was very proud of America and it was with pride and happiness that he had looked forward to raising his children as Americans. The song made me feel better and also my friend's wife. But she cried very hard. I have never forgotten it. (Andrew Kovaly)

Slovakia

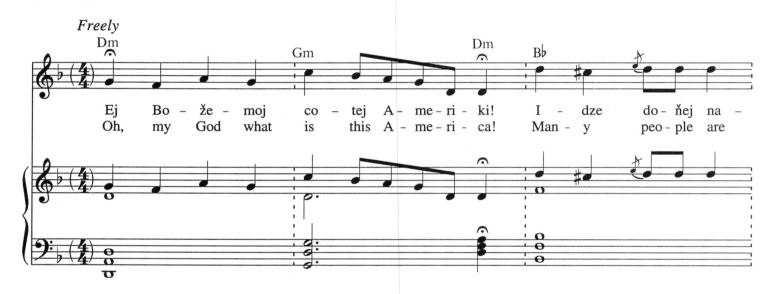

Ej Bo - že - moj co tej A - me - ri - ki! I dze do - ňej na -
Oh, my God what is this A - me - ri - ca! Man - y peo - ple are

rod pre - ve - li - ki, I - ja poj - dzem, šak som mla - di eš - če.
tra - vel - ing to there. I will go there, too, while I am still young.

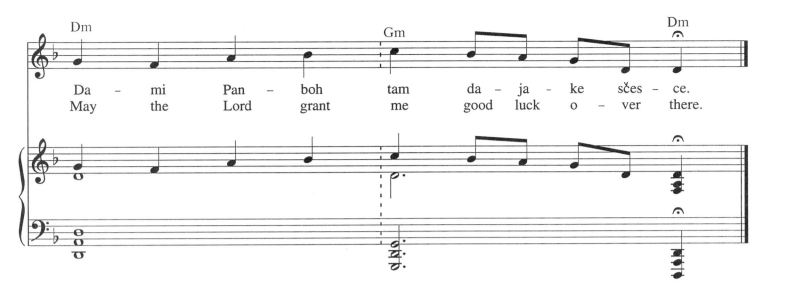

Da — mi Pan — boh tam da — ja — ke sčes — ce.
May the Lord grant me good luck o — ver there.

For the extra two lines in verses 2 and 4, repeat the last two phrases of the music.

Jaše vracim kecme nezabije,
Lem ti čekaj odomňe novinu.
Jak ot domňe novinu dostaneš,
Šicko sebe doporjatku prines,
Sama šedneš navraneho koňa,
Atak pridzeš draha dušo moja.

Ajak vona do McKeesport prišla,
To uš muža živoho nenašla;
Lem totu krev co znoho kapkala
Atak nadnu, prehorko plakala.

"Ej mužumoj co žeši učinil,
Žesi tote dzeci osirocil!"
"Povic ženo tej mojej siroce,
Žeja ležim utej Americe;
Povic ženo najme nečekaju,
Boja ležim v Americkim kraju."

I'll return to you if I don't get killed.
I will send you news from that far-off land.
And when you receive word from me, my dear,
Put your things in order, and do not fear.
Mount a raven-black steed — don't look behind.
Quickly fly to me, oh dear soul of mine.

But when in McKeesport she did arrive,
She did not find her dear husband alive.
All that she could find was her husband's blood.
Bitterly she wept, and her tears did flood.

"Oh, my husband dear, see what you have done,
You have gone and orphaned our little ones."
"To my orphans, my dear wife, you will say
That I lie asleep in America.
Tell them, my dear wife, not to wait for me,
For I lie asleep in America."

327

Hymna Amerických Slovákov
Hymn Of American Slovaks

It is doubtful that this hymn, composed in 1920, ever achieved widespread popularity among American Slovaks. However, the fact that it was written at all attests to the warm feelings that Slovaks felt for their new land.

Slovakia

Words by Grebáč-Orlov
Music by Mikulás Schneider-Trnavský (1881-1958)

My bys-tré de-ti ne-bo-tyč-ných Ta-tier Pro-sí-me Bo-že, do-bro-ti-vý Te-ba Ráč že-naťprá-ci tu i v sta-rom kra-ji, A daťnám zdrav-ia i tej sky-vy chleb-a. Za chleb-om sme pri-šli do

We val-iant chil-dren of the sky-high Ta-tras, To you, oh Lord, we hum-bly ask this fa-vor, Bless ou-r work here, and al-so the old land, And give us health and bread for ou-r la-bor. We came seek-ing bread to this

328

no – vej vlas – ti, O – pust – i – li sme ot – cov dra – hé po – lia:
far – off coun – try, We left the dear fields of our fath – ers, to roam

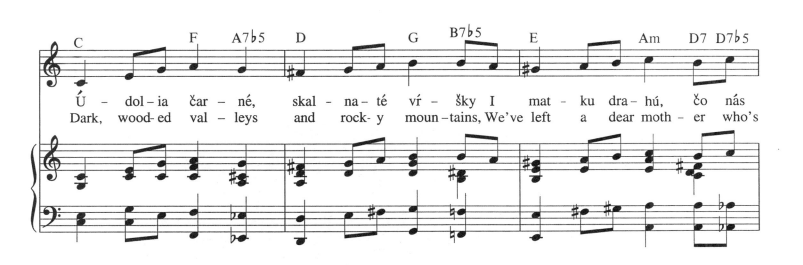

Ú – dol – ia čar – né, skal – na – té vŕ – šky I mat – ku dra – hú, čo nás
Dark, wood-ed val – leys and rock-y moun –tains, We've left a dear moth – er who's

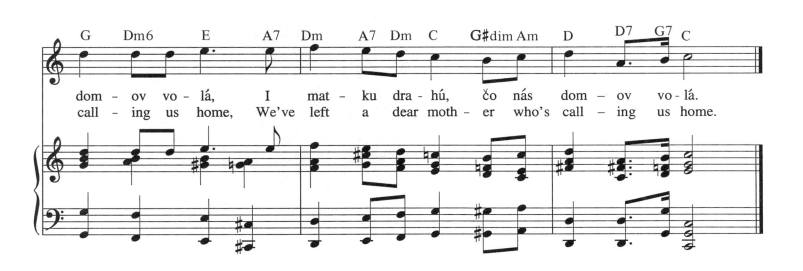

dom – ov vo – lá, I mat – ku dra – hú, čo nás dom – ov vo – lá.
call – ing us home, We've left a dear moth – er who's call – ing us home.

Mysl'ou na rodný kraji otcov rovy
Túžíme sily, rozpíname kriela,
Jak orol pravý trháme okovy
Pri piesni, čo nám u kolísky znela.
Láskou ku matke, ku slovenskej reči,
K národu svojmu vyrvajme verne;
Vo viere otcov žime neochvejne,
Nech z dome nášho zmiznú duše čierne.

Čo Slovák pravý, hor sa každý k činu,
Bystrime ducha, otužujme svaly,
A braňme vieru, pestujme si mravy,
Čo v srdcia naše matky vštepovaly.
Nuž prosíme Ťa, Bože dobrotivý,
Žehnaj nám v práci a daj dopriat' sily,
Posilni vôl'u, povznes našho ducha,
By sme šťastne v svornosti žili.

Thinking of home and the tombs of our fathers,
We stretch our wings out and we yearn for power.
As a true eagle we break the fetters,
Singing the cradle song from childhood's hour.
For love of our mother and our Slovak language,
We'll remain faithful to our native land.
We will live on in the faith of our fathers.
Some day in freedom our country will stand.

As a true Slovak, each of us is ready.
We're growing in strength and sharpening our mind.
Firm in our faith now, we remain steady —
As learned from our mothers, whom we've left behind.
We ask you, oh Lord, to bless our endeavors.
Oh, give us the strength and will to be free.
Keep up our spirit, we ask you to guide us,
So that at last we can live happily.

Naturalization of Aliens

National Park Service

Aja Lejber Man
I'm A Labor Man

In 1899, at age 14, Andrew Kovaly came to McKeesport, Pennsylvania, from Slovakia. He got a job in a steel mill and, in 1947 when he sang this song for folk-song collector Jacob A. Evanson, he was still working at the mill. He recalled hearing it in the early 1900s.

Slovakia

A - ja lej - ber man, Ro - bim ka - ždi den, Vše se - be ra - hu - jem
I'm a la - bor man, Work hard as I can. And I have this crav-ing

ke - lo zo-spo - ru –jem, Ke - lo zo-spo - ru –jem na - ti - dzen.
Al ways to be sav-ing. What's the a-mount I'm sav-ing week – ly?

Pride petnasti,	When comes the fifteenth,
Ta i šesnasti,	Also the sixteenth,
Talara nabaru,	I lay down a dollar
"Daj nam po poharu,	On the bar, and holler,
Naj še napijeme napedu."	Let us all drink a glass on payday.
S kraju list dostal,	Letter came to me
Bim daco poslal,	From the old country.
Šedňem za stoliček,	"Oh, my dearest honey,
Napišem listoček,	Please send me some money."
Poslem žene stovku napedu.	A hundred dollars goes on payday.

331

National Park Service

Slovenia

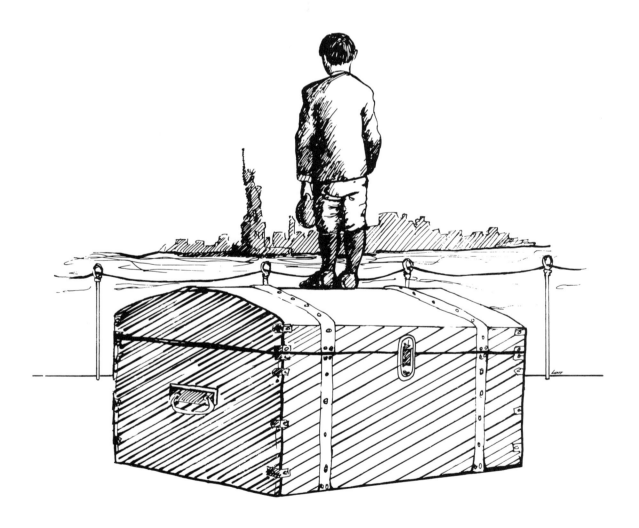

O Mraki
The Evening Bell

As you can see, Slovenian people are very melancholy, especially away from home.
(Fr. Vendelian Spendov)

Slovenia
Gustav Ipavec

Iz stol - pa sem mi zvon do - ni, ko vle - ga mrak se po rav - ni. Le
The steep-le bells to me re - sound, As dusk spreads on the fields a - round. Re-

do - ni, zvon, iz tem-nih lin, le vzbu-jaj mi na dom spo - min! Le
sound, o bell, from the high dome, In me a - rouse the thoughts of home. May

zvo - ni mi ta - ko gla-san in mi - lo poj čez tu - jo, tu - jo plan; Da -
you for - ev - er loud-ly ring. A - cross the for-eign plains so gent-ly sing. Though

si mi v sr-cu pol - je jad, zvo-ne-nje tvo - je slu-šam, slu-šam rad!
you e-voke yearn-ing and pain, when I hear you, I'm hap-py once a - gain.

Ob glasih teh se mi zazdi,
Da v daljni svoji sem vasi,
Kjer ni mi tuj noben obraz,
Pozna me vsak, vsakogar jaz!
    Zato pa, zvon, le svoni mi,
    Na tuji zemlji doni, doni mi
    Ti zvon večerni zvon iz lin,
    Le vzbujaj mi na dom, na dom spomin!

Your sad, sweet tone makes it appear
I'm in my distant village dear,
Where no strange faces one can see;
I'm known to all, and all to me.
    Because of this, dear bell, please ring
    On foreign soil, loudly, loudly sing.
    O evening bell from the high dome,
    Arouse in me the memories of home!

Photo by Z. Vidmar

Danici
To The Morning Star

Slovenia

Gustav Ipavec

Zgod – nja vzbu – je – val – ka, Dne o – zna – nje – val – ka,
Ear – ly ris – er so bright, Her – ald of the day – light,

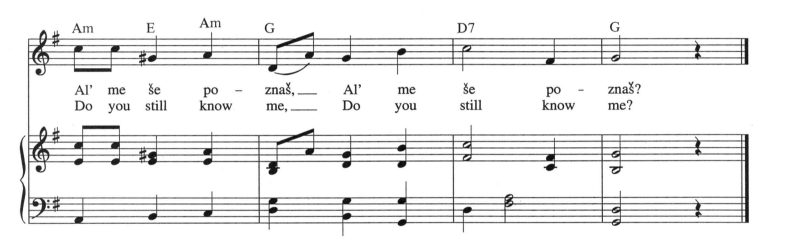

Al' me še po – znaš, ___ Al' me še po – znaš?
Do you still know me, ___ Do you still know me?

Jaz poznam še dobro	O, how well I know thee,
Tebe, zvezdica;	My dear little star,
Stara mati so te	For grandmother showed me,
Mi zaznamila.	Showed me where you are.
Kedar prisvetila,	And your twinkling light beams
S'me iz sna vzbudila.	Woke me often from my dreams.
Daleč tam domá.	Far away, my home.
Daleč tam domá!	Far away, my home!

SLOVENSKI FESTIVAL
MAY 5, 1990

Na Tujih Tleh
On Foreign Soil

I myself am an emigrant who came to America in 1920. As a Slovenian musician, born in 1908, the following is my personal material for your consideration to be used in your book. . . . I moved from Bethlehem, Pa. to New York in 1930 and loved New York ever since. . . . I am also choral director of the "Saint Cyril Slovenian Chorus" in New York. Enclosed is our 1990 Slovenian Festival Program. (Jerry W. Koprivsek)

By Anton Funtek
and Davorin Jenko

Slovenia

Oj, le šu – mi, gozd, nad ma – no, sen – či gozd ___ na ___ tu – jih
Rus - tle, gen - tle woods, a - round me, on the for - eign soil ___ give me

tleh! ___ Zdi se mi, ___ da pe - sem zna - no po – ješ
shade. ___ Yes, you sing a song that I know well, of times

o ___ nek – dan – jih dneh! Da - leč plo – ve mi – sel
past ___ that will nev - er fade In the dis - tance all my

me – ni čez pla – ni – ne in rav – ni: Da, to
thoughts rove, O – ver hills and o – ver vales. Yes, this

gozd je moj ze – le – ni, ki nad ma – no zdaj vr –
is my far – off green grove, And it tells me mourn – ful

ši! Da, to spet___ so tra – te rod – ne, ki jih
tales. O, my na – tive land, o, my mead – ows, I gaze

lep – ših___ ni – ma svet,___ pol – ja zrem___ vr – to – ve
on your beau – ty un – sur – passed,___ Fruit – ful fields___ and fer – tile

339

me – ni, Ko med - lim____ na____ tu – jih tleh!_____
feel – ings, As I lan - guish here on for - eign ground._____

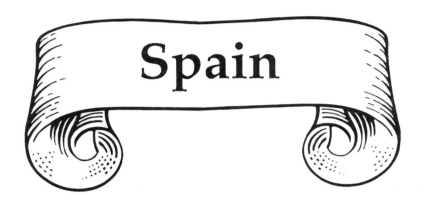

Spain

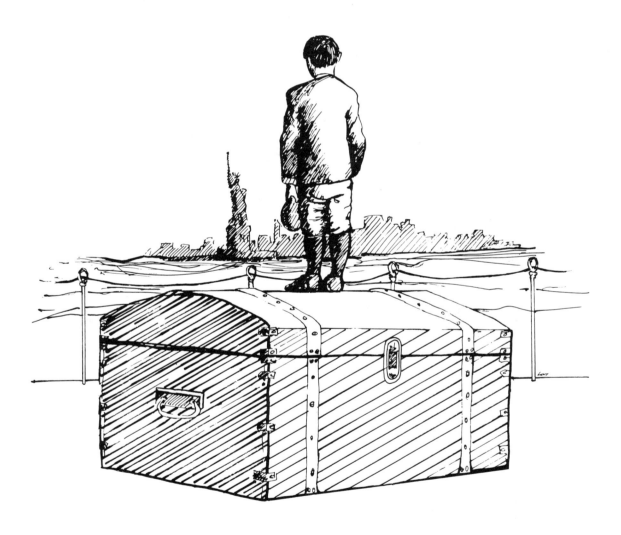

Setesientos Setentaisiete
Seventeen Seventy Seven

This song was collected from the singing of its composer, Irvan Perez, in Poydras, Louisiana (St. Bernard Parish), in 1981. Residents of the region — the "Islenos" — are descendants of the original Spanish settlers who arrived in 1777. The language in which the song is sung reflects over two centuries' separation from the mother country.

By Irvan Perez
Collected by Nick Spitzer

Spain

Set - e - sien - tos set - en - ta - i - siete, _____ va - ri - as fa -
It was sev - en - teen sev - en - ty sev - en, _____ A num - ber of

mi - lias de - ja - ron las Is - las Can - a - rias, _____ Pa - ra la cos - ta de
fam - il - ies left from the Ca - nar - y Is - lands, _____ To go to the coast of

Cu - ba _____ de - ja'ir sur de la Lui - sia - na.
Cu - ba _____ And the south of Loui - si - an - a. _____

* These three beats are found in the first verse only.

Y en sur de la Luisiana,	And in southern Louisiana,
En tierra regalada,	On some land given to them,
Se pusieron de jardineros,	They cultivated gardens,
Para mantenerse estas familias.	To help feed these families.

Varios fueron de soldados.	Some of them were soldiers.
Peliaron por su libertá.	They fought for their liberty,
También salieron victoriosos	And they emerged victorious
Y alcontra Inglatierra.	In fighting against England.

Cuando el tiempo se les puso duro,	And when hard times overtook them,
Cuando no pudían más,	And they just couldn't go on,
Se fueron d'estas tierras,	They left the lands they worked on,
Y con otros españoles se pusieron a la pesca.	And with other Spaniards started fishing.

Y entre el pato y la rata,	And what with the ducks and the muskrats
Entre l'agua y las plerías,	In the waters and the marshes,
Con el ayudo de las mujeres,	With the help of all the women,
Se buscaron la vida.	They tried to make a living.

Con penas y tormentos,	With great hardship and much torment,
Y la voluntar de Dios,	And by the will of God,
Así nace'n pueblo la costa	That's how the coast was settled
De la parroquia San Bernardo.	In the parish of St. Bernard.

¡Viva España y su bandera!	Long live Spain and her banner!
Que con tó mi corazón	But with all my heart I know,
Sé que simos americanos,	Even though we are Americans,
Pero sangre d'español.	Our blood that flows is Spanish.

Malagueñas Al Emigrante
Malagueñas For The Emigrant

Considering that it would be neither just nor equitable to continue maintaining an absolute prohibition that forbids residents of the Canary Islands to seek with security in other countries the sustenance which they lack in their country and to provide an expedient departure of the excess population of said islands . . . Her Majesty, after having heard the opinion of the Royal Council, has decreed that the prohibition of emigration to America, that weighs heavily on the inhabitants of the Canary Islands, should cease. (Queen Isabella II, Royal Order, September 16, 1853)

Spain

By Jerónimo de Francisco

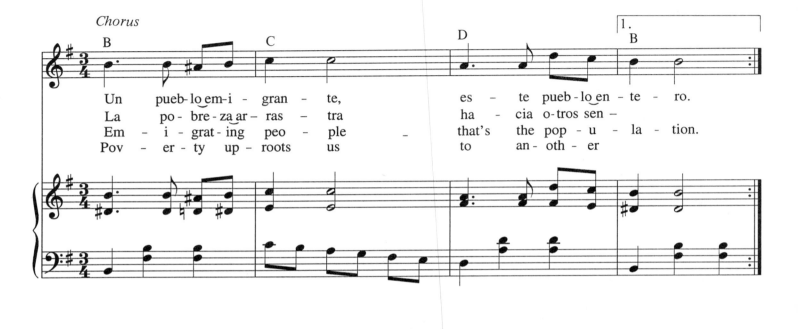

Un pueb-lo em-i - gran - te, es - te pueb-lo en-te - ro.
La po- bre-za ar-ras - tra ha - cia o-tros sen —
Em - i-grat-ing peo - ple that's the pop-u - la - tion.
Pov - er-ty up-roots us to an-oth-er

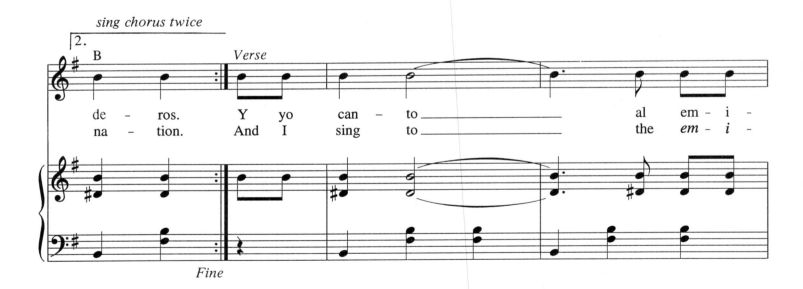

de - ros. Y yo can - to al em - i -
na - tion. And I sing to the *em - i -*

Fine

gran - te,_____

*gran – te,*_____

Y   yo can -

And I sing

to _____   al em- i - gran - te,_____

to _____   the *em- i - gran - te,*_____

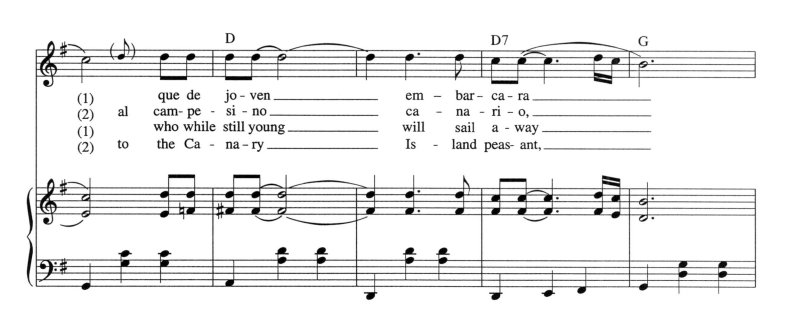

(1)   que de jo - ven_____   em - bar - ca - ra_____

(2) al cam- pe - si - no_____   ca - na - ri - o,_____

(1)   who while still young_____   will   sail a - way_____

(2) to   the Ca - na - ry_____   Is - land peas- ant,_____

a pro- bar nue — va for -
que em- pren- dió un nue- vo ca -
to try and look _____ for his
who un- der- took to change life's

tu - na, _____
mi - no, _____
for - tune _____
high - way, _____

en u- na tier - ra _____
pues la tier - ra _____
in a strange dis - tant _____
for the earth was _____

le - ja - na, Con el su -
__ e- ra un cal- va - ri - o, Y la in- di -
__ coun - try, Crushed by his
__ a cal - va - ry, He had e -

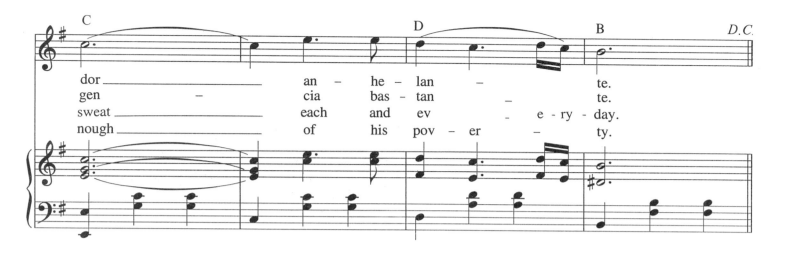

dor _____ an – he – lan _____ te.
gen _____ — cia bas – tan _____ te.
sweat _____ each and ev _____ – e – ry – day.
nough _____ of his pov – er _____ – ty.

Adiós Ríos, Adiós Fontes
Good-Bye Rivers, Good-Bye Fountains

Romantic 19th-century poetess Rosalía de Castro wrote almost all her works in Galician, the language of the northwestern corner of Spain. Guitarist and composer Amancio Prado set this poem of hers to music in 1973.

Spain

Words by Rosalía Castro
Music by Amancio Prado

A – diós, rí – os: a – diós, fon – tes; a – diós, re – ga – tos pe–que–nos; a – diós
Good-bye, ri – vers; good-bye foun –tains; good-bye, springs of crys–tal wa – ter; Good-bye,

vis – ta dos meus o – llos, non _ sei can – do nos ve – re — mos. _____
sights my eyes did gaze on, who–knows when we'll see each oth — er. _____

349

dos cas - ta - ña - res, noi - tes cra - ras de lu - ar, Cam - pa-
mill that ground chest - nuts, moon-light shin - ing in the sky, Chim - ing

ni - ñas tim - bra-doi - ras da i - gre - xi - ña do lu - gar, A - mo-
bells up in the tow - er of the lit - tle church near-by. The black-

ri - ñas das sil - vei - ras que eu lle da - ba ó meu a - mor, Ca - mi-
ber - ries in the bush - es, that we shared, my love and I, And the

ni - ños an - tre o mi - llo, a - diós, pa - ra sem - pre, a - diós!
paths a - mong the corn - fields, for - ev - er, it's good-bye!

351

mos,   Oh.
er,   Oh.

Sweden

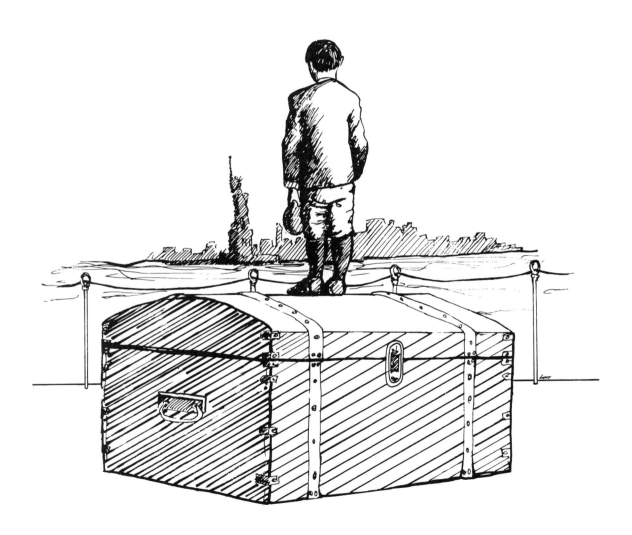

Amerikavisan
Lovsång Över Det Fjärran Amerika
America Song
Love Song For Far-Off America

Crossing over the salty waves from Sweden to America took over three months. When sail-equipped steamships came into service in the 1860s, travelling time was cut to less than one month, with some passages making it in 16 days. By the 1880s the all-steam liners had further cut the time to under three weeks. When direct traffic was inaugurated from Gothenborg to New York in 1915, 13 days was the average crossing time. All this to get to the "pretty girls," "roasted geese," and "cellars bursting with champagne."

Sweden

Brö – der vi   ha långt   att gå   ö – ver sal – ta   vat – ten,
We   must cross   the salt – y waves,   bro – thers get   in   mo – tion,

Och   så finns A – me – ri – ka   in – vid and – ra   strand – en.
And   we'll reach A – me – ri – ca   far   a – cross the   o – cean.

Chorus

In – te är   det mö – je – ligt? Ack   jo,   det är   så fröj – de – ligt!   Ska – da att A –
How   can such   a thing   be so? Ah   well,   it real – ly   is,   you know!   Too   bad that A –

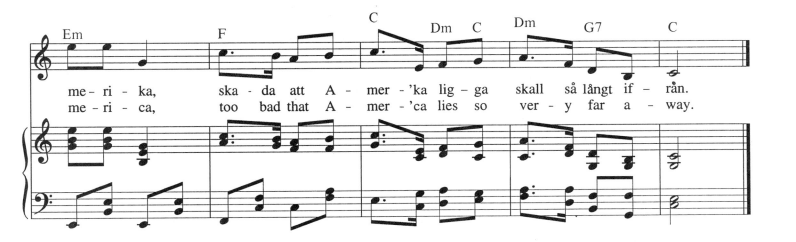

me - ri - ka,   skada att A - mer - 'ka lig - ga   skall så långt if - rån.
me - ri - ca,   too bad that A - mer - 'ca lies so   ver - y far a - way.

Träden, som på marken stå,	Sweet as sugar are the trees,
Söta är som socker,	Growing in the woods there.
Landet är av flickor fullt,	Many are the pretty girls,
Däjeliga dockor. *Chorus*	They are the real goods there. *Chorus*
Önskar man sig en av dem,	If you wish for one of them,
Får man strax en fyra, fem,	Four or five do show up.
Ut' på mark och ängar	In the meadows and the fields,
Växer engelska pengar. *Chorus*	Dollar bills do grow up. *Chorus*
Höns och änder regna ner,	Ducks and chickens fall like rain,
Stekta gäss och ännu fler	They are so enticing.
Flyga in på bordet,	Roasted geese bring their own knives,
Med kniven uti låret. *Chorus*	Ready for the slicing. *Chorus*
Solen, den går aldrig ner,	Cellars bursting with champagne,
Släkt är varje män'ska	Gaiety and song here.
Här är munterhet och sång,	Everyone's related,
Källare full champanje. *Chorus*	And the sun shines all night long here. *Chorus*

Pelles Yankee Doodle
Pelle's Yankee Doodle

This song was collected at the Swedish Home for the Elderly in West Newton, Massachusetts, in the 1930s. In 1937, the Swedish–American newspaper *Svea* included it in an inventory of Swedish immigrant songs. It probably dates from the mid-19th century, the period of the Gothenburg–Boston route. Pelle is a simple country boy who is amazed at the sight of such rare creatures as Catholics (common enough in Boston, but few and far between in Sweden) and the immortal swans (the "swan boats") in the Boston Public Garden.

Sweden

Från Göteborg jag reste hit och stannade i Boston. På
From Gothenburg I voyaged out, To Boston I was going. De-

läckerheter är här rikt, med druvor släckes törsten.
licious food was all about, And how the wine was flowing.

Var flicka här en ängel är, Och engelska kan alla. Fast skorna smala klackar bär De stå — men kan dock falla.	The girls are angels, one and all, And English they all mumble. They balance on their high-heels tall, But can be made to tumble.
De håret uti lockar bär Och därpå sätter hatten, Samt endast bakelser förtär Och dricker sodavatten.	Wear funny hats and fancy curls, You wouldn't know your daughter. They eat rich pastries, lucky girls, While drinking soda water.
Och pojkar kallas "dudar" här Och röka cigaretter. De alltid smala byxor bär Och ögon med lornjetter.	And all the boys are known as "dudes," Smoke evening, night and morn, yet! Wear skin-tight pants, they are no prudes, And each one has a lorgnette.

Här finnas djur av alla slag
Och till och med mosquiter!
Samt sämre folk, i vardagslag
De flesta katoliker.

Här svanor finns som aldrig dö,
De största uti världen,
De simma nere i en sjö
I Boston Public Garden.

Ja, stor är staden, husen se'n,
I Sverige finns ej maken,
Ty vägarna är marmorsten
Och äkta guld på taken.

Och ingenstans jag trivs så väl
Som uppå detta ställe.
Adjö med er och leven väl
Och glömmen inte Pelle!

All kinds of animals abound,
Mosquitoes they do sting here.
All kinds of people running 'round,
And Catholics are king here.

The biggest swans the Lord did make,
My friends, I beg your pardon,
They never die, they swim the lake
In Boston Public Garden.

The city's big, the houses tall,
It's not at all like Sweden.
The marble roads are best of all,
The gold roofs shine like Eden.

In Boston town I want to be,
The whole kit and kaboodle.
And now good-bye, remember me
And Pelle's Yankee Doodle.

361

Hälsa Dem Därhemma
Greet Them At Home

In 1922, Elith Worsing wrote this song, which first was sung in a musical revue in Copenhagen. In addition to its Danish and Swedish texts, it is also sung in Norwegian and English. It has become, over the years, the all-purpose Scandinavian song of nostalgia.

Sweden

By Elith Worsing

Sherman Collection, National Park Service

Chikago, Chikago
Chicago, Chicago

The Swede's love of snuff (*snus*) was such that Chicago Avenue, which ran through "Swede Town," got to be known as *Snusgatan* ("Snoose Boulevard," or "Snuff Street"). Despite the enthusiastic tone of Calle Lindstrom's (1868–1955) song, Swede Town was little more than a slum, known more for its cholera than its high life. This distorted view of life in Chicago is perhaps due to the fact that Lindstrom never visited America.

Sweden

By Calle Lindström

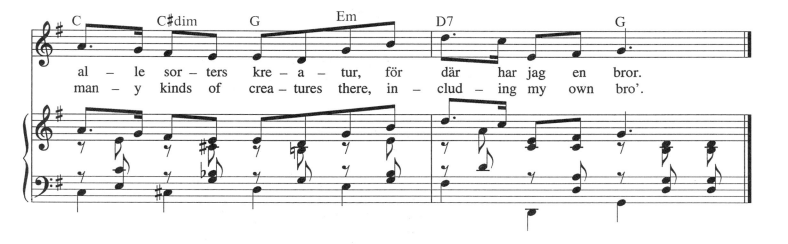

al – le sor – ters kre – a – tur, för där har jag en bror.
man – y kinds of crea – tures there, in – clud – ing my own bro'.

Där finns så store gater, där finns så store hus.
Som ä en mil i höjda och lyser utå ljus.
Där levs det glada livet allt uti sus och dus.
Där rökes det cigarer, för där finns inget snus.

Och högt uppi lufta järnväga går,
Det går så fint te komma opp ifall en vill gå på.
Så många granne saker en skåda där kan få
Och tåget ä så långt som en mil eller så.

Det här har bror min sagt för mig, så nog ä det sant.
Att ingenstans i världa där ä så illengant:
Om natta skiner sola, så fagert och så grannt
Om daga är det ljust ändå, så nog är det galant.

Nu packar ja packaget och sedan hän ja drar,
Ja reser till Chikago och där ja stanner kvar,
För där ja tänker bliva en fin och granner karl.
Ajöss med er nu allihop, för nu iväg ja drar!

They have such wide streets, and the houses are so tall,
They are at least a mile high, with lights in every hall.
The happy life is lived there, and each one has a ball,
And there you smoke cigars because there is no snuff at all.

The railroads, they travel away up in the air,
You get on board so elegantly once you've paid your fare.
There are such pretty sights — and you see them everywhere.
The train is a mile long or so — I can't wait to get there.

This has to be true, for my brother told me so,
And nowhere in the world is it fancier, I know.
The sun, it shines at night with a bright and radiant glow,
It still is light during the day. Amazing! What a show!

Now I'll pack my bags and I'll soon be on my way.
I'm going to Chicago, and that's where I will stay.
A gentleman I'll be there, so what more can I say?
I'm leaving very soon, and I bid you all good day.

Library of Congress

Lincoln-Visan
Lincoln Song

The Swedish view of the assassination of the "emperor" of America, Abraham Lincoln, was somewhat colored by distance and a lack of direct communication. Those Swedes who were here at that time became more directly involved in American life. Of the 20,000 Swedish–Americans scattered throughout many separate communities at the beginning of the 1860s, at least 3,000 enlisted in the Union Army!

Har ni hört den förskräckliga händelsen, Den är
Have you heard the very latest bit of news? And I

sann ty den hände just nu,
tell you ev'ry word is true,

Har som kungan ut av Nordliga A-
How the mighty king of all of North A-

meri-ka Blev skjuten, ja skjuten mitt i tu.
meri-ca Was shot, yes, he was shot right in two.

Chorus

Tjola hopp, tjang tjong, faderal-lan lej, Tjola
Chola hop, chang chong, faderal-lan ley, chola

368

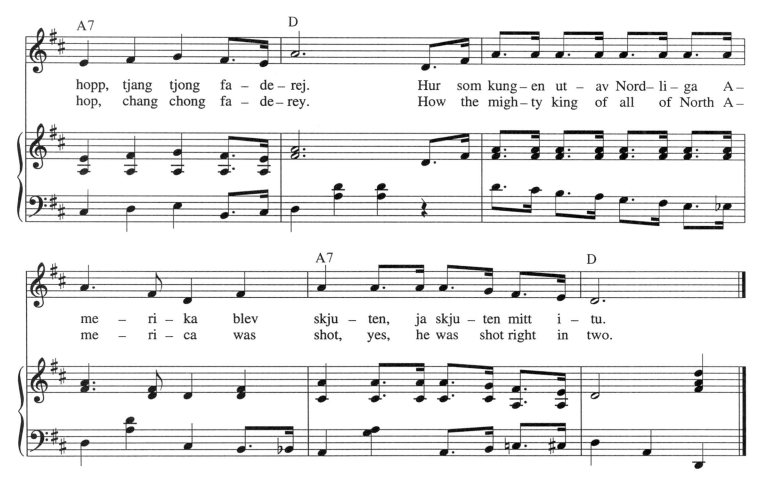

hopp, tjang tjong fa – de – rej.
hop, chang chong fa – de – rey.

Hur som kung–en ut – av Nord–li – ga A–
How the migh–ty king of all of North A–

me – ri – ka blev skju – ten, ja skju – ten mitt i – tu.
me – ri – ca was shot, yes, he was shot right in two.

Han gick ut för at se komedianterna,
Ty det rogade Hans Majestät.
Men inte så kunde han väl tänka,
Att han skulle bli skjuten just för det.

He went out to see the actors in a play,
For he enjoyed that quite a lot.
And he absolutely never did imagine that
For that very reason he'd be shot.

Chorus:
Tjola hopp, tjang tjong, faderallen lej,
Tjola hopp, tjang tjong, faderej.
Men inte så kunde han väl tänka,
Att han skulle bli skjuten just för det.

Chorus:
Chola hop, chang chong, faderallan ley,
Chola hop, chang chong faderey.
And he absolutely never did imagine that
For that very reason he'd be shot.

Han satt uti salongen och tittade,
Hur dom spelte en grann komedi.
Han var klädd i de finaste kläder,
Och stövlar med saffian uti. *Chorus*

Well, he sat there in the theater and he watched
As they played the latest comedy.
He was dressed up in the very latest stylish clothes;
His Morocco leather boots a sight to see. *Chorus*

Each subsequent chorus begins with the same two nonsense lines, as above, and concludes with the last two lines of its respective verse.

Men då kom där en bov genom dörren,
Usch, så hiskeligt ful han såg ut.
Och i handen så bar han sett geväder,
Som var laddat med kulor och med krut. *Chorus*

Then there came a terrible man through the door,
Oh, he was so horrible, in fact.
And a rifle he was holding tightly in his hand —
With powder and bullets it was packed. *Chorus*

Och så sköt han kungen i planeten,
Så att huvudet trilla från hans hals.
Och blodet stänkte på tapeten,
Och betjänten fragte: "Vad befalls?" *Chorus*

Then he shot the king directly in the skull,
So his head, it fell right off his neck.
And the blood made stains upon the theater walls,
And the butler murmured, "What the heck?!" *Chorus*

Och så dog den beskedelige konungen,
Och är salig, jag tänker just nu.
Min Hin Onde må tagen den boven,
Som sköt den kungen mitt itu. *Chorus*

So he died, this great kind-hearted emperor,
And is happy now, I think — don't you?
May the devil take away that murderer
Who shot the emperor in two. *Chorus*

Switzerland

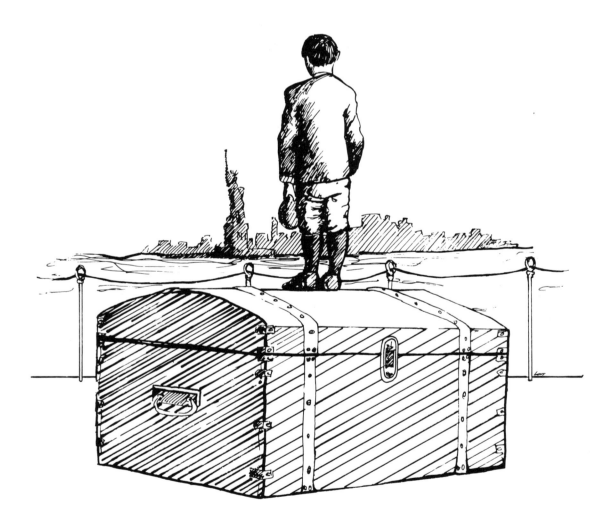

Der Obersimmentaler In Amerika
The Obersimmentaler In America

The Simmental is the valley cut by the river Simme, which flows into Lake Thun south of Berne. On New Year's Eve in 1835, a certain "J. R.," who had lived in the heights above the valley ("Obersimmental"), found himself in Buffalo, New York. He undoubtedly had drunk a little schnapps and was feeling homesick, for he wrote this epic ballad that night. It has been handed down to us in the Swiss–German Obersimmentaler dialect.

Switzerland

Gät acht, i will ech öp — pis zel — le vom neu — e
I hat das jetzt scho lang geng wel — le u ha's de
Lis — ten, I have some-thing to tell you, Of the new
It's a thing I've long want — ed to do; I have — n't

Land A — me — ri — ka.
neu — e geng la gah.
land A — me — ri — ca.
had the chance so far.

Es ist jetzt de es Jahr gly scho,
Al—most a full year has gone by,

dass mir von öch hi Ab — schied gno,
dass mir von öch hi Ab — schied gno.
since all of us did say good–bye,
Since all of us did say good–bye.

372

Wo mir vo ech ewäg sy 'gange,	When from you we did take our leave,
Do het's is weh tah nit e chly;	It hurt us, you know that is true.
Mer sy vor Härzweh fast vergange	With great heartache all of us did grieve,
Bis mer es Mal sy von ech gsy;	Until we had lost sight of you.
Danah sy mir bi Paris für	Paris was the next place we found,
Und über's Meer, dur ds Wasser dür. (2)	Then across the sea we were bound. (2)
I muess ech z erst no öppis brichte	There is something I must first tell you
Vom Meer und vo de Wälli druff,	About the ocean waves that roared,
U was das mängsmal cha verrichte	And what the ocean may sometimes do
Mit Lüt u Guet, da obe druff.	To people and the things on board.
Es het mi mengist Wunner gno,	I had often wondered before,
Jetzt bin i usem Wunner cho. (2)	But now I will wonder no more. (2)
Es ist e grüselichi Glunte —	It is the worst water, I've heard said,
Wer's nit gseh het, der gloubti's nit —	You won't believe this, I'll be bound.
Und tüüf ist's, dass me cha kei Chlumpe	It's so deep that even with a lead,
Ganz z Bode lah am länge Siil.	A long rope cannot touch the ground.
Dir chöht e Jahr druff ummi gah,	One year you can travel on it,
Dir gseht no numme Bitz derva. (2)	And see only just a small bit. (2)
A Himmel uehi und y ds Wasser,	Into the water or in the air,
Da cha me gugge, wenn es ist;	You look around — what can you spy?
Sust gseht me nit viel schöni Sache,	One does not see things of beauty there,
As hie u da e grosse Fisch.	But now and then a fish swims by.
U mengist sy da Wälli cho,	We were struck with waves of such size,
Die ds Schiff hi ganz u d Syte gno. (2)	I thought that the ship would capsize. (2)
Eh bhüetis Gott, wie het es gwalpet!	May God save us, how the ship did heave,
Gly wänes z uangerobe ghyt.	As if it would turn upside down.
Da het me rächt gsit: «Gott es walti!»	Then one truly prayed God us to save,
U diecht, es müessi gstorbe sy.	And each one thought that he would drown.
E Tiil hi Ängste übercho,	A great fear did overcome us.
U ds Lache het's is alle gno. (2)	Laughter was soon taken from us. (2)
Fast all, die uf em Meer wei ryte,	Almost all who sail the ocean,
Die wärde chrank die ersti Stund.	Within an hour are in a fog.
Das Waggle spürt me scho bi Zyte,	They become dizzy by its motion,
U chotze muess me wie ne Hun.	And start to vomit like a dog.
Mi sälber het es tüechtig gno;	I myself was thoroughly hit;
I ha my Tiil fast übercho. (2)	I thought I would kick the bucket. (2)
Chei Wunner, dass me albe inist	It is no wonder that night and morning
Öpp use gugget über d Wan,	One stood and looked out on the sea.
U da su trurig stiht und gihnet	And as one stood there sadly yawning,
U deicht: o chämi numme Lan!	Thought, "Oh, if I on land could be."
Langwylig ist es, das ist wahr,	It is boring — that is so true.
U macht ihm ds Hihmweh sunnerbar. (2)	He feels homesickness through and through. (2)
Öpp inist amme Morge gscheht es,	Then on one morning it comes to pass,
So säge die, wo's chenne, ihm:	So say the ones who know the score,
«Jetz rückt es de, un üarstig' giht es	"It won't be long now — it will go fast,
Mit üs zum neue Ufer hin!»	And we'll soon see the foreign shore."
Vor Freude wird's ihm da schier bang,	Our feelings we cannot command,
Un eismal tönt es: «Lan, Lan, Lan!» (2)	When we hear the cry: "Land, land, land!" (2)
Me gseht's no numme im Blaue usse,	One sees it only there in the blue,
Grad wie nes Wülchli näher cho.	Just like a cloud — we understand.
Doch giht 's nit lang, so cha me wüsse,	But it does not last long. Now in view
Dass 's Lan ist, mi gseht Hüble scho.	We see the hills, we know it's land.
U gly druf hie u da nes Hus:	And then we see a house on shore —
Gott Lob! jetzt hört de ds Walpen uf. (2)	Thank God, the heaving is no more. (2)

Me fährt gschwin yhi zu der Luke,
Wo ds Meer da numme chlys meh ist.
Da bist am Lan, du chätzers Trucke!
Me packt si drus, was hest was gist.
Da steit me uf der neue Wäl
U seit scho englisch: wäriwell.   (2)

Me giht u gschuet afe d Gägni
Un öppe d Städt u lost o d Lüt.
Da «helf ju self» so seit der Jenggi,
U «hilf dir selber», deicht der Dütsch.
Wer gnue Gäld het, ist obe druff.
Wer keis meh het, ist hie o uff.   (2)

Die Meiste wotte gäng bas yhi;
As gfallt ne neue niene rächt,
U wott ne si nit schicke z blybe.
'S guet Lan ist z tüer u d Lüt sy z schlächt.
Z lötscht anhi chuft me denn e Bitz
Des Gstrüpps und buut si druf e Sitz.   (2)

Das Buue ist es gspässigs Wäse
Für dä im Busch, wo's chuum vermah;
Me schleppt e Hufe Trömmle zamme,
Öpp i der Längi so ugfahr.
Danah so bstellt me d Lüt e Tag,
Und lüpft si uf und leit si grad.   (2)

De bruchts nüt meh as Dach u Bode,
Zwi Pfester dry und öpp a Tür,
U de no d Chleck mit Dräck z verschoppe,
Susch blast ihm ganz der Luft dedür;
Und hindenahi es Kamin;
Das tuet's de fast und ghyt nit yn.   (2)

Verwiche hani afe Schlange,
De was der numme schö's wiit gseh,
In üser Stube inne gfange;
Me schücht se nit — es soll o gscheh,
Dass gwüssni Lüt ne no expräss
In ihrne Stube hi es Näst.   (2)

Me het hie Vieh und milcht und metzget,
Me gugget öppe und zicht si hi.
Me nimmt e Achs u giht u bäzget
Im Holz a mängem grobe Buum.
Es git ech Arbit nit für Gspass,
Hie zmitts im Wal, uf frischem Platz.   (2)

We ds Vieh furtluft, so muess me flueche —
Das ist e tusigs Tüfels Gschicht!
Viel lieber wett i no ga sueche
Bi öch uf d Allmit euers G'richt;
Denn diesi Allmit giht ech no
Vo Grenland bis nach Mexiko.   (2)

One quickly moves into the harbor.
The sea is narrow here at last.
The ship was landed — at sea no more,
And we unload it very fast.
Here in the New World one feels swell,
And says in English: "Wäriwell."[1]   (2)

One goes down and walks along the wharf
To hear and see what may occur.
The *Jenggi*[2] he does say: *"Helf ju self."*[3]
The German thinks: *"Hilf dir selber."*[4]
Money is king here, there's no doubt.
If you have none left, you are out.   (2)

Most of them want to go here and there,
They really do not like it here.
They do not want to stay anywhere;
People are bad — the land is dear.
And finally one buys a piece
Of bushes and builds a small place.   (2)

Building really is a strange affair,
One has no money — only strength.
One drags many logs from everywhere,
And cuts them off in equal length.
You hire people for a day,
One lifts them up and lays them straight.   (2)

Then one needs just a roof and a floor,
And then you fill the cracks with mud.
Cut two windows and, perhaps, a door,
But the wind will surely freeze your blood.
And in the back goes a chimney.
That's it. It stands. Here is your key.   (2)

It's many a big snake I have fought.
Whatever nice you want to see,
In our living room I have caught.
We're not afraid. People tell me
That certain people do their best,
And at home they do keep a nest.   (2)

One here does milk and slaughter cattle.
He drags them home by twos and threes.
One takes an axe and goes to battle
Out in the woods against the trees.
There is work here for you — no joke.
In the woods you work or go broke.   (2)

When the cattle run away, you curse.
A thousand devils' story now.
Searching for them here could not be worse.
They're in the alp — but where and how?
For the alp reaches, even so,
From Greenland to Mexico.   (2)

---

1. "Very well."
2. Yankee
3. "Help yourself."
4. "Help yourself."

'S ist nadisch nit, wie viel Lüt meine
Hie allz so söfli fadegrads.
Wär's rächt grad will, ist bas dahinne
No öppe uf sym alte Platz.
Doch flinggi Lüt, die werhe meu,
Die chömme numme, we si cheu.   (2)

Öpp ine söllti Glogge bringe
U no nes Wüschli Gäld derzue;
Hie Chüeh ha u ne Matte dinga,
Der Schwyzerchäs, der gälti gnue.
Es wär nes lustigs Läbe da
Für ine, dä rächt juchze ma!   (2)

Dir sölltit chönne dürhi gugge
U sälber gsch grad wie nes ist;
Es würdi viellecht mänge gluste,
U mängi siiti: «Ni, ni gwüss —
Wenn's sy muess, will i lieber no
Hie um my lötschte Chrüzer cho!»   (2)

I chan ech wäger nit rächt rate
U säge: chömit — oder nit.
Denn üsers Läbe ist e Schatte,
Bis dass mer gah y d Ewigkiit.
Dert finne mer enannere scho,
Will's Gott, doch öppe frisch und froh. (2)

It is not the way we did believe:
Here everything so clear and straight.
He who wants it straight did never leave,
But stayed behind in his old place.
Workers here that we latch on to,
They come only when they want to.   (2)

Maybe one should bring along a bell,
And lots of money in the clear.
Go rent a cattle farm — all is well,
For Swiss cheese is well thought of here.
Life here would not be bad at all
For one who wants to have a ball.   (2)

You should be able to look around,
And judge independently.
Still more willing people might be found,
While some would say, "No, certainly —
If I must face sure bankruptcy,
I'll stay to lose my last penny."   (2)

Thus, I can't tell you if you should go,
Or tell you stay, or come with me,
Because our life is but a shadow,
Until we reach eternity.
There surely we will meet again,
Fresh and glad in the Lord's domain.   (2)

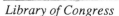

Library of Congress

Havre Ist Ein Schönes Städtchen
Havre Is A Pretty City

In the early 1880s, a certain Herr C. Bienggeli from Schwartzenburg composed this realistic, if somewhat depressing, account of his trans-Atlantic passage. Its last verse is strikingly similar to the hard-times song of the American cotton farmer, "The Boll Weevil":

> Now, if anybody should ask you,
> Who was it sang this song,
> It was the poor old farmer,
> With all but his blue jeans gone. . . .

Switzerland

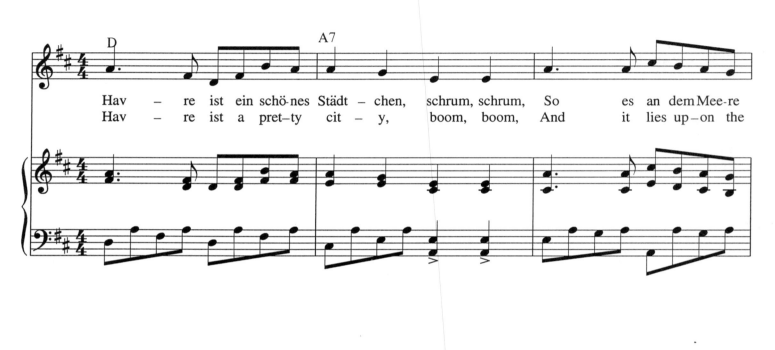

Hav — re ist ein schö-nes Städt – chen, schrum, schrum, So es an dem Mee-re
Hav — re ist a pret–ty cit – y, boom, boom, And it lies up – on the

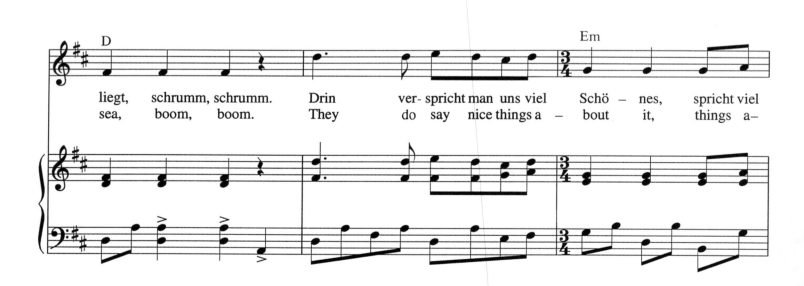

liegt, schrumm, schrumm. Drin ver- spricht man uns viel Schö — nes, spricht viel
sea, boom, boom. They do say nice things a — bout it, things a—

Schö – nes,   A —   ber halt – en tut's man nicht, schrumm, schrumm.
bout it,   But   to stay here, that can't be, boom, boom.

Und ein Schiff, das heisst «la France» (schrumm, schrumm),
Führt uns nach Amerika (schrumm, schrumm).
Drinnen gibt es schlechtes Fressen (schlechtes Fressen),
Und eine Schweinerei ist da (schrumm, schrumm)!

Wer viel frißt, der muss viel kotzen (schrumm, schrumm),
Kotzt bei Tage und bei Nacht (schrumm, schrumm).
Drum sind all schon unsre Kammern (unsre Kammern),
Nun zum Schweinestall gemacht (schrumm, schrumm).

Morgens gibt es braune Brühe (schrumm, schrumm),
Die zum Spott man Kaffee heißt (schrumm, schrumm).
Mittags Fleisch so zäh wie Leder (zäh wie Leder),
Dass man sich die Zähn ausbeisst (schrumm, schrumm).

Auch der Wein ist wenig nütze (schrumm, schrumm),
Bette, die sind ziemlich hart (schrumm, schrumm).
Das hat ja schon manchen Schweizer (manchen Schweizer),
Bei seiner Wasserreis geplagt (schrumm, schrumm).

Den Herrn Doktor sicht man selten (schrumm, schrumm),
Selten auch den Kapitän (schrumm, schrumm).
Weil die Herren Offiziere (Offiziere),
Gar kein Wörtchen deutsch verstehn (schrumm, schrumm).

Wenn euch nun die Leute fragen (schrumm, schrumm):
«Wer hat denn dies Lied erdacht?» (schrumm, schrumm),
«Ei, so sollt ihr ihnen sagen (ihnen sagen):
«Ein Passagier hat es gemacht» (schrumm, schrumm).

On a ship that's called *La France* (boom, boom),
To America we go (boom, boom).
There the grub is simply awful (simply awful),
Fit for pigs, I'll have you know (boom, boom).

He who eats a lot must vomit (boom, boom),
Vomit all day and all night (boom, boom).
Therefore, very soon our cabins (soon our cabins)
Smell like pigsties — what a sight (boom, boom)!

Mornings they give us brown "gravy" (boom, boom),
Coffee! It would make you choke (boom, boom).
Noontime — meat as tough as leather (tough as leather),
Many were the teeth that broke (boom, boom).

And the wine is good for nothing (boom, boom),
Beds — they give us all a pain (boom, boom).
That has caused many a poor Swiss ('ny a poor Swiss)
Of his voyage to complain (boom, boom).

O, we seldom see the doctor (boom, boom),
And the captain's not at hand (boom, boom).
While the officers on board ship ('cers on board ship),
German do not understand (boom, boom).

Now, if anyone should ask you (boom, boom)
Who it was that made this song (boom, boom),
Just you turn to them and tell them (them and tell them):
A passenger who came along (boom, boom).

An Einen Auswanderer
To An Emigrant

In the early 1850s the lure of California gold proved irresistible to a great many Swiss. If things didn't pan out the way they were hoped for in the goldfields, they tried their hands at farming. Most returned to Switzerland after 10 to 15 years in America.

Switzerland

Und willst du hier nicht län-ger wei – len, Im __ grü – nen Tal, am blau-en
So is it true that you are leav – ing Our __ moun – tain lakes and vales be–

See? Du willst der Hei-mat Los nicht tei – len, Nicht
low? The des – ti – ny the fates are weav – ing, Your

dein – es Vol-kes Wohl und Weh? So wan – dre nach A–me–ri–
peo – ple's wel-fare and their woe? Go to A – me–ri–ca, you

ka. / say.
Ich bleib' in Land der Al–pen da. / Here in the Alps I'll al–ways stay
So / Go

wan — dre nach A-me-ri–ka, / to A–me-ri-ca to–day.
Ich bleib' in Land der Al-pen da. / Here in the Alps I'll al–ways stay.

Die Schweiz, die dich mit Mutterhänden,
Als Kind gepflegt so treu, so gut,
Ihr kannst du kalt den Rücken wenden,
Durchwallt dein Herz kein Schweizerblut? *Chorus*

Du willst den Bürgerbrief zerreissen,
Den dir das freie Hochland gab?
Du willst nicht länger Schweizer heissen,
Schwörst unserm Bund auf ewig ab? *Chorus*

Die Väter, die in Unglückstagen
Nie feig aus ihrer Heimat floh'n,
Die Tell und Winkelriede klagen
Um dich, um den verlor'nen Sohn. *Chorus*

So wähl' ein Grab im gold'nen Sande,
Verschmacht' am Sakramento nun!
Im schönen, freien Schweizerlande,
Bei meinen Vätern will ich ruh'n.

Final chorus:
Fahr' hin, fahr' nach Amerika,
Als Schweizer leb' und sterb' ich dah! (2)

Our Switzerland, with loving kindness,
To raise you, she took many pains.
Can you now turn our back in blindness
While Alpine blood flows through your veins? *Chorus*

Will you tear up the old agreement
That gave this highland free to you?
Have you forgot what living free meant —
Renounce our land? It can't be true. *Chorus*

Our fathers, who their watch are keeping,
Did never from their homeland run.
The Tells and Winkelrieds are weeping
For you, for their departed son. *Chorus*

So dig a grave in golden sand,
And you'll pine by Sacramento's stream,
While here in my fair Switzerland,
With my ancestors I'll remain. *Chorus*

Final chorus:
America's the course you steer,
As a Swiss I'll live and die here. (2)

Bald Ist Die Zeit
Soon Is The Time

The Alpine town of Arosa is in the heart of modern ski country. In the 19th century, long before people thought of sliding down a mountain in the winter for pleasure, emigrants from Arosa sang this song as they left for America.

Switzerland

Bald ist die Zeit und Stun – de da, Wir
Soon is the time and soon the hour, We

rei – sen nach A – me – ri – ka. Der Wa – gen steht schon vor der
tra – vel to A – me – ri – ca. The wag–gon is pre – pared to

Tür, Mit Weib und Kin – dern rei – sen wir.
start, With wife and chil – dren we de – part.

Die Rosse sind schon eingespannt,
Wir ziehen aus dem Vaterland.
Das Schifflein führt uns auf die See.
Wir seh'n uns heut und nimmermehr.

Drum Mädchen, gib mir einen Kuß,
Weil ich von Dir jetzt scheiden muss.
Und reich mir deine zarte Hand,
Es geht jetzt fort ins fremde Land.

Ade, ihr Freunde und Verwandt'
Reicht mir zum letzten Mal die Hand.
Ade und weinet nicht so sehr,
Wir seh'n das Bündnerland nie mehr.

Und wenn das Schiff auf'm Wasser schwimmt,
Und sich kein andres mit sich nimmt,
Wir fürchten keinen Wasserfall,
Und denken: Gott ist überall!

Und wenn wir kommen in das Land,
Da heben auf wir unsre Hand
Und rufen laut: Victoria,
Jetzt sind wir in Amerika!

See how the horses ready stand,
We're going from our fatherland.
The boat is leaving from the shore,
We'll see you now and nevermore.

So maiden, kiss me one last time,
For now I must leave you behind.
And give to me your precious hand —
I'm off now to a foreign land.

Good-bye, you relatives and friends,
My time here now is at an end.
Good-bye, and do not weep for me,
Though Switzerland no more we'll see.

And when the ship is on the sea,
Without the one who's dear to me,
The stormy seas we do not fear,
Because we know our God is near.

And when we get to that far land,
Then we will raise up our hand,
And cry aloud, *"Victoria,*
Now we are in America!"

Der Auswanderer
(Soldatenlied)
The Emigrant
(Soldiers' Song)

Another "go if you must" song. Ships from every nation negotiated the heavy passage around Cape Horn. Sailors and passengers alike had but one thought in mind:

Then blow, boys, blow,
For Californi-o.
There's plenty of gold,
So I've been told,
On the banks of the Sacramento.

Switzerland

Willst du dein Dienst-büch-lein zer-rei-ßen, Das
So will you tear up your old ser-vice book, That

dir die teu-re Hei-mat gab? (zwei,drei) Willst nicht län-ger Schwei-zer-bür-ger
your dear home-land gave to you? (two,three) Will you leave your land with-out a

hei-ßen? So reis in Land A-me-ri-ka! (zwei,drei) Ja, ja, das land, das land A-
back-ward look? So trav-el to A-me-ri-ca! (two,three) Yes, yes, the land, the land A-

Chorus

Dich locken Kaliforniens Felder,
Wo man das Gold im Flusse wäscht (zwei, drei).
Was nützen dir die vielen Felder,
Wenn du die teure Heimat nicht mehr häscht (zwei, drei)?
Chorus

So leb denn wohl, ich wünsch dir gute Reise,
Vergiß das teure Hochland nicht (zwei, drei),
Wo sich der Fremde Edelweiße
Und Alpenrosenkränze flicht (zwei, drei)! *Chorus*

Es pfeift, die Ankerketten stöhnen!
Am Sprachrohr steht der Kapitän (zwei, drei),
Bei solchen schauervollen Tönen
Hält's schwer, nach Amerika zu gehn (zwei, drei). *Chorus*

Grab dir dein Grab im Wüstensande,
Verdirb am Sakramentostrom (zwei, drei)!
Ich bleib im lieben Schweizerlande,
Bei meinen Vätern will ich ruhn (zwei, drei). *Chorus*

California's fields are calling to you,
Its streams, where men pan for bright gold (two, three).
The fields at home no longer woo you,
And you, our homeland can no longer hold (two, three).
Chorus

So fare you well, I wish you a good journey,
And don't forget this land of thine (two, three),
Where edelweiss is growing in the mountain,
And alpine rosy garlands twine (two, three). *Chorus*

Whistle blows, the anchor chains are groaning!
The captain bellows his command (two, three);
And with such a horrible intoning,
It is hard to leave one's native land (two, three). *Chorus*

So dig your grave out in the desert sand,
In Sacramento's stream decay (two, three).
I'll remain in my beloved Switzerland —
Among my people I will stay (two, three). *Chorus*

383

Syria

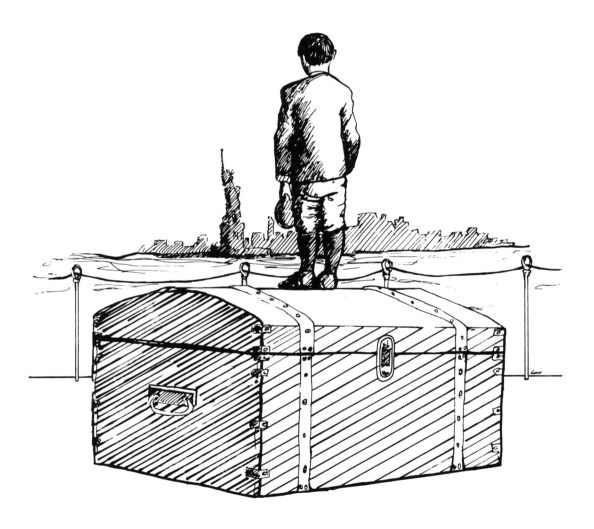

Thelenna Be Rass'l Babor W'nzilna
We Got On Board The Ship And Sailed Away

To one just come from the Occident, from somewhere in New York, a descent upon the Syrian quarters is like a dream travel. It is as if some undreamed-of means of transportation had suddenly been realized, and we could at will, in a few minutes, land across the seas into some remote, outlying district of Damascus; Damascus, referred to by the Syrians of the desert as the Paradise on Earth; Damascus, the city that has remained as ancient as it was two thousand years ago.

Take the Sixth Avenue Elevated at Forty-second Street, or wherever you happen to be, and in a few minutes you are in Rector Street; walk a block westward to Washington Street and you are in Syria. . . . From underneath the table one of the women pulled out an instrument which was a cross between a mandolin and a guitar, and began to pluck its strings. And then, with eyes fixed on me, the other woman stood up and began to move slowly. Her feet remained in one place. Only her body moved and swayed; at first slowly and languorously; then, as the music became faster and faster, she brought her arms and hands and fingers into the dance. . . . I later asked Malouf what the two women had danced. It was "Going Away And Coming Home.". . . (*Around The World In New York* by Konrad Berkovici, 1924)

Syria

The – len – na be ras – s'l ba – bor w'n zil – na, W'
We got on board the ship and sailed a – way, Our

d'moo il im___ rah mu'_____ na. Nih – na ba – lud – na
moth – ers' tears went with us that sad___ day. Our home – land we'll___ not

386

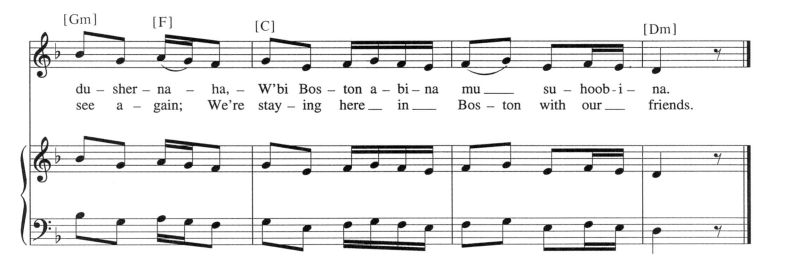

du – sher – na – ha, – W'bi Bos – ton a – bi – na mu____ su – hoob-i – na.
see a – gain; We're stay – ing here _ in __ Bos – ton with our __ friends.

Ya Souria shifthek dum'ee ala chudoodee.
Rohithna dushernaha wurrana.
W'aimthain b'shoofek, ya uchthee,
Allah b'yufreh; ah, ya dounya.

Oh, Syria, I picture you and cry.
Our souls we've left behind, and who knows why?
My sister, when will I see you again?
Only God knows — such is the fate of men.

National Park Service

387

Trinidad

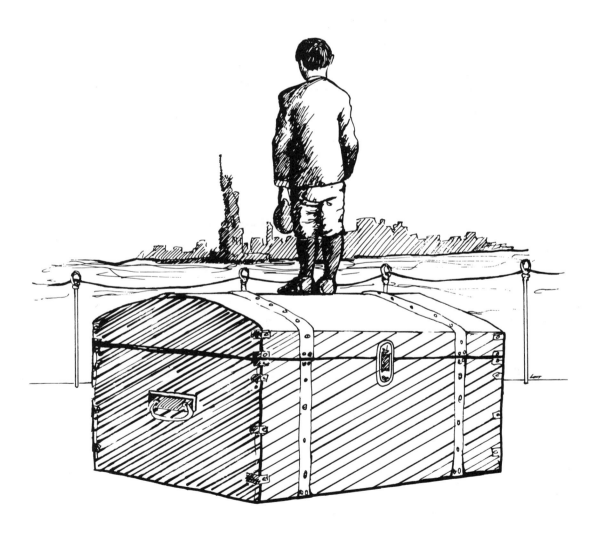

Workers' Appeal

True calypso music carries biting social commentary, often couched in witty, complicated rhymes and carried forward with an infectious rhythmic bounce. This song was sung and recorded by a number of calypsonians in the 1930s and 1940s, including Neville Marcano (The Tiger) and Wilmoth Houdini. Each singer put his distinctive stamp on the song. Houdini's version concludes:

I'm not the crooner Rudy Vallee,
Or the songbird Mister Bing Crosby.
People, I want you to understand,
I am not Guy Lombardo or Paul Whiteman.
This is plain Papa Houdini,
The calypso king of the West Indies;
And every man was born to be free and to be happy
From suppression and misery.

Trinidad

Kind-heart-ed em-ploy-ers, I ap-peal now to you: Give us some work to do.

We are not asking for equality,
To rank with the rich in society,
To visit their homes in their motorcars,
Or to go to their clubs and smoke their cigars.
We are asking for a living wage
To exist now and provide for old age.
Our kind-hearted employers, I appeal now to you,
Give us some work to do.

Many a day, persons haven't a meal.
They were too decent to beg, too honest to steal.
They went looking for work mostly everywhere,
But saw signboard marked "No hands wanted here."
The government should work the wastelands and hills,
Build houses, factories and mills,
Reduce taxation and then we would be really
Emancipated from slavery.

The legislators only quarrel and fret
About unemployment but haven't relieved us yet.
There is no visions that we can see
To take us out from tribulations and misery.
We can't fight physically for we wouldn't prevail
On account of ammunition, cruel laws and jail.
But every man was born to be free
From this oppression and tyrannic slavery.

Sherman Collection, National Park Service

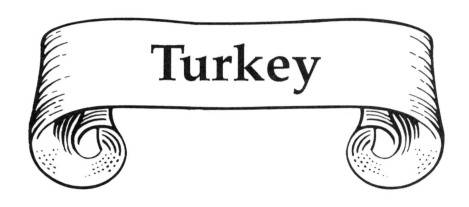

Turkey

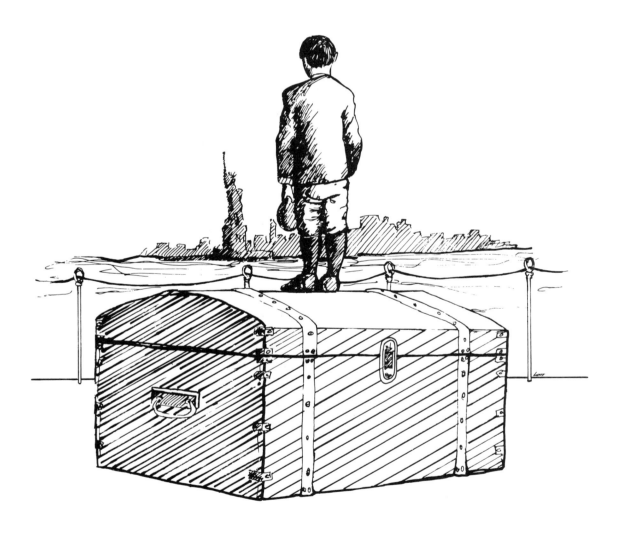

Amerika Dilberi
American Beauty

Just before the Great Depression, the majority of Turkish immigrants collected their personal effects and what money they had saved and returned to their Anatolian villages. Those who stayed married or carried on as bachelors, maintaining the lifestyles they had developed since their arrival. . . . Turks who had married slowly assimilated into America's mainstream. . . . (*The Turkish Times*, July 15, 1991)

Turkey

Yar ge – lir gü – le gü – le, _____ Saç – la – ri lü – le lü – le. _____
My be – lov – ed smiles at me, _____ And her hair is flow – ing free. _____

Bir ö ___ pü –
When she _____ is _____

cük a – lin – ca, Ne – dir _____ çek – tin-gin _____
steal – ing a kiss, She _____ asks _____ me to say,

ben – den _____ der.
"What _____ feel – ing is this?"

tacet chords

394

Chorus

Yürüyüşü edali,
Bakişi pek havali.
Şivesine doyulmaz,
Bir gecelik sarmali. *Chorus*

She has such a charming walk,
And I love to hear her talk.
Her looks were born up above —
O, for one little night of love! *Chorus*

Neden Geldim Amerikaya?
What Brought Me To America?

Between 1900 and 1920 approximately 400,000 immigrants whose "country of last residence" was recorded as Turkey entered the United States. A great many of these new arrivals settled in New England, where the Turkish coffee house soon became an integral part of this transplanted society. Walnut Street in Peabody, Massachusetts, had the highest concentration of these coffee houses in New England. It got to be known locally as "Ottoman Street," and the neighborhood was referred to as "The Barbary Coast."

Turkey

Ne – den gel – dim A – me-ri – ka – ya? Ne – den gel – dim A –
What brought me to A – me – ri – ca? What brought me to A –

me-ri – ka – ya? Tu – tul – dum kal – dim a – ma – ne, Tu –
me – ri – ca? I've sunk in – to a deep sor – row, I've

tul – dum kal – dim a – ma – ne. Şim – di bin ke – re piş –
sunk in – to a deep – sor – row. And now I suf – fer a

ma — — nim, Şim-di bin ke-re piş – ma – nim, _____ Fa-
thou — sand re-grets, And now I suf – fer a ____ thous-and re – grets. But

kat geç – ti_____ ah he ça — re, Fa-kat geç – ti_____ ah ne
there is noth – ing I can do_____ now, But there is noth – ing I can

ça — re. _____ Ah! Gel – mez o lay —
do_____ now. _____ Ah! I wish I had-not-

dim. Ah! Gel – mez o lay – dim.
come. Ah! I wish I had not come.

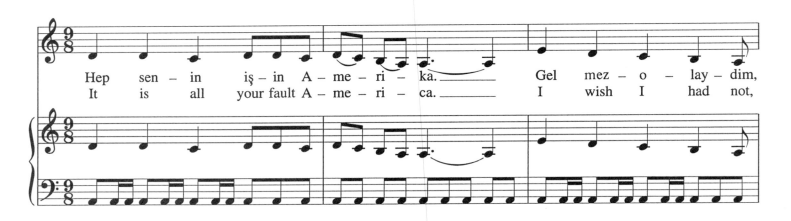

Hep sen – in iş – in A – me – ri – ka._____ Gel mez – o – lay – dim,
It is all your fault A – me – ri – ca._____ I wish I had not,

Gel – mez o lay – dim.
I _____ wish I had – not_____ come.

Bandirmanin kiş denizi, (2)	The winter sea of Bandirma, (2)
Gemileri dizi dizi. (2)	The ships are lined up in a row. (2)
Merhametsiz, insafin yok mu? (2)	Without mercy, is there no justice? (2)
Ne tür mahsun ettin sen bizi, (2)	You made us all feel so unhappy. (2)
Ah! Kaçmaz olaydim,	Ah! I wish I had not come.
Ah! Aşmaz olaydim.	Ah! I wish I had not sailed.
Hep senden ileri Bandirma,	Away from you, my own Bandirma,
Aşmaz olaydim. (2)	I wish I had not sailed. (2)

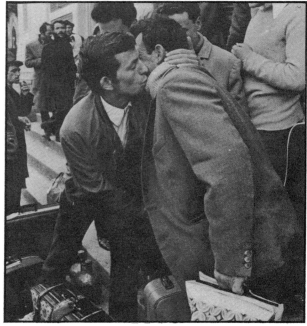

Seeing Friends Off to America from Istanbul
New York Public Library Picture Collection

New York Public Library Picture Collection

Ukraine

In 1972, a song book was published in Kiev entitled *Ukrainian Folk Songs From The Lemkian Region.* It contains a number of songs, in the Lemkian dialect, dealing with going to America — four of which are included here.

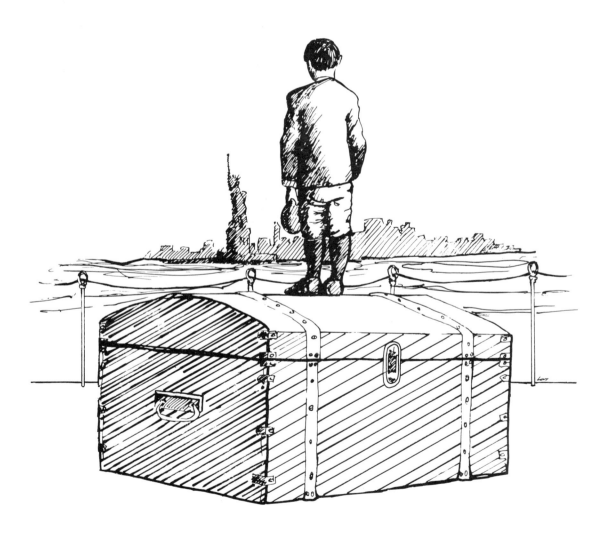

Oy Nema To Na Svetse
What A Most Delightful Life

Collected, along with other songs, in the years 1940–43 from Maria Makara, age 41,
in the village of Vysova.

So reads the note to this song in the appendix of the Kiev publication. It is of more than passing interest to note that in the Nazi-occupied, war-ravaged Ukraine of the early 1940s, people were singing about America and collectors were on hand to copy down their songs!

Ukraine

Oy ne – ma to na sve – tse,   yak mo – lo – diy ne – ves – tse,
What a most de – light – ful life   for a young and pret – ty wife;

Muzh i v Ha – me – ri – tsi, Muzh i
Her man's in A – me – ri – ca, A –

v Ha – me – ri – tsi, O – na ro – bit shto khtse.
me – ri – ca, And she does as she pleas — es.

Oy muzh i v Hameritsi,
Ey, robit na talyari. (2)
A ona kupuye (2)
Paribkim tsigari.

Oy, kupuy, zheno, kupuy,
Lem ked mash zach kupuvats. (2)
Idye tam ti stivka (2)
Mozhesh yei skel'tuvats.

Oy, vikhod zhe, miy muzhu,
Do svoyoho krayu. (2)
Nai tya tvoyi diti (2)
Til'ko ne chekayut.

Husband's in America,
Working hard for money there. (2)
While at home she is a-flying, flying, (2)
Young men fancy cigars buying.

Oh, my wife go out and buy
What you can afford for them. (2)
If you have the money, (2)
Spend to the last penny.

Oh, come back, my dearest man,
Come back to your native land. (2)
Your children are crying, (2)
How the time is flying.

401

Dobri V Hameritsi
It's Good In America

Another song from the repertoire of Maria Makara.

Ukraine

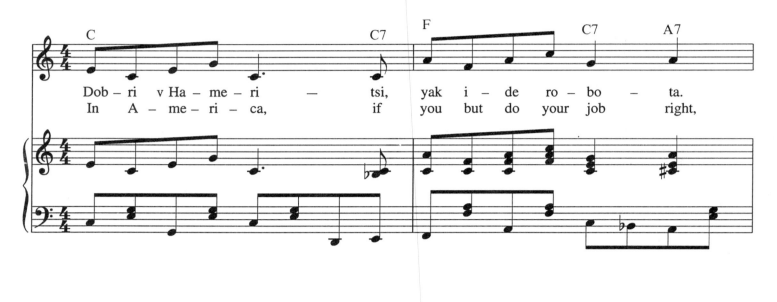

Dob — ri v Ha — me — ri — tsi, yak i — de ro — bo — ta.
In A — me — ri — ca, if you but do your job right,

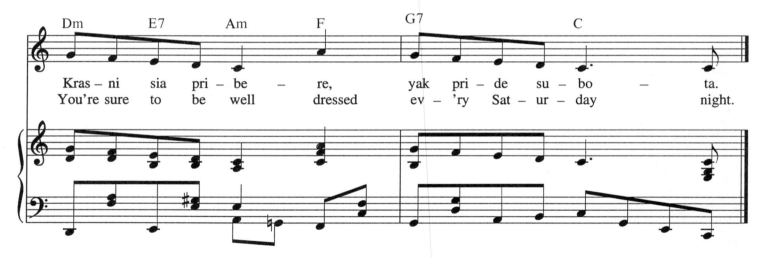

Kras — ni sia pri — be — re, yak pri — de su — bo — ta.
You're sure to be well dressed ev — 'ry Sat — ur — day night.

Krasni sya pribere,	You will be well dressed,
Krasni sya umiye.	Well groomed like in a contest.
Bo vin sya ne starat,	And you needn't worry
Zhe mu v poli hniye.	'Bout a rotting harvest.
Zhe mu v poli hniye,	What rots in the fields
Voda mu zabepe,	Is washed away by water.
Bo yomu privezut	Here the farmers bring you
Do havzu farmere.	Everything you order.
Do havzu privezut,	To your house they bring it,
Platsu ne pitayut,	And don't ask for money.
Azh na pyatnastoho,	They wait 'til the fifteenth —
Yak peydu dostayut.	Really, it's too funny.
Yuzh na pyatiy rochok,	For the past five years
Yak ya v Hameritsi,	America's my story.
Tak tyazhko pratsyuyu	I've been working hard
V tiy noviy fabritsi.	In a brand-new factory.

402

Zheno moya lyuba,	Tell me, my dear wife,
Zheno moya dobra,	Oh, write me a long letter.
Yak ti tam gazduyesh	How are all the children?
Z timi ditmi doma?	Is life any better?
Gazduyu, gazduyu,	I am hanging on,
Yuzh lipshe ne mozhu.	And the children kiss you,
Tebe z Hameriki	Life is very hard —
Dochkatsya ne mozhu.	Come back soon, we miss you.
Dochkashsya ti, dochkash,	I'm sure you'll succeed,
Moya zheno, dochkash.	My dearest, do not worry.
Yak ya pridu domiv,	And when I get home,
Lichko mi poboskash.	You'll kiss me in a hurry.
Lichko mi poboskash,	You will kiss my cheek,
Pravu ruchku podash.	My right hand you'll hold, honey.
Budesh sya mya pitats:	Then you'll ask of me:
Duzhe pinyaziy mash?	Do you have much money?
Ne mam ya pinyaziy,	I don't have a penny,
Bo ya lem sluhuvav.	There is nothing to it.
A shto ya zasluzhiv,	As I worked I spent it,
I toto-m prohulyav.	Every cent, I blew it.

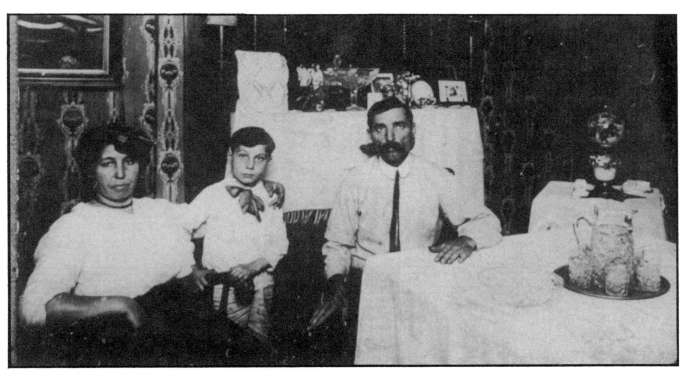

National Park Service

403

V Hameritsi Brama Maliuvana
In America's A Golden Portal

From the singing of Olena Hatalia, age 35, in the village of Vysova in 1944.

Ukraine

v Ha – me – ri – tsi bra – ma ma – liu – va – na.
In A – me – ri – ca's a gold – en por – tal.

O – tve – rat yei ha – me – rits – ka pan – na.
O – pened by a la – dy who's im – mor – tal.

O – tve – rat yei, O – tve – rat yei ha – me – rits – ka pan – na.
O – pened by a, O – pened by a la – dy who's im – mor – tal.

Yak ya ishov, otvorena bila,
Sama ona mi yei otvorila.
Sama ona,
Sama ona mi yei otvorila.

Ishchi sya mya, vera, zapitala:
De ti idesh, moya dusho draha?
De ti idesh,
De ti idesh, moya dusho draha?

Tsi ti idesh pinyazki shparuvats?
Tsi ti idesh divchata lyubuvats?
Tsi ti idesh,
Tsi ti idesh divchata lyubuvats?

Ne idu ya pinyazki shparuvats,
Lem ya idu divchata lyubuvats.
Lem ya idu,
Lem ya idu divchata lybuvats.

Pri pinyazkakh mozhe boh zdrav'ya zbits,
Pri divchatku mozhe boh zaplatits.
Pri divchatku,
Pri divchatku mozhe boh zaplatits.

A yak bude divcha khloptsya mati,
Bude to tya listochki pisati.
Bude to tya,
Bude to tya listochki pisati.

Yak ti budesh tot listok chitati,
Budesya tya otets mats pitati.
Budesya tya,
Budesya tya otets mats pitati.

Shto ti, sinu, shto novoho chitash,
Sivi ochka slezami prolivash?
Sivi ochka,
Sivi ochka slezami prolivash?

Stala mi sya prevelika shkoda,
Syav ya zhitko, vzyala mi ho voda.
Syav ya zhitko,
Syav ya zhitko, vzyala mi ho voda.

Vzyala mi ho do Chornoho Morya.
Zato plachu, stara mamo moya.
Zato plachu,
Zato plachu, stara mamo moya.

Open was the gate I saw before me,
She herself did open it wide for me.
She herself did,
She herself did open it wide for me.

She gazed down on me and then demanded:
Where are you bound, dear soul, now you've landed?
Where are you bound,
Where are you bound, dear soul, now you've landed?

Will you try to save all of your money?
Or will you call all the girls your honey?
Or will you call,
Or will you call all the girls your honey?

No, I don't think I will save my money,
I would rather call the girls my honey.
I would rather,
I would rather call the girls my honey.

Work for money, God won't keep you healthy.
With the girls, God just might make you wealthy.
With the girls, God,
With the girls, God just might make you wealthy.

When the girl does tell you she's a mother,
She will write you letters like no other.
She will write you,
She will write you letters like no other.

When you read her letter full of pleading,
Then your parents ask you what you're reading.
Then your parents,
Then your parents ask you what you're reading.

What's that news that sets you so to sighing,
Turns your grey eyes red with all that crying?
Turns your grey eyes,
Turns your grey eyes red with all that crying?

I have suffered a great loss, I stated.
My new-seeded fields were inundated.
My new-seeded,
My new-seeded fields were inundated.

To the Black Sea all my grain went flying.
That's why, my old mother, I am crying.
That's why, my old,
That's why, my old mother, I am crying.

Moyi Mamtsia Doma
My Mother Is At Home

Written down in 1957 from the singing of Teodora Marchyk, age 54, in the village of Mokhnachka Nizhnia.

Ukraine

Mo – yi mam – tsia do – ma, a ya v A – me – ri – tsi,
My moth – er is at home, I'm in *A – me – ri – tsi,*
(ca)

Rob – liu ya v Nev –Yor – ku, v ty no – viy fab – ri – ki.
Work– ing here in New York, in a new fac – to – ry.

Yak mashinu pushcham,	I switch on the machine,
Nitki sya torhayut.	The thread begins to go.
A moyi mamusya	While mommy far away,
O nichim ne znayut.	She really doesn't know.
A ta Amerika	Here in America
Yest to prevelika.	Life can be really fine.
Nayitsya ho bida,	English you've got to speak,
Khto ne zna yazika.	Or you'll have a hard time.
Mene sya nayila	I had my troubles here,
Za dvanatset tizhniv.	Twelve weeks I cursed my fate.
Nizh sya mi ne zderli,	I couldn't understand,
Ti krayivski tsizhmi.	I lost a lot of weight.

Tsizhmi sya mi zderli, Lashki z mya spadali. Khtovdi mya anhliki Do roboti vzyali.	My dresses didn't fit, I was becoming thin, When finally the English People took me in.
Obitsyali meni Pivtalyara na den. Ishchi sya smiyali: Robi, griner blazen!	They promised that they'd pay Half a dollar a day. They held me up to scorn: Work, you crazy greenhorn!
Yak ya to pochula, Shto oni sya smiyut, Ne budu robila, Bo mi ruchki mliyut!	And when I understood That they were poking fun, My hands were growing weak, I thought — my work is done!
A ruchki mi mliyut, Slezi me spadayut. A moyi matusya O nichim ne znayut.	My hands are weakening, My eyes are turning red. My mother doesn't know How I am earning bread.
Vikhovali-ste mya, Na svoyikh kolinakh. Ne budu robila Na vashikh polyanakh.	You held me on your knees, You were my staunchest shield. But I will never work At home on your broad field.
Vikhovali-ste mya, Yak yednu yahodu. Vipravili-ste mya Za shiroku vodu.	Like some delicious fruit, You raised your own daughter. And then you sent me off, Over the wide water.
Za bodu shiroku, Za more gluboke, Teraz banuyete: Ditya moye lyube!	Over the waters wide, Over the ocean wild. How sorry you must be, My precious only child!

National Park Service

407

United States
of America

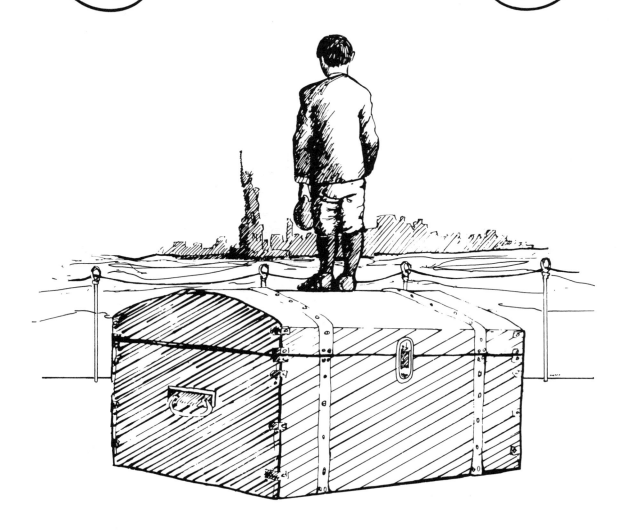

To Come To America

In June 1991, I conducted a week-long folk song workshop with third- and fourth-grade children at the Coman Hills School in Armonk, New York. The children came from many different ethnic backgrounds, and we discussed the reasons why immigrants came to America. We put many of those reasons into verse form and set them to the tune of the Irish immigrant song "Paddy Works On The Railway."

United States of America

Chorus

Fi - li - mi - oo - ri - oo - ri - ay, fi - li - mi - oo - ri - oo - ri - ay,

Fi - li - mi - oo - ri - oo - ri - ay, To come to A - me - ri - ca.

Fine

Verse

It was per - se - cu - tion that made us leave, It was per - se - cu - tion that

made us leave, It was per-se-cu-tion that made us leave, To come to A-me-ri-ca.

2. We didn't want to be pushed around, (3)
   To come to America.

3. We wanted to get away from war. . . (3)

4. We came to America to get good land. . . (3)

5. I came to America to join my love. . . (3)

6. We went from place to place to place. . . (3)

7. We wanted to vote for a President. . . (3)

8. We left our homes because we were poor. . . (3)

9. It was Adolf Hitler that made us leave. . . (3)

10. We wanted to have freedom there, (3)
    So we came to America.

National Park Service, Ellis Island Immigration Museum

Uncle Sam's Farm

The United States itself has made many contributions to the repertoire of songs dealing with immigrants and immigration. Not all of them have been of the "welcoming" variety. Fear and insecurity in the face of strangers is an all-too-common human emotion. Balancing these negative feelings are the songs inviting the downtrodden people of the world to come build and share in America's bounty.

The singing Hutchinson Family of New Hampshire was the most popular vocal ensemble during the 30-year period preceding the Civil War. They are remembered particularly for their anti-slavery and Abolitionist songs. It was during this turbulent era in American history that some 20 million people responded to America's "general invitation to the people of the world" to come to these shores and build a new life. The Hutchinsons wrote this song around 1850.

United States of America

Words by Jesse Hutchinson
Music by the Hutchinson Family

Of _____ all the might – y na – tions in the East or in the West oh, the
room for all cre-a – tion, and our ban – ner is un-furled, With a

glo – ri – ous Yan – kee na – tion is the great – est and the best. We have
gen – e – ral in – vi-ta – tion to the

peo–ple of the world. Then come a–long, come a–long, make no de–lay,

Come from ev – 'ry na – tion, come from ev – 'ry way. Our___ lands they are broad e–nough, don't be a–larmed, For___ Un – cle Sam is rich e–nough to give us all a farm.

St. Lawrence is our Northern line, far her waters flow,
And the Rio Grande our Southern bound, way down in Mexico;
While from the Atlantic Ocean where the sun begins to dawn,
We'll cross the Rocky Mountains far away to Oregon. *Chorus*

While the South shall raise the cotton, and the West the corn and pork,
New England manufactures shall do up the finer work;
For the deep and flowing waterfalls that course along our hills
Are just the thing for washing sheep and driving cotton mills. *Chorus*

Our fathers gave us liberty, but little did they dream
The grand results to follow in the mighty age of steam;
Our mountains, lakes and rivers are now in a blaze of fire,
While we send the news by lightning on the telegraphic wire. *Chorus*

While Europe's in commotion and her monarchs in a fret,
We're teaching them a lesson which they never can forget;
And this they fast are learning, Uncle Sam is not a fool,
For the people do their voting and the children go to school. *Chorus*

The brave in every nation are joining heart and hand,
And flocking to America, the real promised land;
And Uncle Sam stands ready with a child upon each arm,
To give them all a welcome to a lot upon his farm. *Chorus*

A welcome warm and hearty do we give the songs of toil,
To come to the West and settle and labor on Free Soil;
We've room enough and land enough, they needn't feel alarm —
Oh! Come to the land of Freedom and vote yourself a farm. *Chorus*

Yes we're bound to lead the nations, for our motto's "Go ahead,"
And we'll carry out the principles for which our fathers bled;
No monopoly of kings and queens, but this is the Yankee plan:
Free Trade to Emigration and Protection unto man. *Chorus*

The New Colossus

This poem by New York-born poet Emma Lazarus (1849–1887) is inscribed on a tablet at the base of the Statue of Liberty. She was a member of the oldest Jewish congregation in New York. The Russian pogroms of 1880 and 1881 were a trumpet call to her, and many of her poems reflect her reaction to these tragic events. She witnessed the beginnings of the mass immigration of Russian Jews. "The New Colossus," however, speaks to all humanity.

United States of America

Words by Emma Lazarus
Music by Jerry Silverman

Not like the bra — zen gi - ant of Greek fame, With con - quer-ing limbs a – stride from land to land, Here at our sea – washed sun – set gates shall stand A might – y ____ wo – man with a

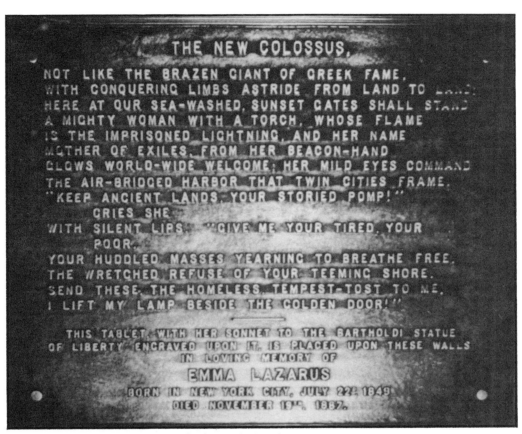

National Park Service, Statue of Liberty National Monument